Ethics and Cultural Policy in a Global Economy

Also by Sarah Owen-Vandersluis

POVERTY IN WORLD POLITICS: Whose Global Era? (*co-edited with Paris Yeros*)
THE STATE AND IDENTITY CONSTRUCTION IN INTERNATIONAL RELATIONS

Ethics and Cultural Policy in a Global Economy

Sarah Owen-Vandersluis

First published 2003 by
PALGRAVE MACMILLAN
Houndmills, Basingstoke, Hampshire RG21 6XS and
175 Fifth Avenue, New York, N.Y. 10010
Companies and representatives throughout the world

PALGRAVE MACMILLAN is the global academic imprint of the Palgrave
Macmillan division of St. Martin's Press, LLC and of Palgrave Macmillan Ltd.
Macmillan® is a registered trademark in the United States, United Kingdom
and other countries. Palgrave is a registered trademark in the European
Union and other countries.

ISBN 0–333–98197–9

This book is printed on paper suitable for recycling and made from fully
managed and sustained forest sources.

A catalogue record for this book is available from the British Library.

Library of Congress Cataloging-in-Publication Data

Owen Vandersluis, Sarah, 1974-
    Ethics and cultural policy in a global economy / Sarah Owen-Vandersluis.
        p. cm.
    Includes bibliographical references and index.
    ISBN 0–333–98197–9 (cloth)
        1. Culture—Economic aspects. 2. Cultural policy—Moral and ethical
    aspects. I. Title.

HM621.O9 2003
306—dc21   2003048064

10 9 8 7 6 5 4 3 2 1
12 11 10 09 08 07 06 05 04 03

Printed and bound in Great Britain by
Antony Rowe Ltd, Chippenham and Eastbourne

For my parents

Contents

Acknowledgements

This book arose out of my PhD research at the London School of Economics and Political Science. I wish to gratefully acknowledge the financial assistance of the Social Sciences and Humanities Research Council of Canada, the Overseas Research Students Award Scheme, the Canadian Women's Club and the Scholarships Office of the London School of Economics.

This project began with my editorship of *Millennium: Journal of International Studies*. Looking back, it is clear to me that my prolonged involvement with the *Millennium* community and the continued friendship of successive generations of editors and business managers has been invaluable. In particular, several friends and colleagues have willingly devoted much of their own time to reading and commenting on portions of this book. I owe a special debt of gratitude to Paris Yeros, Eivind Hovden, Amru Al-Baho, Hakan Seçkinelgin, Nick Bisley, Per Hammarlund, David Macdonald, and Julius Sen. Their assistance has been invaluable, as has their companionship.

James Mayall has been encouraging me and challenging me intellectually since he first became my undergraduate tutor in 1991. Without his help, there is no question that I would not have achieved first-class results in 1994, nor would I have felt the motivation to pursue postgraduate studies. Throughout the writing of my PhD and then this book, he has always been available when I have needed his counsel, and his thoughts and comments have always forced me to think things through more carefully.

That this book has reached fruition is, above all, a credit to my parents, Bob and Lesley Owen. Both have sacrificed a great deal to encourage and support me throughout this project. Without their intellectual, emotional and financial support, I would never have arrived at the LSE in the first place, nor could I ever have hoped, 10 years later, to be publishing my completed PhD.

Finally, I am grateful for the constant support of my husband, Bob Vandersluis. He has read and discussed many parts of this book and has often frustrated me greatly by challenging my assumptions and forcing me to better defend my ideas. He has also willingly allowed my research to take over a good portion of our house and our lives over the past seven years. I could not have finished this book without his support and companionship and, in all respects, it is a much better product because of his involvement.

Responsibility for the ideas expressed here is, of course, entirely my own; the argument does not necessarily reflect the views of any organisations with which I am affiliated.

1
Introduction

Neoclassical economics and IPE

Introductions to international political economy (IPE) invariably begin from Adam Smith's conception of absolute advantage and its modification in David Ricardo's tale of British cloth and Portuguese wine.[1] Not surprisingly, this story has been retold and refined over the years. Nonetheless, the fundamental idea that there are demonstrable welfare gains from free markets has continued to guide economic thinking.

As Chapter 2 will show, a great deal of economic analysis has demonstrated that intervention in cultural 'markets' is inefficient and can lead to domestic and international market distortions. As a result, they argue that all countries should abandon culturally 'protectionist' measures. If there is sufficient demand for culture as a distinct product, then the industry will survive and market distortions arising from protection will be eliminated. If not, then the market will shift towards stronger producers, who enjoy the economies of scale provided by the size and vitality of their domestic market.

This economic approach has much in common with numerous IPE approaches. As Susan Strange has described it, 'a great deal of the literature in IPE written in the United States has displayed a marked tendency to imitate the methods and concepts of liberal or neo-classical economics'.[2] For these analysts, the desirability of freer markets is not open to debate – its advantages have already been demonstrated by the economic model. The central question of this type of IPE analysis is how to create and maintain the political preconditions for mutual gains from freer markets to be achieved. In Craig Murphy and Roger Tooze's words, 'the first political problem is that of assuring that a liberal trade regime is maintained'.[3] Specifically, as James Mayall has noted, this has been posed as a question of will: 'since liberal trade theory is well-grounded and well-understood, why is it that … governments … repeatedly fail to deliver what they profess?'[4] The assumption clearly is that states must be helped, as much as possible, from taking actions that would hurt their own – and their citizen-consumers' – economic interests. These claims have generated reams of analysis concerned with understanding and predicting relationships between actor behaviour and system management, including hegemonic stability theory and regime theory.[5] More importantly, however, such approaches assume that the role of politics is to facilitate the smooth running of the economy. As Stephen Rosow has put it, the effect of such an assumption 'is to reduce the interpretation of civil society in modern states to an echo of commercial practice'.[6]

Importantly, not all IPE scholars have been so keen to embrace the primacy of neoclassical economic theory. Many differing critics of neoclassical trade theory, for example, have focused on the impediments to trade inherent in a system of sovereign states. Mayall has described the importance of national defence for the liberal system, arguing it constitutes 'a major concession to realism'.[7] Taking the idea of national security to its neorealist extreme, Joseph Grieco has claimed that the relative gains of one state may often override the absolute gains of all.[8]

Some of these scholars have also focused on concerns beyond a limited idea of national security. Indeed, many have focused on the more general ties of obligation between nation and citizens and have offered more scope for the state's role in protecting the national community. According to E.H. Carr, 'the first obligation of the modern national government, which no obligation will be allowed to override, is to its own people'.[9] Similarly, Mayall has claimed that '[n]o one has ever successfully challenged the claim that the first duty of a state is to its citizens'.[10] As a result, 'economic policies which are adopted to defend and strengthen the state against foreign competition are adopted for explicitly nationalist reasons'.[11] In a similar vein, Strange has argued that all governments are faced with the task of trading off four different values, namely, wealth, order, justice, and freedom. As a result, '[e]fficiency never has been and never can be the sole consideration in the choice of state policies'.[12] Indeed, Joan Robinson sums it up when she claims that economists ignore the fact that there are some good national arguments for protection.

Importantly, however, the case that is made by Strange, Mayall, and Robinson is hardly the simplistic one decried by economists as mere lobbying for particular interests. All three have a profound sense of the metaphysics at work in the legitimation of neoclassical claims.

Not surprisingly, then, all three also stress the importance of ethical considerations in IPE. In Mayall's words, 'the major economic problems in international relations in one way or another all raise the question of justice'. However, this is no simple concept of allocative justice: '[t]o talk about justice, of what is owed by men to each other, is necessarily to examine the nature, purpose and possibility of human community'.[13] Similarly, Strange argues that IPE scholars must abandon realism and liberalism and 'start again at the beginning'. For Strange, this means 'starting with what used to be called moral philosophy. ... [M]oral philosophers were concerned with fundamental values – how they could be reflected in the ordering of human society and how conflicts between them might be resolved.'[14] At an even deeper level, Robinson makes a case for revealing the very roots of the ethical system that we take for granted. Such a task is clearly relevant to IPE, not least because, in her words, '[a]ny economic system requires a set of rules, an ideology to justify them, and a conscience in the individual which makes him strive to carry them out'.[15]

This book is sympathetic to these nationalist and statist criticisms of neoclassical economic theory. In fact, one important task of this research is to investigate some of the non-commercial motivations for government intervention in cultural 'markets'. Furthermore, the purpose of this book is to heed calls for an ethical renewal in IPE, by exploring what an ethical analysis might entail in the specific case of cultural policy. In so doing, however, I will question the ideas of community and the good life which underlie both neoclassical and nationalist approaches. I will suggest that to read the politics of culture from exclusively an economic or a nationalist approach is to miss something fundamental about culture and cultural products. In this regard, I aim to bring an IPE argument to bear on considerations of cultural policy; though, as will become clear, heeding the calls for ethical theory results in analysis quite different from very many other accounts of IPE. A preview of what this entails is set out below.

What role for critical theory? Moving beyond neo-Gramscianism

The past few decades have witnessed the steady rise of critical theorising in international relations (IR). In less than 20 years, critical theory has moved from the periphery of enquiry to a position where it can claim some significant gains, not least in terms of the reinvocation and rearticulation of cultural concerns. Even though culture is not always itself a direct subject of theorising, the return of culture and identity as key concerns in IR was a crucial element in the process of reflection on the discipline's motives, methods, and achievements. However, in contrast to the proliferation of approaches in IR, IPE has shown a marked reluctance to stray from the dictates of scientific methodology. This tendency is often not directly admitted. Indeed, most IPE theorists have refused to engage in metatheoretical debate, preferring to draw their legitimacy instead from the fact that they remain within the confines of accepted, 'normal' science.[16] As Murphy and Tooze have noted, 'orthodox IPE has accommodated "paradigmatism" only to a limited extent'.[17] Stephen Krasner, however, is one traditional IPE theorist who has acknowledged and responded to the methodological challenge posed by critical theory. In an article entitled 'The Accomplishments of International Political Economy', Krasner directly addresses the methodological question in IPE. He claims that IPE 'has been guided almost exclusively by the... assumption that reality exists independently of the way in which it is represented by humans and that the truth of a statement depends on how well it conforms with this independent reality'.[18]

If this claim is accepted, the key points of difference between approaches to IPE can be characterised as existing *within* a broad agreement on positivist epistemology.[19] In other words, approaches can be distinguished according to the positions they take on, for example, the possibilities for interstate cooperation under anarchy. In this way, as Murphy and Tooze note, 'although at one level the frameworks are contesting (liberalism versus nationalism versus Marxism), at another they... maintain and reproduce a particular form of knowledge'.[20] Indeed, this triad, along with domestic politics approaches, is seen by Krasner and others as defining the range of approaches to IPE. To his credit, Krasner does acknowledge that positivist theorising has numerous faults, not least that it only rarely is able to show policy-makers what the best course of action is. However, he nevertheless concludes by endorsing conventional methodology because any other method would be anti-foundationalist, 'lead[ing] directly to nihilism'.[21]

It should be clear that Krasner's defence of (what he terms) 'Western Rationalism' is based on a gross overstatement of the dangers of alternative approaches. It delegitimises all non-conventional approaches and in so doing, excludes the possibilities held out by critical and post-structuralist approaches that fall short of full-fledged anti-foundationalism or nihilism.[22] Indeed, as Chris Brown stressed in his 1994 article, there is no 'mythical beast called "post-modern (or critical) international relations theory".... [T]here are only critical theories in the plural.'[23] More importantly, as this introduction has already suggested, these theories are not simply marginal contributors to an already existing debate, but are flourishing and have already succeeded in making important contributions to our understanding of IR. In IPE, however, the variety of new approaches has been more limited. One approach that clearly occupies this critical space between 'normal' science and radical postmodernism is neo-Gramscianism. Because of its central position in the critical IPE debate, a discussion of neo-Gramscianism is a crucial first step in orienting the position taken by this book.

There is, of course, no unified view on what constitutes the 'Italian school' or the new 'Gramscian approach'. Indeed, many theorists who have been labelled neo-Gramscians have rejected the characterisation as one-sided and inaccurate.[24] However, it is nonetheless possible (and important) to speak of the numerous historical materialist (and post-Marxist) approaches to IPE that have been spawned by Robert Cox's now famous comment that 'theory is always *for* someone and *for* some purpose'.[25] As Randall Germain and Michael Kenny have noted, the notion of a school 'is useful to the extent that it highlights how a particular set of ideas has come to exert an important influence within the discipline'.[26] Indeed, while acknowledging the impossibility of faithfully discussing a single 'school', we can nonetheless summarise the main invocations of these Gramscian-inspired approaches.

First, and contrary to structural Marxism, Antonio Gramsci stressed the role of human consciousness in historical development. Indeed, 'he consistently argues for a more empowering self-understanding in which humans are actively self-constitutive in the process of consciously reconstructing their internal relation with society and nature'.[27] In other words, not only are humans conscious of their involvement in the natural and social world, but they are further able to consciously affect the course of history.

Second, while human consciousness is central to historical development, this consciousness does not have influence independently of material conditions. In particular, Gramsci stressed the importance of specific historical circumstances as the inescapable context of historical struggle. As Cox has claimed, '[i]n Gramsci's historical materialism, ... ideas and material conditions are always bound together, mutually influencing one another, and not reducible one to the other'.[28]

Third, Gramsci identified a conception of social power that is complex and not easily reducible to economic, political, or cultural factors alone. Ideology, for example, is central to hegemonic leadership and distinguishes it from material dominance. In particular, a hegemonic class can only become so by 'combining the interests of other...groups...with its own interests so as to create a national-popular collective will'.[29] Further, 'there must be a cultural–social unity through which a multiplicity of dispersed wills...are welded together with a single aim'.[30] Revolutionary struggle, then, must take place on both ideological and material grounds.

Finally, we must note Gramsci's political goals, namely transcending the divisions of capitalist society and creating a new historic bloc based on proletarian leadership. In Mark Rupert's words, 'Gramsci's radical politics envisions a comprehensive transformation of social reality through the creation of an effective counter-culture, an alternative world view and a new form of political organization.'[31]

The specific *methodological* contribution made by Gramscian-inspired approaches has been summed up by Stephen Gill. In particular, Gill argues that neo-Gramscian approaches do not accept 'symmetry between the social and natural sciences with regard to concept formation and the logic of inquiry and explanation'.[32] Further, unlike the natural scientist, the social scientist cannot be a neutral, distant observer. The separation of observer and observed which is so central to positivist accounts is rejected by neo-Gramscian approaches. In other words, 'the Gramscian approach is an epistemological and ontological critique of the empiricism and positivism which underpin the prevailing theorisations'.[33] According to Gill, neo-Gramscian approaches provide this critique through historicism, methodological holism, dialecticism, and a deliberate involvement in both theorising and bringing about human emancipation.[34] Indeed, Gill even claims that Gramsci's work is overtly ethical, displaying 'something akin to the Aristotelian view of politics as the search to establish the conditions of the good society'.[35] As a result, 'questions of justice, legitimacy and moral credibility are integrated sociologically into the whole'.[36]

Neo-Gramscian political economy has been attractive precisely because of the methodological claims just described. In particular, neo-Gramscianism is often seen to offer the possibility of reconciling subject and object, material and ideal, theory and praxis.[37] It is perceived as the ultimate alternative to the individualism of liberal IPE and the rigid structuralism of Marxist IPE. However, as Germain and Kenny are correct to point out, such an interpretation hardly does justice to the inherent contradictions and irreconcilable tensions within Gramsci's own work. In particular, Germain and Kenny are not convinced that Gramsci's thought holds the possibility of overcoming the subject–object dualism.[38] In response, they call for a careful reconsideration of Gramsci's concepts and their applicability to IR and IPE. Although I agree that such a reconsideration is necessary, this book does not aim to undertake this type of critical engagement with neo-Gramscianism. However, it originates in a similar unease about the methodological claims made on behalf of neo-Gramscianism and shares the view that alternative, critical theories must be developed.

In particular, the method taken by this book developed out of a sense of the ethical inadequacy of neo-Gramscian approaches. As noted above, neo-Gramscians are apt to make claims about the capacity of their theory to transcend the subject–object divide, or the gulf between theory and praxis. This transcendence is intimately connected to the process by which a proletarian historic bloc will gain power and legitimacy. However, this vision is problematic for two reasons. First, the neo-Gramscians are quick to show the political and normative implications of 'normal' science, but they rarely acknowledge that their own vision is also only a singular and contestable vision of a particular moral order. They gain great moral purchase by portraying themselves as the liberators of IR from the shackles of problem-solving theory. The reason that they succeed in this offers the second reason that neo-Gramscianism is ethically inadequate. In particular, neo-Gramscians often refer to the goal of emancipation, but rarely specify what emancipation might actually entail. It is not clear if they wish to see a new hegemony grow out of subaltern forces or if they are striving for a post-hegemonic order. In other words, they fail to set out and defend their specific vision of the good life. This is highly problematic for a theory which purports to assume the critical mantle in IPE and which seeks to dethrone conventional methodologies for their inability to recognise the role of theory in serving particular political ends.

However, the ethical critique of neo-Gramscians runs even deeper than this. It is not merely the case that neo-Gramscians refuse to elaborate on the content of their new world order, but rather that they are actually incapable of doing so without violating some of their central assumptions. In particular, if the role of human consciousness is to be taken seriously, then a theorist can hardly presume to dictate the actual shape of any future social organisation. Indeed, Gill goes further than any other neo-Gramscian theorist in outlining the desired characteristics of a new order: rational, democratic, and open. However, even he stops short of further explanation or justification, claiming that he 'offers no promises or prescriptions for the form that such a society might take'.[39] According to Gill and Cox, Gramsci described 'a normative force, but not a normative plan or set of normative criteria'.[40] As a result, although neo-Gramscians are consistently emphasising the importance of emancipation as a goal of their theory, they remain fundamentally incapable of thoroughly elaborating or justifying this vision of the good life. This is a serious ethical shortcoming that prevents neo-Gramscianism from offering any useful conceptualisation of what constitutes the good and, more importantly, the terms on which we can understand one theory or state of life as better than any other.

In this context, one aim of this book is to further exploit the space for counter-discourse that has been opened in IPE by neo-Gramscian approaches. Indeed, paralleling the neo-Gramscians, this book aims to expand considerations of IPE beyond the liberal/realist/structural Marxist triad. However, it seeks to chart a different course from that of the 'Italian school'. In particular, since I have found the problems of neo-Gramscian ethics to be their most significant failing, this book adopts an explicitly normative approach. In other words, it begins with an IPE problem – the extent of legitimate government intervention in the cultural arena – but then considers it normatively, focusing on many of the cultural and critical questions that have informed recent discussions within IR. In so doing, it seeks to extend our ways of understanding IPE, thereby expanding the range of questions that may legitimately be asked about IPE and the range of reasons for action that may be taken as legitimate. In this sense, then, the book seeks to comprehend what a normative approach to IPE might entail.

In light of the discussion above, the choice made to rely upon normative theory should be clear. Indeed, for some time already, IR theorists have made the claim that normative theorising is not simply desirable. It is unavoidable. Indeed, as has been often repeated in IR literature, even the most scientific observer cannot hope to be neutral in his starting assumptions, methods, and desires for the future. In Isaiah Berlin's words, '[s]uch men are in the first place students of facts, and aspire to formulate hypotheses and laws like the natural scientists. Yet as a rule these thinkers cannot go any further: they tend to analyse men's social and political ideas in the light of some overriding belief of their own.'[41] The central problem, then, centres around a need for what Mark Neufeld has referred to as reflexivity or 'theoretical self-consciousness'. Reflexivity entails '(i) self-consciousness about underlying premises; (ii) the recognition of the inherently politico-normative dimension of paradigms and the normal science tradition they sustain; and (iii) the affirmation that reasoned judgements about the merits of contending paradigms are possible in the absence of a neutral observation language'.[42] Without a neutral language, 'judgements about contending paradigms are possible by means of reasoned assessments of the politico-normative content of the projects they serve, of the ways of life to which they correspond'.[43] Without such reflexivity, we are ill-placed to recognise that 'to engage in paradigm-directed puzzle-solving is – intentionally or not – to direct one's energies to the establishment and maintenance of a specific global order',[44] nor can we question the methods and conclusions of normal science. Indeed, as Berlin has noted, only where society is dominated by a single goal can scientific methods be of use, since 'there could in principle only be arguments about the best means to attain this end – and arguments about means are technical, that is, scientific and empirical in character'.[45] Where there is no total acceptance of any single end, then we cannot avoid a 'critical examination of presuppositions and assumptions, and the questioning of the order of priorities and ultimate ends'.[46] Despite having so far avoided the question of reflexivity, IPE embodies no greater agreement on the goals of society and the purposes of theorising than any other social science discipline. In this respect, the aim of this book is to take one very modest step towards this theoretical self-awareness in IPE.

It should be noted, however, that the idea of normative theory has developed a radically new meaning in the context of the developments in IR theory that were detailed in the first paragraphs of this introduction. Indeed, the connection between critical theory and culture has completely altered the meaning of ethics for those who see themselves in the critical tradition. Most importantly, ethics is no longer considered as a realm of inquiry that is *separable* from the considerations of IR theorists. In other words, ethics is not a domain of external questions that can either be heeded or ignored by IR. Indeed, if, as Cox noted, theory is always for someone or something, then the task of theorising itself cannot be considered morally or culturally neutral. In consequence every act of theorising is considered to embody, if implicitly, normative claims about the nature of the individual and the appropriate ends of human endeavour. Method and meaning are no longer clearly separable. In this context, critical theory takes on many roles. One task, in particular, is to ask, 'what constitutes good theory with regard to world politics?'[47] Providing a preliminary and contestable answer to this question in the realm of IPE is one goal of this book.

Importantly, in light of this shift in understanding normative theory, the question of good theory is no longer separable from questions of value and meaning. Moreover, and as a result, cultural issues have clearly returned into view. For normative theory, the result is that justice is no longer understood primarily as an end-state between individuals. Instead, justice is often conceived of as a process, in which the establishment of adequate intercultural dialogue is key. The rise of cultural concerns, then, has forced a reconsideration of the ethical premises and implications of different theories in an effort to establish their capacity to seriously endorse and enable value pluralism. For IPE, a concern for processes and institutions as well as outcomes has meant a challenge to traditional notions of distributive justice.

In this context, another purpose of the book is to show how an adequate understanding of social life and an adequate emancipatory method for IPE entail taking seriously the meaning and importance of culture. In other words, culture as a moral referent, however it is conceptualised, is an inescapable element of critical theory. In this light, this book asks (i) what are the ethical premises underlying the conventional approaches to cultural policy, and (ii) what legitimate alternatives can we envisage? The purpose is not to refuse the merit of conventional approaches, but to re-evaluate their centrality or obviousness and to make a case for an alternative, culturally informed way of understanding and legitimising government policy. Indeed, the book is intended, in part, to challenge the economic notion that state activity is only legitimate if it is 'adjusting national economic activities to the exigencies of the global economy'.[48] However, as we will see, the position taken here nonetheless remains very distant from the realist notion that the national interest is the ultimate justification for any policy.

Answering these questions will require a serious consideration of the normative bases of different approaches to cultural policy. More importantly, it will demand a wide-ranging and often theoretically dense discussion of the importance of culture in the constitution of identity and moral personality, and the relevance of this relationship for considerations and evaluations of government action. The book will proceed by questioning the normative foundations of different approaches, enquiring whether these premises are adequate for our task and for society. The book will then seek to build an alternative picture based on normative premises that, according to the argument, better reflect our values and self-understandings. In taking such an approach, I must begin by being clear about my own values and foundations. This work is clearly located within the broad spectrum of critical theory (small c, small t) that developed out of Western Marxism. It is, however, post-Marxist, in the sense that it seeks to go well beyond the narrow and often teleological considerations of class and production that have dominated much Marxist analysis. In particular, the book must be understood as taking a broadly interpretive or hermeneutic approach to culture, drawing on insights developed most recently by Taylor and Young.[49]

Culture and critical theory

But why focus on culture? In one sense, an ability to accommodate the relevance of cultural pluralism is now perceived by theorists of all stripes to be important to understanding the post-Cold War world. Indeed, the re-emergence of identity politics in IR has clearly posed a challenge to realist conceptions of power and interests. Moreover, for critics of neo-realism, cultural factors are an important element of theorising which can conceptualise difference and change in the international system.

However, as this introduction has highlighted, cultural issues are also inextricably intertwined with the project of critical theory itself. By questioning the dominance of scientific epistemology, critical theorists have forced open the question of what constitutes good knowledge. They have challenged the universality of Western rationalism as the only standard by which knowledge can be evaluated. The recognition of fundamental differences between cultures and the consequent problem of cross-cultural understanding have thus come to dominate the epistemological landscape. In this sense, prioritising metatheory and taking an interpretive approach are in one sense to already have accepted a focus on culture.

But what understanding of culture underlies such a position? Craig Calhoun has noted that there are numerous ways in which sociologists have attempted to understand culture. However, many of them, including the idea of culture as a commodity or as an intervening variable, represent attempts to 'scientise' the study of culture. In other words, many studies of culture have felt 'obliged to interpret the social world as one in which meaning was not problematic'.[50] However, unless meaning is taken as problematic, there is little opening for the insights of hermeneutic approaches. Or, to consider the problem from a different point of view, hermeneutic approaches both require and generate a culturalisation of social science. As a result, the only sense of culture that fully accords with the methodological imperatives of interpretive social science is one that 'starts with the recognition that social life is inherently cultural, that is, inherently shaped and even constituted in part by differences in the ways in which people generate ... meaning'.[51] This is the type of definition of culture adopted by this book, which follows Taylor in defining culture as 'the background of practices, institutions, and understandings which form the langue-analogue for our action in a given society'.[52] In this regard, Taylor has been significantly influenced by Clifford Geertz, whose anthropological, symbolic, and interpretive approach to culture has received a great deal of attention throughout the social sciences.[53]

Argument of the book

Having delineated the context in which this book is located and the methodology to which it adheres, the only remaining task for this introduction is to outline the argument which follows. Chapter 2 analyses the existing literature on cultural policy. This literature is divided into two categories corresponding to the two main approaches, namely market-based approaches and community-based approaches. Market-based approaches begin from a very firm commitment to the free market. When the market is functioning properly, it is seen to provide the best guarantee of individual welfare. Moreover, although very few market-based authors define culture, it is clear from their analyses that it is both possible and desirable for culture to be understood through a market paradigm. They view culture as essentially like any other good, with a market for its creation, its sale, and even its subsidisation. As a result, the question of adequate cultural policy resolves itself into the question of when government can legitimately interfere in the free market. 'Good' policy, in this context, is that which uses (measurable) welfare effects to guide government intervention in the free market. Community-based approaches to cultural policy all begin from the premise that cultural activity fulfils important social functions. They stress the benefits to the community of cultural production by, for, and representing that community. In turn, the good of the community, broadly defined, is the ultimate justification for policy. Beyond this premise, however, there are many differences between community-based approaches, not least in their assessments of what constitutes the community and what constitutes the 'good', as well as in their ideas of how this good can be promoted. Within the literature, there emerge six different dimensions through which culture can be seen to contribute to the 'good' life of the community. These are identity, unity, sovereignty, prosperity, democracy, and artistic fulfilment. These themes are each drawn out in detail.

Chapters 3 and 4 will begin the process of ethical critique. Chapter 3 focuses on the market-based approach, with particular attention to its ethical premises and implications. The chapter discusses the core values of market-based approaches, namely, individual well-being and freedom. Each value is discussed in turn, demonstrating that the manner in which market-based approaches deal with culture is flawed in two related ways. First, proponents of market-based approaches do not recognise that their values are particular. In other words, they do not acknowledge that their own assertions are culturally grounded and have both moral premises and implications. Because proponents of these approaches perceive their values to be universally accepted (or at least universally acceptable), they have great difficulty in understanding that cultural particularity may be *morally* significant. As a result, and second, the conception of social justice suggested by market-based approaches is fundamentally incapable of conceptualising the moral relevance of culture.

Chapter 4 addresses the question of whether and in what ways it is possible to provide a moral justification for community-based approaches to cultural policy. In other words, are there good ethical reasons why the state should intervene to support culture, and, if so, what might these reasons be? This chapter argues that, in considering community-based approaches, we can and ought to distinguish between community-based approaches which are morally acceptable and those which are not. Having made this distinction, this chapter focuses on those community-based approaches which are *not* ethically justifiable, delineating the reasons why these community-based approaches are unacceptable as a basis for cultural policy.

Building on this discussion, Chapter 5 offers a detailed delineation of an ethics which can support the acceptable forms of community-based approach. The first part of this chapter sets out Taylor's ontology and especially the main points of his understanding of culture and its relationship to identity.[54] The second part of the chapter focuses on the cultural ethics which is generated by Taylor's work. It also addresses several criticisms of Taylor which are the most relevant for the application of Taylor's work to cultural policy. The chapter concludes by suggesting the most important connections between Taylor's work and the policy debate on culture.

Chapter 5 also sets out the foundations of the approach that this book takes towards cultural policy. It establishes the value of Taylor's ontology, even though it argues that his ethical and political positions contain serious difficulties and are inappropriate for this project. In this light, Chapter 6 shows how Taylor's ontology can be developed to produce a different and more useful ethics for cultural policy. This is achieved by drawing on the work of Young. In terms of the concerns of this book, Young's ethics clearly have value. Her work builds upon the many attributes of Taylor's ontology, developing a sound and useful statement of how culture should be accommodated in social theory and practice. Her conception of social justice and its manifestation in radical democracy will be taken up by this book as the ethical basis for its claims about adequate cultural policy.

Chapters 6 and 7 seek to understand how the ethical claims developed above can be applied to particular instances of cultural policy.

These chapters attempt to show the relevance of the market-based and community-based approaches in understanding actual cultural policies. Additionally, these chapters build upon the ethics developed in earlier chapters to critique existing policies and offer suggestions for improvement.

Chapter 6 shows how market-based and community-based approaches have been relevant in Canada–United States disputes relating to trade in periodicals. It highlights an instance in which Canadian attempts to implement a policy protecting Canadian periodicals resulted in disputes between the Canadian and American governments. An examination of the positions taken by the governments, opposition groups, publishers, and advertisers demonstrates the precise ways in which the market-based and community-based approaches have played out in practice. The chapter claims that US publishers and policy-makers rely very heavily upon market-based assertions, even when their actions are not consistent with free market logic. Similarly, the Canadian government has trumpeted the rhetoric of community-based positions (national identity, in particular), even when, in practice, it has sometimes balanced these concerns against economic or other policy interests. In conclusion, this chapter will argue that Canadian magazines policy must be as enabling, participatory, and, ultimately, democratic as possible. The particular implications of these demands will be discussed in detail.

Chapter 7 seeks to use the analysis developed in earlier chapters to understand European Union cultural policy. The main goals and instruments of this policy are set out and examined in light of the market- and community-based approaches. The chapter argues that European cultural policy demonstrates a very particular form of community-based approach, backed up by key functionalist assumptions. In conclusion, suggestions are made for ways in which European cultural policy could be made more ethically justifiable.

The conclusion to the book sums up the arguments made throughout the chapters and discusses the implications for IPE and cultural policy more generally.

2
Contending Views of Culture and the Good Life

This chapter will discuss the competing claims of market and community-based approaches to cultural policy. It will first outline the claims of several key proponents of market-based approaches. Subsequently, it will draw out the key features of these approaches by examining the claims of its proponents on two central issues: definition of culture, and criteria for 'good' policy. A critique of market-based approaches will be offered. The chapter will then turn to community-based approaches. It will discuss the main claims of these approaches, paying particular attention to the same two central issues. A limited critique of these approaches will also be discussed.

Market-based approaches

Market-based approaches to cultural policy can be identified primarily by an ideological commitment to the free market. All of the approaches described below seek to apply the tools of welfare economics to generate a better understanding of culture. Nonetheless, within this framework there remains much room for debate. The two most important positions are set out below.

First, there are those cultural economists who believe that there are few, if any, grounds for government intervention in the cultural market. Steven Globerman is one of the foremost proponents of this approach. In several books and articles, he has repeatedly challenged the assumption of cultural nationalists and policy-makers alike that the sphere of culture must be insulated from the constraints of economic theory. He argues that if policy is to be effective and if limited resources are to be efficiently used, cultural policy must be subjected to economic analysis. Thus, in his 1983 study of Canadian cultural policy, Globerman sets out to critically address the justifications and the instruments of Canadian government intervention in the cultural marketplace.[1] Not surprisingly, Globerman concludes that the rationales for intervention are either insufficiently defended at a theoretical level (for example, the idea that national culture is required to preserve national identity) or are empirically irrelevant (for example, the argument that intervention is necessary to remedy externalities).[2] Moreover, he argues that the instruments chosen for government intervention are, at best, 'hardly contributory to alleviating obvious market failure problems'.[3] Combining this assessment with a public choice approach to the formation of domestic policy, Globerman concludes by arguing that '[i]n the absence of an identification of genuine market failure problems, one would anticipate the imposition of policies that serve no obvious social function but, rather, benefit a small number of individuals who assume certain costs associated with lobbying for their favoured policies'.[4] Globerman makes some very important points, not least of which is that the assumptions of cultural nationalists should not be immune from critical and popular assessment. However, his approach also has serious limitations, as will become apparent in the final section of this chapter.

Like Globerman, the second type of market-based approach to culture, the market-failure school, begins with a firm commitment to the free market. However, proponents of this approach use the arguments of welfare economics to show why culture should be considered an exception to the free market.[5] These are often theorists who have some sympathy with the arguments of arts groups and cultural nationalists, but have sought to justify government support for culture in terms acceptable to most economists. As Abraham Rotstein has noted, '[t]he intellectual challenge as they see it, is to find a suitable rationale for such intervention within the parameters and concepts that economics establishes'.[6] Like Globerman, these theorists examine the concepts of merit goods, public goods, market failure, and externality as exceptions to the market rule. However, compared to Globerman, these cultural economists are more supportive of the legitimacy of government intervention in the cultural sphere. However, even though they might advocate cultural protection, these cultural economists remain firmly part of the market-based school. This is because they agree with Globerman in accepting that the justifiability of *reasons* for cultural policy derives from considerations of market efficiency. The problems with this assertion will be drawn out in Chapter 3.

The above approaches can be analysed according to their views on several important dimensions of cultural policy. These views will be addressed in the following sections.

Conception of culture

Within the literature of cultural economics, there is surprisingly little attention paid to the definition of the terms 'culture', 'cultural industries', or 'the arts'. In fact, most analyses use these words interchangeably and as though there already existed a commonly agreed meaning of them. Nonetheless, a careful reading of the work of the cultural economists reveals that, with few exceptions, they use a very narrow definition of culture. Several characteristics of this definition are immediately obvious. In the first place, in order for an economic analysis of culture to make sense, culture must be understood in supply and demand terms; it must be something that can be bought and sold. Moreover, culture must have a price, which, in turn, is seen to reflect its value to consumers. Finally, those who produce, buy, and sell culture must be seen as sovereign economic agents who are presumed to act in the interests of their own individual welfare.

Remarkably, these three characteristics say nothing about the substantive nature of culture. One commentator explains this as follows: '[i]t is not the economist's task to provide a definition of culture; in a paradigm dominated by consumer sovereignty, the necessary and sufficient conditions to identify culture are to be determined by each individual, according to his experience and preferences'.[7] Given the invocation of consumer sovereignty, this statement can only be understood to mean that no policy-maker or scholar should dictate to the consumer which types of activities should be considered culture and which are merely leisure activities or entertainment. Nonetheless, this still presumes that, at a fundamental level, we all share an idea of what is implied by the term 'culture'. Clearly, this approach avoids the difficult issues involved in defining culture. However, as will become clear in Chapter 3, it also artificially limits the ways in which we understand and legitimate cultural activity.

Globerman is one of the few cultural economists who attempts to define the subject which he is discussing. He initially argues that 'there is no one universally accepted definition of culture industries'.[8] However, after reviewing several options, Globerman eventually chooses a definition of culture as 'the creative and expressive artistic activities generally referred to as the performing, visual and creative arts and those functions related to their preservation and dissemination'.[9]

This definition of culture is typical of that implicitly used by many others and notable for several reasons. First, although it claims to be a definition of culture, it focuses mainly on cultural activities and products. It says nothing about the relationship of these discrete activities to other, broader understandings of culture as a social force or as a way of life. This is not surprising, given that Globerman and other cultural economists would want to define culture in a way that would allow them to quantify its social and economic effects. However, because it ignores the broader social context of cultural activities, this is a very limited definition for the purposes of evaluating policy-making. Moreover, to complicate matters further, Globerman uses the terms 'culture', 'cultural sector', and 'culture industries' interchangeably throughout his work. The implication of this loose use of terms is that culture is not relevant beyond its 'industrial' or commercial manifestations. For Globerman, culture is essentially like any other good that can be bought and sold on the open market; it is a commodity with no social role apart from the generation of national income and the satisfaction of wants.

The market-failure school takes a substantively similar position, although (like with most cultural economists) culture is rarely explicitly defined. Nonetheless, a survey of the main texts on the subject quickly confirms the supposition that culture must be defined in a fairly limited sense for the application of economic tools to be fruitful. In this context, economic analysis has been applied to explain the costs and benefits of government intervention as well as such diverse topics as the demand for opera tickets, the market in fake art, artists' income, and taste formation. In all of these cases, for economic analysis to make sense, culture must be defined as a product, with a market for its creation, its sale, and even its subsidisation. As James Heilbrun and Charles M. Gray attest, '[w]e have suggested that the arts share most attributes of ordinary consumer goods, and that the standard tools of demand analysis can usefully be brought to bear on them'.[10] Cultural economists do often recognise that their subject of study has social or individual value. However, this value is usually understood quantitatively, manifesting itself through the price mechanism. In this sense, cultural goods play the same role as all other commodities in society – they satisfy consumer wants.

Criteria for 'good' policy

For both types of market-based approaches, the question of what is good policy can be answered by addressing the question of what constitutes a strong economic argument for government support of cultural activities. This is because market-based approaches agree that the free market is the best guarantee of individual welfare. 'Good' policy, in this context, is that which uses (measurable) welfare effects as its guide to government intervention in the free market.[11] For example, Globerman describes the object of his book as to 'set out clearly and explicitly the conditions under which government intervention into cultural activities might improve...welfare', using neoclassical economics as a tool 'for evaluating the efficiency with which resources will be used under alternative institutional arrangements'.[12] Thus, government intervention can only be justified when it will produce a more optimal allocation of resources than the market. Indeed, market-based approaches see their own task as the very limited one of providing analysis so that intervention occurs only when it is justified. In this context, Mark Schuster has set out the constraints on any explanation which seeks to interfere with the free market:

> [a] strong economic argument would demonstrate that financial resources other than government support are not likely to support the arts. ... [It] would specify the amount of support necessary. It would also specify the form of support necessary and would be able to cite research demonstrating that this type of government support would be *effective*.[13]

In other words, market-based approaches agree that welfare economics is the ultimate source of legitimacy of intervention. In other words, as we will see in Chapter 3, the ends of society are presumed to be settled. However, their conclusions as to the legitimacy of individual policies differ. These differences will become apparent in the following discussion of the three main economic justifications for government intervention: market failure, equity, and merit goods.

(i) Market failure

A first economic justification for government intervention relates to cases of market failure. It is acknowledged by most economists that, in some cases and for fairly specific reasons, the market will fail to produce optimal economic outcomes. In these cases, the government should intervene to rectify the particular market failure. Several types of market-failure arguments have been applied to the case of culture. First, market failure may arise due to imperfect information. For the market to produce the optimum allocation of resources, it is presumed that both consumers and producers have cost-free access to all the available information. However, in many circumstances, this is not the case, leading to a diversion of resources from more productive activities into less productive ones. In these cases, government intervention is justified. In the particular case of the arts, David Cwi has argued that a taste for art may never be developed without the opportunity to sample it. Similarly, Globerman has highlighted the argument that many people are ignorant of the net benefits of the arts and therefore do not consume cultural goods.[14] In these cases, government subsidies have been called for to lower ticket prices, to increase the number of performances available, and to aid with advertising. However, as Globerman has argued, it is not clear that there actually is an information problem. According to Globerman, although potential consumers of the performing arts do consistently overestimate ticket prices, many do not attend due to lack of interest, rather than poor information or lack of opportunity.[15]

The second example of market failure in cultural industries relates to William Baumol and William Bowen's 'cost disease'. This is an example of market failure particular to the labour-intensive cultural industries, in particular the performing arts.[16] In essence, they argue that the labour-intensive nature of the performing arts means that these industries cannot substitute capital for labour at the same rate as other industries. As a result, they will not experience the same rates of productivity growth as other sectors. Moreover, the production costs of performing arts organisations will increase relative to other industries and their relative prices will consistently rise. Baumol and Bowen conclude that government subsidy is therefore necessary just to maintain the existing level of cultural output. The Baumol and Bowen thesis has been refuted many times over by proponents of both types of market-based approach. Dick Netzer, for example, has argued that, even in the performing arts, there are significant opportunities to increase technical efficiency. Moreover, he claims that consumer demand is not highly sensitive to increases in ticket prices. Nonetheless, he tempers his criticism by reminding us that '[p]ublic intervention to prevent economic pressures from causing *any* change whatever in the arts is a reductio ad absurdum of the Baumol–Bowen thesis'.[17] In other words, the thesis has limited relevance and can justify government subsidy only in certain specific cases. Globerman, however, is far less charitable in his analysis of the Baumol–Bowen thesis. He claims that there are significant opportunities for arts organisations to market more effectively, to increase earned and charitable revenue, and to reduce fixed costs without significantly damaging the quality of production. He acknowledges that 'some contraction of arts activities would result from a significant real reduction in government support to the arts'. Nonetheless, 'such a contraction would not be *per se* evidence of market failure'.[18] In sum, according to cultural economists, the Baumol and Bowen thesis alone does not justify increased government subsidy to the arts. It is even less relevant to more technology-intensive cultural activities such as book or magazine publishing and television broadcasting.

Third, markets are also acknowledged to fail in the provision of public goods. These goods are defined according to two characteristics: non-excludability and non-rivalry. In other words, people cannot be excluded from consuming them once they have been produced (or the costs of collecting payment would be prohibitive) and one individual's consumption does not preclude another's.[19] General examples of such goods might include national defence, crime prevention, and public parks. The market failure arises because of the free-rider problem: no individual will agree to pay for the service if the benefits of it can still be achieved when it is paid for by others. Thus, payment for this 'social infrastructure' must be secured through government intervention, usually in the form of taxes. Following a strict interpretation of the idea of public goods, most cultural products do not qualify: for the most part, individuals can easily be excluded from consuming them.[20] Nonetheless, it is possible that culture could be seen as a public good by virtue of its connection to broader social values or national defence. The question of broader social values will be addressed in the next chapter.

National defence is widely acknowledged to be the 'classic example' of a public good.[21] It is non-excludable and non-rival in consumption and is acknowledged by most to be crucial to the public interest. Many cultural advocates have claimed that culture should rightfully be considered an element of national defence.[22] Clearly, however, many people would disagree. Globerman, for example, questions whether culture actually establishes national identity and therefore contributes to a more easily defended nation.[23] What this illustrates, however, is that what actually comprises the public good called 'national defence' cannot be taken for granted. There are, of course, certain elements of defence which we would all agree are meritorious. Nonetheless, the question of whether culture can be considered an element of a public good like national defence is a political one. It is for this reason, along with the difficulties of classing cultural goods as public goods, that the national defence argument for cultural protectionism will be treated more extensively in the following chapter on community-based approaches to cultural policy.

A fourth source of market failure involves the presence of externalities. Externalities can be defined as 'the unintended social effects, desirable or undesirable, of production or consumption'.[24] Whether positive or negative, it is an entailment of externalities that the exact cost or value of the good in question is not reflected in consumer choices or in price. In some cases, this disparity occurs because part of the value of the good in question is unquantifiable, such as the appreciation of scenic country-side. In other cases, however, such as the common example of industrial pollution, externalities arise because the polluting firm is not responsible for the costs of clean-up and so these 'costs to society' are not reflected in the price of the good being produced.

Arguments relating to externalities have often been applied to justify cultural protectionism. Four specific arguments are relevant here. In the first place, it has been argued that production in one cultural field has important spillover effects for other fields.[25] In particular, it is argued that valuable training and employment opportunities may be provided for some industries by others. As Netzer argues, by way of example, '[v]irtually all the musical art forms tend to support one another. ... Thus the consumer of one form of music is likely to derive some benefit from the flourishing of another form even if he does not actively patronize it.'[26] These benefits are not realised in the market for cultural goods, it is argued, and, pursuing Netzer's example, '[i]f that form [of music] cannot flourish on its own, it may have a legitimate claim to public subsidy'.[27] Not surprisingly, Globerman has argued against this justification, questioning the extent to which there is cross-fertilisation between art forms. Moreover, he has suggested that, to the extent that interdisciplinary training improves the marketability of the artist, its costs can be internalised and thereby reflected more accurately in the cultural market-place.[28] In any case, the spillover argument entails limited and specific support for the arts on the grounds of artistic development. It could not provide a firm justification for the wide-ranging cultural measures undertaken by some governments.

Another common example of externalities in cultural production is the argument that government should support experimental cultural endeavours. Many of these undertakings will fail, or at least, they will be very high risk, and so the market support for them is limited. However, without the benefit of such experiments, future creative efforts will be less well-informed and, more importantly, some cultural products might never materialise.[29] As Netzer has argued, '[f]ailure may cause a theater company to go out of business or a writer to stop writing, but other artists and society at large may learn a lot from the failed experiment'.[30] Moreover, in Netzer's view, given that no one can convincingly assert which art will be valuable to society, support for risky endeavours is necessary to counter the weight of government support for conventional artistic projects.

A third example of externalities in cultural markets relates to the benefits accruing to future generations as a result of the preservation and nurturing of cultural activities in the present. It is usually argued that subsidy is necessary to preserve 'continuity and access in future years to the product of current artistic endeavour'.[31] It is also sometimes argued that cultural skills will be forgotten and therefore lost to future generations if particular industries are allowed to flounder. There is an element of this argument in the claim that culture is necessary to preserve particular social values and traditions, and to keep these alive for future generations. A version of this argument also appears as the 'option demand' claim, namely that cultural activities should be supported so that they are available for consumption by existing consumers at a later date. Globerman dismisses all of these arguments in relation to the performing arts, on the grounds that the art of performing is not likely to disappear with the bankruptcy of a few performing companies. Moreover, new technologies allow particular performances to be recorded and stored indefinitely.[32] However, this argument may not be so persuasive in the context of other cultural goods, particularly if it is deemed important that a certain culture remain a 'lived' culture. This latter argument, however, depends on a strong connection being drawn between cultural products and the preservation of certain traditions and values. This link will be addressed in greater detail in Chapter 4.

The final externality which is commonly discussed in relation to cultural protectionism is what Cwi has called a public externality.[33] He argues against the assumption that cultural goods are public goods on the grounds that there is both excludability and rival consumption in the cultural goods markets. However, he also points out that the private consumption of cultural goods produces public externalities. Government support could be justified on the grounds that these goods 'redound to the acknowledged benefit of the general public; that these goods are generally desired; and that additional benefits can only accrue if the private market is augmented by public support'.[34] Such public benefit could accrue in an economic form, such as positive national income and employment effects, or it could be purely social. Netzer supports such subsidisation, but argues that it should not be justified on the grounds of economic development, since this development can better be achieved through other means.[35] Globerman has dismissed the public externalities argument on the grounds that it leads to a tendency to overstate demand, especially when the taxpayer will foot the bill.[36]

Nonetheless, this argument has much appeal if it is understood that the public benefits arising out of cultural consumption may include national identity. In the case of most national cultures, however, it is not universally agreed that cultural goods are to the benefit of the general public (as opposed to a large minority), nor that these goods are generally desired. Both of these measures are highly political and, in this respect, are more usefully dealt with under the 'merit goods' justification below.

(ii) Equity

A second economic argument for government intervention is some-times made on the grounds of equity. For example, Schuster argues that '[i]f, from society's point of view, it is determined that people who deserve to enjoy artistic output cannot because it is too expensive, over-coming that barrier needs to be considered as a part of public policy'.[37] Netzer further argues that '[m]ost economists would agree that market processes, if left to themselves, will result in a distribution of personal income that is unacceptably unequal'.[38] Moreover, he draws attention to the fact that a primary goal of many cultural granting bodies and a common condition of government support is that the arts are made more widely available.

Globerman also discusses government intervention to fulfil one of its democratic responsibilities, namely to 'assure equitable treatment for all individuals in society'.[39] According to Globerman, this is a legitimate reason for intervention. However, he dismisses this justification in cul-tural cases on the grounds that 'the "rationale" for income redistribu-tion must be found in the operations of political markets, whereby policies directed at redistributing income are, in turn, largely the out-come of supply and demand forces in the "market" for government intervention'.[40] By treating the political process as itself a market, Globerman is able to conclude that government intervention to support distributional outcomes will 'reduce allocative efficiency in the culture industries'.[41] Netzer, however, is more optimistic. He acknowledges that government subsidies have not been very successful in making the arts more accessible.[42] Nonetheless, he maintains committed to the princi-ple that income barriers to arts consumption must be overcome and argues for 'long-term subsidies for audience development ... which provides initial exposure to the arts to large numbers of people'.[43]

As we will see in Chapter 3, considerations of equity rest uneasily with the market-based approach. In particular, it is difficult to achieve greater equity without sacrificing well-being or freedom. Clearly, such a trade-off has been accepted in many spheres. However, market-based approaches have, in general, been loath to accept equity as a legitimate justification for cultural protectionism. In particular, for reasons discussed in Chapter 3, market-based approaches are unlikely to consider access to cultural forms as sufficiently important to justify the negative effects of such a policy for allocative efficiency.

(iii) Merit goods

A third and final economic justification for government intervention falls under the heading of 'merit goods'. There exists no single agreed-upon definition of a merit good. The most useful definition, from the point of view of analysing cultural protectionism, is that provided by David Austen-Smith. He argues that a merit good is one which is intrinsically good, and is thereby necessary for the good society.[44] Moreover, to justify state support, this good must not only be meritous, but must be unable to be financially self-supporting within the free market. The argument that culture deserves protection because it is intrinsically good is an attractive one, particularly for those who already have a natural or financial interest in the cultural industries. Not surprisingly, the merit good argument has been applied frequently to urge or justify state support for the cultural industries.

Despite, or perhaps because of this public attention, the merit goods argument has been extensively criticised by both types of market-based approach. The essence of these criticisms relates to conceptions of consumer sovereignty. Alan Peacock has argued that the central premise of consumer sovereignty, and the linchpin of welfare economics, is that the individual is presumed to be the best judge of his or her own interests.[45] Not only is this principle crucial to the functioning of the economy as a whole, it is linked to a faith in individual judgement and acts as an endorsement of individual free will. However, a questioning of individual preferences is implicit in the merit goods argument. In some cases, these preferences are challenged on the grounds that people do not know what is good for them, while in others, consumers are presumed to have poor, but alterable, tastes.[46] In all cases, however, the merit goods argument entails that someone must be allowed to judge what has merit. Following Austen-Smith, Globerman has argued that 'if there is no consensus within society on what constitutes "the good society" with a high degree of arts activity, then the argument can be reduced to a claim that some tastes are "better" than others'.[47]

In this understanding, the merit goods justification would only be valid if it could be shown that it is supported by the majority of the population. Many surveys have been conducted in an attempt to substantiate the merit goods case. Ironically, however, even if it were the case that the majority agreed with state support for cultural activities, then the merit goods argument would reduce to a case of market failure and the question would become how to encourage the market to reflect the desires of these consumers. Even so, as Schuster argues, 'the strong [economic] argument essentially *requires* as its first step a determination that the arts are a merit good. ... But it is impossible to imagine this argument being made in solely economic terms; and so, from an economic perspective, the first link in the argument may also be the weakest.'[48]

The discussion above has focused on the question of the circumstances in which government may intervene in the free market. In market terms, however, as was noted above, a description of 'good' policy must go further, to show also how such intervention should be undertaken and to what magnitude. There are many debates, particularly within welfare economics, but also within cultural economics, about the efficiency of subsidies as opposed to tax breaks, or tariffs, and about the appropriate extent of government support.[49] These latter arguments reinforce the measurable welfare criteria for 'good' policy described above. However, the terms of the cultural policy debate for market-based approaches are, in the first place, defined by the question of whether government should intervene and so this has been the primary focus of this section.

From the above arguments, it should be clear that for market-based approaches, 'good' policy for culture is defined primarily by whether it will promote consumer welfare, defined in measurable, if not strictly economic terms. Differences exist between proponents of the market-based approach as to whether or not government intervention in cultural markets can be justified. Moreover, even though they rely on the same conceptual apparatus, different analysts come to different conclusions about the allocative and distributional effects of the same policies.

Community-based approaches

Community-based approaches to cultural policy all begin from the premise that cultural activity fulfils important social functions. They stress the benefits to the community of cultural production by, for, and representing that community. In turn, the good of the community, broadly defined, is the ultimate justification for cultural policy. Beyond this premise, however, there are many differences between community-based approaches, not least in their assessments of what constitutes the community and what constitutes the 'good', not to mention how this good can be promoted. The parameters of these debates will become clear in the following sections.

Conception of culture

There is little disagreement within community-based approaches about the definition of culture to be applied. Proponents of community-based approaches do not deny the validity of the market-based understanding of culture as an industry. However, for community-based approaches, this is only one of several aspects of culture. All community-based approaches also see culture as an artistic process, while many go even further, understanding culture as the way of life of a people.

All proponents of community-based approaches see culture as a process of artistic creation. However, this creation is not understood as autonomous individual production. Instead, it is perceived to be inseparable from its social context. Cultural products, in this sense, are responses to the artist's interaction with the social and material reality around him. The process of cultural creation and the cultural artefact which results serve to give meaning to this reality, both for the artist and for society at large. In this sense, for all community-based approaches, cultural artefacts are the result of an individual and social process of meaning creation; they arise out of and reflect the community from which they emanate.

Most proponents of community-based approaches to culture also make a further step in their understanding of the term. They argue that culture must be also understood as a 'way of life' of a particular people. Moreover, for these community-based approaches, all of the meanings of the term 'culture' – as industry, as artistic process, and as a way of life – are inextricably linked. In other words, they see cultural goods as manifest forms of cultural expression, inescapably bound up with their broader cultural origins. Culture, as Bernard Ostry has famously put it,

> is central to everything we do and think. It is what we do and the reason why we do it, what we wish and why we imagine it, what we perceive and how we express it, how we live and in what manner we approach death. It is our environment and the patterns of our adaptation to it. It is the world we have created and are still creating;

it is the way we see that world and the motives that urge us to change it. It is the way we know ourselves and each other; it is our web of personal relationships, it is the images and abstractions that allow us to live together in communities and nations. It is the element in which we live.[50]

For community-based approaches, then, culture is much more than an undifferentiated commodity. At the very least, it is a representation of a community; potentially, it is an integral element in the very constitution of the community. In either case, culture is a much broader (and more complicated) concept than it is for market-based approaches.

Criteria for good policy

In general, for all community-based approaches, 'good' policy is that which contributes to the good life of the community. Within this broad school, differences arise over the definition of community and over the primary dimensions through which culture can be seen to contribute to the good of the community. Six different aspects of community are highlighted in the literature: identity, unity, sovereignty, prosperity, democracy, and artistic fulfilment. Obviously, these themes overlap quite substantially, especially as they are all, in one respect or another, tied to the preservation and enhancement of the community. Nonetheless, each of them stresses a different element of the relationship of culture to the good life and each embodies a different conception of the community.

(i) Identity

The conception that cultural activity is crucial for the development and maintenance of community identity is very popular, whether such identity is presumed to be based around the nation, the state, the ethnic group, the region, or any other collectivity. Most of the arguments dealing with culture focus on the nation as the primary locus of cultural identity. The work of A.W. Johnson, for example, emphasises the connection between culture, cultural products, and national identity. He defines culture broadly, as 'the whole complex of knowledge and beliefs and attitudes and practices which are embodied in the society, and in its social, political and economic arrangements'.[51] In this definition, he refers to society generally, but it soon becomes clear that his primary point of reference is specifically the nation. For example, Johnson draws a connection between culture and cultural industries in specifically national terms: '[t]he cultural industries are simply the vehicles by which the *expressions* of a nation's culture are "published" '.[52] Moreover, he argues that the appreciation of the quality of a work stems, in part, from an understanding of the cultural roots of that work. These roots, for Johnson, are nationally based. Because members of a certain group will necessarily have a greater appreciation of the value of their own cultural expressions, national ownership is crucial to the survival of national culture and therefore national identity. Discussing the Canadian case, he comments that '[t]here is, in short, such as thing as an intrinsically Canadian work, and it should, as a generalization, be judged by Canadians'.[53] Thus, Johnson argues that culture is rooted in and reflects the natural and social realities faced by the nation. Moreover, if culture is taken to include values and beliefs, as Johnson intends, then it is clearly a defining element of national identity. 'Good' policy is therefore that which supports culture and, hence, buttresses national identity.

Similarly, Allan Smith focuses on the importance of national self-knowledge in linking cultural policy to nationalist ideas. In particular, he relies on the idea that the state, as a national community, is 'held together by the ability of its people to communicate with and understand one another'.[54] Moreover, he argues that contact with one's own culture is a 'normal attribute of national life' and it 'makes life in definable and self-conscious communities possible'.[55] In this context, he shows how the ideas of romantic nationalism, including the connection between culture and nation, have underlain many cultural policies. He argues that a proliferation of cultural activity can be 'stimulated by the seriousness with which cultural producers viewed the need to equip their new national society with what they saw as a key attribute of national life', namely an indigenous national culture with a consciousness of its own.[56] In this sense, Smith argues that a culturally interventionist policy is essential for the development of national identity. Since Smith places a high value on national identity for the good life of the community, then this cultural policy provides an example of 'good' policy.

Ostry, too, has a very definite understanding of the relationship between culture and national identity. At the heart of Ostry's understanding of culture is its basis in human imagination. In this context, he argues that '[i]t is with the eye of imagination that we perceive [the nation], and perceive it as belonging to us and ourselves as belonging to it'.[57] In this sense, it is culture which provides the 'image of the nation' by demonstrating the 'best that has been thought and felt and imagined by its artists and writers, its scientists and historians' and by turning the territory of the nation into an emotional symbol.[58] Moreover, it is culture which highlights the common history and destiny of a people and thereby allows them to 'connect' and to understand the 'things we cherish in common'.[59]

However, for Ostry, culture goes further than simply representing a national identity to the people. First, culture is more than just a finished work – it is an active and ongoing process. As a result, all of the members of the nation may potentially be agents in their own cultural development. Thus, allowing for the importance of culture means also 'giving a society the ability to create its own life and environment'.[60] Second, however, cultural participation plays the role of critic in society, challenging people's views and continuing 'to feed the sources of change'.[61] In other words, culture not only reflects a nation, but it also creates and continuously recreates it. Thus, policy which supports cultural activity is 'good' policy.

Finally, several authors are notable because they include non-national identities in their analysis. Paul Audley, for example, focuses on the relationship between culture and identity, though his conception is broadened to include identities beyond the national. In relationship to national identity, he stresses the role played by culture in recreating and keeping alive the past experiences of the nation. He argues that '[c]ommunities and nations whose past is not reflected in publications, broadcast programs, films, and video and audio productions are as handicapped as individuals afflicted with amnesia'.[62] Indeed, for Audley, the principles outlined in this section also apply to describe the role culture plays in promoting other, non-national identities. He does not spend much time developing this strand of argument, although he does cite government publications which discuss the way in which broadcasting reflects who we are and thereby contributes to national, regional, and local identities.[63]

Abraham Rotstein makes similar points when he discusses community or social identity. For him, culture can be understood as a 'domain of discourse that links seemingly autonomous individuals into a coherent and living entity, that is, a society cognizant of its past and in control of its future'.[64] Culture, in this sense, comprises many social activities, but at its broadest, is a language which provides unity and coherence to a society, '[i]t is the essential binding feature without which any semblance of orderly discourse and interaction would disappear'.[65] In this sense, it is the framework through which people are shaped but also in which they come to recognise themselves. Without culture, there could be no common identity, whether national or non-national, and, in the words of Raymond Breton, 'individuals feel like social strangers'.[66]

Whether the identity under discussion is national, regional, or local, all of the above commentators agree that identity is essential to the 'good' life of the community. They also agree that culture is an essential element in the formulation and contestation of identities. 'Good' policy, in this context, is one which supports the development of culture towards these goals.

(ii) Unity

National unity has appeared often as a concern of cultural policy. It has appeared most explicitly in the Canadian policy arena – no doubt in part because of the salience of questions about independence for Quebec. Owing to the significant and explicit discussions of unity in the Canadian case, this will be used as an example of the types of discussions present in many sites of cultural policy debate. On this basis, a few observations can be made about the relationship between culture and national unity.

The first way in which culture can contribute to the goal of national unity can be found in the work of those scholars who emphasise the uniqueness of Canada's political culture, especially as it compares with the United States. They argue that specifically Canadian political institutions are a reflection of national needs and interests as well as an important factor in the development of a distinctive Canadian sense of self.[67] In this context, it is argued that a tradition of state intervention to build an East to West oriented economy as well as a national communications and transportation network has been crucial to the creation of a Canadian nation from such a vast territory and disparate population. Public cultural institutions have also been crucial in this regard. Moreover, state intervention has created national social programmes whereby society as a whole takes responsibility for the health and welfare of even the poorest. Finally, government intervention has ensured a net shift of income from the most prosperous regions and provinces to the most needy. All of these actions, it is argued, are seen as justifiable interventions by government into the private sphere and the values which underlie them are seen as reflections of a distinct Canadian political culture. Moreover, all of these actions contribute to the maintenance of the Canadian federation. In this sense, the promotion of culture is crucial to national unity, where the nation is understood to be the sum of all the Canadian provinces and territories.

Secondly, culture can contribute to a *sense* of national unity if cultural products are understood as a means to promote a common or even singular vision of Canadian identity. In this understanding, the community is accepted as the state, but there is also an attempt to create a coterminous sense of nationhood. Taken to its extreme, this vision of cultural politics would imply the direction and/or censorship of all cultural activity, so that only an acceptable vision of the nation or community would be available. Because of these connotations, cultural groups are rightly wary of such policies. Moreover, viewed in this extreme way, there is an inevitable conflict between the ideals of cultural diversity and those of national identity or unity in federal cultural policy. Nonetheless, these goals need not be completely incompatible, as we will see below, if any kind of cultural expression by Canadians is accepted as the nationalist premise. Despite all of this, however, there is still room for the argument that culture promotes national unity, whatever the nation, by reminding the nation of its common past and future and by interpreting the natural and social challenges faced by the nation as a commonality of experience.

Despite their differences about what is implied by national unity, commentators who support the above positions all agree that 'good' policy is that which supports culture and therefore contributes to the maintenance of national unity.

(iii) Sovereignty

Some scholars maintain that the primary contribution of culture to the 'good' society is through its role in buttressing and defending the sovereignty of the state. Most often, these arguments refer to sovereignty as the freedom of the people (or their government) to choose what is best for them. In these understandings, the territorial state is clearly the primary embodiment of community.

Franklyn Griffiths makes a connection between culture, sovereignty, and defence, arguing that the defence of sovereignty increasingly requires a vibrant cultural life. Griffiths begins by distinguishing between two types of threats to sovereignty. Type One threats are those which challenge the right of the state to exercise exclusive jurisdiction within a given space. These are traditional military threats. In contrast, Type Two threats are transboundary processes that threaten the quality of life, environment, or government within a country. By way of illustration,

Griffiths describes how processes of economic globalisation are creating new governance issues for all nation-states despite the fact that their territorial integrity remains intact. To a certain extent, this has always been the case. Nonetheless, Griffiths perceives that these threats are now superseding traditional military threats. The result is that conceptions of national defence must be rethought. In so doing, the defence of sovereignty must have as a key element the defence of a national cultural life. As Griffiths writes, 'defence of sovereignty comes down to our ability to nourish the processes that hold us together as a people with purposes and a destiny of our own. ... Defence of sovereignty is, *au fond*, a matter of culture – political culture very much included.'[68] Griffiths clearly draws upon the themes discussed in the previous sections on identity and unity. However, he builds on these to argue for the importance of having a defence policy that includes expenditures for cultural policy in the order of current spending on military security. In this sense, as Griffiths himself argues, '[t]he state of our cultural life becomes a key variable in our security, in our survival as a people with the capacity to decide for ourselves in an interdependent world'.[69]

'Good' policy, in this context, is that which supports culture as a means to the preservation of state sovereignty.

(iv) Prosperity

Since the early 1980s, cultural lobby groups have increasingly tried to demonstrate the economic advantages provided to society by their activities. Essentially, these cultural groups attempt to use the rhetoric of economics to justify state cultural support for the arts. They have emphasised that culture is an industry which employs increasing numbers of people, contributes to GDP, and generates sales and export revenues.[70] These arguments, however, are not based on the free-market premises of neoclassical welfare economics. They are strategic industry-specific claims made in an attempt to secure revenues during a decade where fiscal restraint generally has become the government's 'order of the day'. What is most interesting about these arguments, however, is that they are based on the presumption that the economic policy of governments is oriented towards increasing the wealth of the *nation* (very broadly defined), even if this comes at the expense of a completely free market. In this sense, while the actual arguments may be interpreted as nothing more than self-interested rent-seeking, they betray a perception that governments value national prosperity as an element of the good life of the community.

(v) Democracy

The argument that culture is necessary for any democracy to function effectively is expressed mainly in the work of the cultural development school, although it is implicit in many other analyses, particularly those which focus on high culture. In all cases, the community is perceived to be embodied in the liberal democratic state, while its members are defined by the established norms of citizenship. The argument is set out best by Marc Raboy, Ivan Bernier, Florian Savageau, and Dave Atkinson in their 1994 article.[71] First, however, the work of Matthew Arnold will be discussed.

Arnold's ideas are key to understanding the early roots of the cultural democracy argument. Writing in the late nineteenth century, Arnold sought to defend high culture on the grounds that the values which it naturally produced were essential to the proper functioning of liberal democracy. In particular, he argued that culture provided a 'source of concern for the common good', which would act as an antidote to the more selfish values which Arnold perceived to have accompanied the liberal progress of the nineteenth century. Arnold saw that there was a tendency in Victorian society to confuse 'political liberalism with purposeless freedom, economic liberalism with selfish materialism, and liberal progress with mere technological innovation'.[72] Culture would balance these tendencies and aid democracy by producing a concern for the common good.

This was further reinforced by Arnold's second claim on behalf of culture, namely, that it was intrinsically a force for freedom. This was a liberal humanist conception of freedom which emphasised that man was never truly free until his intellectual, moral, and spiritual qualities were fully developed.[73] Moreover, this was a very elitist conception of freedom, stressing the civilisational and educational virtues of high culture in contrast to the more pluralistic conceptions of culture and freedom emphasised more recently. For Arnold, the importance of culture was not primarily a matter of self-awareness, of communication among the members of society, or of social criticism. His was a defence of high culture and its relevance to a civilised democracy. In particular, the social function of culture was 'the pursuit of our total perfection by means of getting to know, on all the matters which concern us, the best which has been said and thought in the world'.[74] Only with this insight could people be effective citizens of a democracy.

In a more recent context, Raboy et al. contend that government should support cultural activities because these contribute to cultural development, namely, 'the process by which human beings acquire the individual and collective resources necessary to participate in public life'.[75] The goals of cultural policy, in this context, should be oriented towards increasing access to the 'means of cultural production, distribution and consumption' both in absolute terms and also to generate a greater equality of cultural opportunity within society.[76] This vision of culture as an instrument of democratic development is explained and buttressed by a Habermasian concept of the public sphere. In essence, the public sphere comprises 'all types of information, communication, and symbolic exchange – in sum, ... the entire sphere of culture'.[77] The social role of the public sphere is to provide a forum which is 'free, transparent, and accessible to all, where citizens can discuss and be informed about the social and political issues that concern them'.[78] Thus, a focus on culture and specifically a cultural development approach is crucial in that it promotes an enlightened public. Moreover, 'the values it generates constitute the best insurance that basic democratic rights will be exercised intelligently, and that democratic behaviour spreads throughout the society'.[79]

Audley also picks up on the increasing concern of government for the needs of consumers at the expense of the needs of citizens. In particular, he highlights the work of Mark Starowicz. Starowicz defines culture as the aggregate values of the national group, however diverse (and even incompatible) these may be.[80] In this context, Starowicz argues that television is an instrument of the process by which such national culture is continuously being made and remade. Starowicz clearly draws on the arguments linking culture and national identity which were discussed above. Nonetheless, his work has important implications for democracy. In particular, he argues that '[t]elevision has become essential to the maintenance and functioning of any body politic today', in the sense that it is integral to 'the power to set the national agenda in all fields, not just entertainment'.[81] Moreover, he shows how 'foreign' programming does not deal adequately with 'national' realities. He argues that 'our problems and the solutions are not those we are watching on our screens. Our mirror is showing us someone else's reality.'[82] For Audley, this is an issue of democracy. In his words, '[s]ocieties whose current realities are not adequately explored, reflected, debated, and contested through works that are widely available, and create a substantial body of shared knowledge, will increasingly become democratic in name only, with propaganda, social management, and manipulation becoming ever easier'.[83] Notably, for these approaches, good policy furthers democracy, but does not necessarily prioritise national identity.

(vi) Artistic fulfilment

Finally, there is a group of scholars who maintain that culture is good for society because it provides a channel for artistic and creative fulfilment. Often, these arguments are referred to as 'intrinsic' justifications for cultural subsidy, because they argue that it is the intrinsic properties of cultural activity which are valuable, rather than its potential political uses.[84] In one sense, however, this is a false distinction, since most of these 'intrinsic' justifications ultimately justify cultural subsidy in terms external to cultural activity. Nonetheless, in most artistic fulfilment arguments, the external referent is not a political actor, such as the nation or the state. Instead, the external referent is usually society as a whole. Society, in these understandings, is a fairly open-ended concept. It is not necessarily defined by any political, national, or economic criteria (although it may be). At its broadest, it refers to all bonds of human association. Correspondingly, these arguments are inherently sceptical of the potential for government interference in culture in support of political aims. Moreover, they believe that cultural activity, on its own terms, can make a substantial contribution to the good life.

Some of the arguments for the social value of artistic and creative fulfilment are reflected in the arguments for a cultural contribution to democracy. However, there are a few scholars who make the case specifically on the grounds of artistic fulfilment. The most notable example of this argument is probably the 1982 *Report* of the Canadian Federal Cultural Policy Review Committee (the Applebaum–Hébert Committee). The sympathy of this Committee for intrinsic justifications for cultural subsidy was noted in the previous chapter's discussion of merit goods. More specifically, however, the Committee placed priority on a view of 'the manifest value of cultural activity in releasing the creative potential of a society, and in illuminating and enriching the human condition – celebrating its strengths and exposing its frailties'.[85] It argued very vehemently against any attempt to subjugate the arts to political purposes, commenting that '[t]he well-being of society is threatened if the state intrudes into the cultural realm in ways that subordinate the role and purposes of the latter to the role and purposes of government itself'.[86] For the Committee, the prior and most important variable in cultural policy must be the creative artist and, in turn, the relationship between that artist and his audience. This relationship must be facilitated by government, but it must not be subjected to political aims. In order to achieve this, the Committee re-emphasised the government's commitment to 'arm's length' support for cultural activities. The report also argued for the principle of diversity in national cultural experience, including support for increased participation by women and minorities, an increased priority for native peoples, and increased exposure to arts and culture for Canadian youth.

Audley also reflects this concern for the intrinsic social value of artistic activity. Specifically, he argues that 'communities in which talented individuals lack opportunities to create works of the imagination that grow out of their character and knowledge will atrophy – losing vitality, energy and depth of understanding'.[87] For Audley, however, this is only one element of the social importance of culture. The other elements, namely, its national and democratic potential, are mentioned first in his work and take priority throughout his analysis.

From the above discussion, it should by now be clear that for community-based approaches to cultural policy, 'good' policy is that which places the best interests of the community at the forefront. These best interests, and the community in question, differ substantially within the community-based school. Nonetheless, and especially in comparison to market-based approaches, all of the approaches described above have a relatively strong sense of community to which all policy must be addressed if the 'good life' is to be achieved for its members.

Conclusion

This chapter has outlined the basic approaches to cultural policy and highlighted the key points of contestation. While each is concerned with improving human conditions, market- and community-based approaches nonetheless represent two fundamentally different ways of looking at the relationship between the individual, the market, the state, and society. Moreover, each prioritises different values, institutions, and processes in its quest to improve the human lot. In essence, they comprise very different visions of the good life. These visions will be drawn out and interrogated in the following two chapters. In practice, however, it is important to note that these two approaches are not mutually exclusive. In defining any given cultural policy, every government is influenced by concerns both for the community which it represents and for its budgetary restrictions and its relations with other countries. The concluding chapters of the book will examine in greater detail how these approaches have been manifest throughout several decades of discussion between Canada and the United States regarding their mutual trade in periodicals, and also in the development of a pan-European cultural policy.

3
Welfare Economics and the Moral Relevance of Culture

The last chapter set out the framework within which this book will discuss cultural policy. In that chapter, I argued that the central claims being made in the debate about culture can be categorised as market-based and community-based approaches. This chapter and the next will move on to show how these are actually ethical positions, stemming from different conceptions of individual self-understanding, of the location of value in society, and from different visions of the good life and how it can be achieved.

This chapter will focus only on the market-based approach, with particular attention to its ethical premises and implications. In particular, it will discuss the core values of market-based approaches, namely individual well-being and freedom. The chapter will discuss each value in turn, demonstrating that the manner in which market-based approaches deal with culture is flawed in two related ways. First, market-based approaches do not recognise that their values are particular. In other words, they do not acknowledge that their own assertions are culturally grounded and have both moral premises and implications. Because market-based approaches perceive their values to be universally accepted (or at least universally acceptable), they have great difficulty in understanding that cultural particularity may be *morally* significant. Second, and as a result, the conception of social justice suggested by market-based approaches is fundamentally incapable of conceptualising the moral relevance of culture.

Establishing these claims is fairly straightforward for the first value, namely individual well-being. However, the second value, freedom, is so rarely discussed by market-based approaches that much more interpretive work must be done before its importance can be firmly established. As a way of bridging this interpretive gap, the chapter discusses an approach that parallels the claims of market-based approaches, but originates in moral philosophy and highlights the importance of freedom, rather than efficiency, as the core value that sets the limits to state intervention. This approach is drawn out through an examination of the work of F.A. Hayek. The chapter concludes by arguing that even when the moral assumptions of welfare economics are brought to the fore and defended, they remain incapable of consistently conceptualising the moral relevance of culture.

Ethics and economics

An analysis of the literature on ethics and economics reveals several ways in which ethics is considered to be relevant for economics. First, some scholars focus on what constitutes ethical economic practice. This entails asking what morals should govern our personal economic or business transactions.[1] Second, others ask what norms and values are necessary in order for the capitalist economy to function. Analyses in this vein might highlight, for example, the idea that trust is a social and moral precondition for economic life as we know it.[2] Finally, many authors have considered the justice of the outcomes of economic activity. Here, a crucial debate has centred around how we may judge distributions of wealth to be just or unjust.[3]

The enquiry of this chapter touches upon all three approaches, but its central question is somewhat different. Whereas the three examples above concentrate exclusively on norms as they relate to economic *practice*, this chapter will shift the focus of inquiry towards the ethical importance of market-based approaches as *theory* – as a proposal for the ordering of human relations that has considerable influence over our understanding of what is both possible and desirable.[4] The task of this chapter is to make explicit the normative framework relied upon by the market-based approaches set out in Chapter 2 and, moreover, to suggest a way of comprehending why this framework is inadequate as a basis for our understanding of social life. This framework is often not acknowledged by the proponents of market-based approaches, but is nonetheless crucial to the legitimacy and intuitive force of their proposals – perhaps all the more so *because* it is never openly acknowledged and debated.

The obvious moral claim: individual well-being

The objectives and techniques of all types of market-based approaches can be best categorised under the broad heading of neoclassical welfare economics. Indeed, as one commentator has noted, '[m]ost economists look to welfare economics for principles to guide government when it concerns itself with resource allocation'.[5] In essence, welfare economics is defined by the view that the conceptual and analytical tools of neoclassical economics can be applied to determine the desirability of different policy outcomes. More specifically, 'the performance of economic institutions can and should be judged according to whether they provide economic goods in quantities that accord with people's relative desires for those goods'.[6] In this regard, welfare economics is the central framework through which market-based approaches seek to make public policy recommendations. For these two reasons, welfare economics is the focus of ethical argument in this chapter. Moreover, as we will see, it differs substantially from both utilitarian and Keynesian theories.

Broadly speaking, welfare economics evolved out of earlier utilitarian theories.[7] Like utilitarianism, it understands the welfare of society in terms of individuals' subjective senses of satisfaction, and perceives that 'satisfaction is best achieved by letting individuals' preferences determine the use of societal resources'.[8] However, utilitarians and welfare economists differ substantially in their views of the additive properties of individual preferences. Utilitarians seek to maximise the sum of all individual happiness, thereby arriving at an unambiguous societal optimum. Welfare economists, on the other hand, are extremely reluctant to make interpersonal comparisons of utility, claiming that a social summation approach neglects the ethical integrity of the individual and could lead to gross violations of elementary justice.[9]

Refusing to sum individual utilities, many welfare economists instead use a variation on Pareto optimality as the 'bridge' between individual and social welfare. Pareto optimality dictates that '[t]he community becomes better off if one individual becomes better off and none worse off'.[10] However, since most policy options will entail some harm to someone, Pareto conditions are nearly impossible to satisfy. Instead, most welfare economists have come to rely on an alternative standard for judging welfare states. This is referred to as the compensation principle, since it suggests that if the gainers from any policy change could, in principle, compensate the losers, then the policy would be a good one. It is important to note that the winners need not *actually* compensate the losers for the principle to hold. In this regard, the compensation principle is akin to choosing between policies based on their predicted results in overall social surplus creation. It should be noted that although this principle does not require a summation of individual utility functions, it reaches its social conclusions through a summation of individual demand curves.[11]

Welfare economics devotes much attention to judging different economic states according to their efficiency in allocating resources. Except in unusual circumstances, the free market is the best means of ensuring allocative efficiency and it is for this reason that welfare economists support the market so strongly.[12] More specifically, natural market equilibrium, when it does occur, is considered to be a Pareto optimal condition. In cases of disequilibrium, policies are favoured that minimise deadweight loss, or, in other words, that maximise efficiency. Despite the importance of efficiency, however, it alone does not provide the moral vision for welfare economics. In fact, welfare economists do not value efficiency for its own sake. Efficiency is desirable primarily because it contributes to one of the central goals of welfare economics – maximising individual well-being. Well-being, however, is a huge concept, with many different possible meanings. It is by no means uncontroversial. In this light, it is imperative to interrogate the conception of individual well-being espoused by welfare economics.

For welfare economists, the important facts about individual well-being can be summed up by two tenets. First, well-being consists in having one's preferences satisfied. Preferences, in turn, simply represent what the individual wants. The relative strengths of different preferences, or their value to each individual, are understood in terms of what she is willing to pay for something. In turn, then, people's preferences can be revealed by what they choose to buy. Moreover, if they do not buy something at a particular price, then it can be assumed that this good was not valuable enough to them vis-à-vis alternative goods. So strong is this claim that it applies even to those who have no means of purchasing anything. For example, if a starving man had no endowments with which to pay for food, it would be assumed that he did not value this food enough to pay the price offered. In this context, as Neva Goodwin has argued, ' "[u]tility", "satisfaction," and "happiness" are thus identified with the *purchase* of marketed goods and services'.[13]

The second important tenet underpinning individual well-being is that the individual is the best judge of her own interests. This entails that welfare economists refrain from any evaluation of the merits of what people prefer. As Lionel Robbins famously put it, '[e]conomics is not concerned with ends as such. It assumes that human beings have ends. ... The ends may be noble or they may be base. ... Economics takes all ends for granted.'[14] Equally, welfare economists do not place any relevance on an understanding of how preferences are determined. People may prefer a variety of things for a great variety of reasons.

The task of welfare economics is to show how social resources can be marshalled so as to satisfy these preferences.

Owing to their focus on individual well-being and preference satisfaction, welfare economists are often considered to be among the economists most aware of normative concerns. Nonetheless, they consistently refuse to acknowledge their own normative inclinations, vehemently claiming that their approach is morally neutral.[15] Their stated purpose is simply to provide value-free technical information to decision-makers. Clearly, however, the understanding of individual well-being described above is not value free. It is underpinned by certain very particular assumptions about human nature and values, namely individualism, subjectivism, and value commensurability. An exploration of these assumptions helps to explain the particular understanding of human well-being that is endorsed by welfare economics.

This section will first discuss these values, showing how the welfare economists' conception of well-being is a very particular one, before discussing its supposed moral neutrality. Finally, it will discuss how the combination of moral particularity and claims to neutrality act to exclude consideration of the moral relevance of culture. In particular, the discussion below will show how, once adopted, these three assumptions act to preclude an understanding of the relevance of culture in any non-commercial sense.

Individualism

First, it should hardly be contentious to claim that welfare economics is underpinned by a radical individualism. This was evident, above, in the discussion of welfare economists' refusal to aggregate individual welfare functions. Economists do admit the relevance of the social sphere, as is shown by their desire to maximise overall surplus. However, even here, they believe that the social level can only be understood as a function of individual welfares. In this context, even the way that individual and social welfare are related indicates the depth of commitment to individualism. The importance of this methodological individualism is that it leaves no room for a conception of the social which is something more than a function of its individual parts. Most obviously, this means that welfare economists cannot understand that a community or other social group may have welfare needs that are not captured by the revealed preferences of individuals.

More importantly, however, this view does not capture the ways in which the individual's needs, desires, and understanding of himself as an agent (moral or otherwise) are constituted by and through the culture of which he is a part. In other words, it fails to capture the importance of the social in establishing our moral frame of reference. Indeed, the same concerns can also be applied more broadly to enquire into the cultural preconditions of welfare economics' conception of the individual. In the words of Charles Taylor, 'the free individual of the West is only what he is by virtue of the whole society and civilization which brought him to be and which nourishes him; that our families can only form us up to this capacity because they are set in this civilization'.[16] To be fair, economists have always recognised that their conception of the person is an unrealistic abstraction.[17] In spite of this, it has consistently been supported because of its usefulness as a foundation for theories that would make 'useful and meaningful predictions'[18] and, less overtly, because of its perceived centrality for freedom. As this section will continue to show, however, one's starting assumptions have important implications for the limits of the possible in the theories which they support. The following section will address the relationship between individualism and liberal freedom.

Subjectivism

Second, there is the assumption that individual preferences are given. Economists would not deny that different individuals may have different motivations, including moral ones, for making certain choices. However, in order to accommodate ethical motivations, welfare economics must characterise them as having been the self-interested choice of the individual. Coupled with the claim that each individual knows what he wants (and therefore what is good for him), this assumption resonates with our intuitive sense of the importance of individual freedom and so provides a very powerful justification for non-interference in the market. The importance of freedom in legitimating the market will be discussed in the following section. First, however, this subsection will address the claim that preferences are given. In particular, this claim is by no means morally neutral or uncontroversial. In terms of understanding culture, it is especially problematic for several reasons.

In the first place, this claim relies upon a very strong moral subjectivism. It assumes that since there is no objective way of supporting any one judgement as against any other, preferences must be seen as equally valid. *Within* the framework adopted by welfare economics, such subjectivism is clearly important. After all, observation which purports to be scientific must also be objective. More specifically, welfare economics sees its task as helping individuals to fulfil their wants, whatever these may be. Radical individualism, then, demands neutrality between values. However, it will become clear below that, in this case, subjectivism is only plausible because it is located within a theory that has *already accepted* a certain framework of values as given. In other words, the deeper moral issues (and questions about the good life) have already been resolved by the existing framework. The semblance of subjectivism has important ramifications for culture that cannot adequately be drawn out until freedom is discussed in the following section.

Second, as Russell Keat has argued, this approach assimilates ethical choices to well-being choices. As a result, it fails to capture the possibility that ethical choices may have dimensions and ramifications that cannot be understood as choices about consumption preferences. Even more starkly, this approach cannot understand that people might make ethical choices that actually conflict with their preferences or well-being. Indeed, making an ethical choice may not in fact reflect 'what the person concerned wishes to achieve for his or her own well-being'.[19] In this sense, the analysis of human behaviour which results from conflating ethical and well-being choices will simply not be able to conceptualise a whole range of *reasons* for human action. Broadly understood, the reasons for action are clearly relevant since it is these which give the action meaning, which characterise it in a particular society as a certain type of action with a certain intent and significance. In this respect, welfare economists are clearly ill-equipped to understand the ways in which culture may itself provide much of the meaning behind certain reasons. Indeed, in this sense, welfare economics cannot understand that culture may be morally relevant.

This argument can be taken even further. In particular, it is only within the context of social interaction that we can understand certain actions as self-interested. As Taylor has pointed out, the individual and subjectivist approach taken by welfare economics cannot understand that 'all acts and choices ... are ... only the acts and choices they are against the background of practices and understandings'.[20] Once this is accepted, the cultural background of all action is brought forward and it becomes very difficult to maintain a full ethical subjectivism. After all, if social understandings give acts meaning as self-interested, rational, or charitable, then they also unavoidably bestow culturally informed judgements about the goodness or badness of these actions. If nothing else, the introduction of cultural concerns forces us to recognise that no action (economic or otherwise) takes place outside of a moral context.

Valuations

Finally, welfare economics entails particular claims about *how* individuals value things. Indeed, the value of something to an individual can only be understood in terms of what he would be prepared to trade off for it. Indeed, rarely do welfare economists understand that the way in which we value things may be radically at odds with a question about how much we would pay for them. In this sense, as Amartya Sen, among others, has noted about mainstream welfare economics, '[n]ot only is there a unified and complete view of ethical goodness (weighing the different objects of value vis-à-vis each other), but even the objects of value must be all of the same type'.[21] As we will see below, the implications of this for culture are important.

Most particularly, welfare economics is poorly equipped to describe intrinsic value or social value, not to mention the connection between them. As John Foster has argued, to see something 'as mattering in itself is to yield to a kind of involvement in value – or better, a kind of involvement in the world *through* value – to which the comparative and arbitrative posture that goes with optimising is profoundly alien'.[22] Many commentators have noted that such values as friendship, honesty, and love are actually stripped of their value if we could imagine placing a fixed money price on them.[23] The argument here is not the simple one that some things cannot be bought, but rather that our lives are comprised of an extensive diversity of values which cannot be indexed to the same scale. Indeed, it is even possible that 'goods are plural in that the authentic evaluative standards they meet are fundamentally diverse'.[24] In this context, where economists are apt to argue that in making decisions, we do in fact rank our preferences (and so our values),[25] critics claim that we make decisions through a process of weighing which need not entail any commensurability between values at all.[26]

Moreover, once the individualism and subjectivism of welfare economics are taken into account, it is clear that economists have no means of understanding that some values may be irreducibly social. As Taylor has argued, welfare economics understands that things 'are goods to the extent that people desire them'.[27] What they neglect is that 'these things can only be good in that certain way, or satisfying or positive after their particular fashion, because of the background understanding developed in our culture'.[28] Or, as Elizabeth Anderson has claimed, 'I am capable of valuing something in a particular way only in a social setting that upholds norms for that mode of valuation.'[29]

Clearly, welfare economists rely upon a very particular conception of social justice. As we have seen, they understand social justice as a Pareto optimisation of individual well-being. Short of this, a good outcome is realised by a maximisation of total surplus and therefore a maximisation of efficiency. This vision is radically individualist. It is also subjectivist in the sense that it recognises no source of value beyond the revealed preferences of individuals. Its resulting conception of value is poorly equipped to understand the importance of the intrinsic or social worth of things. In this context, it is not a coincidence that market-based approaches conceptualise culture as a good, whose value to people can be determined by their consumption choices.

What is clear from the above discussion is that welfare economics *is* based on some very particular value judgements. It may be even-handed in its considerations, but, as a theory, it is definitely not morally neutral. Given this highly particular ethical stance, it is important to question the implications of the claim that welfare economics is morally neutral. In making this claim, welfare economists essentially mean that they do not wish to judge the goodness or badness of different ends. It is not the case that the economist is denying that he has ethical views or principles. Instead, a position of moral neutrality implies that the economist does not bring these views to bear on his analysis. Indeed, the welfare economist perceives himself to be the neutral observer of the social world. To be fair, this is actually quite possible in one respect. As was discussed above, welfare economists are very strict in taking individual preferences as given. Revealed preferences, and never the economist's own feelings, are the basis of value in such an analysis.

To understand, however, why such an analysis cannot be *consistently* considered morally neutral, it is helpful to refer to Robert Cox's often repeated distinction between problem-solving and critical theory.[30] In this regard, welfare economics provides an excellent example of problem-solving theory. In Cox's words, such theory 'takes the world as it finds it, with the prevailing social and power relationships ... as the given framework for action'. Within this context, problem-solving theory aims 'to make these relationships and institutions work smoothly by dealing effectively with particular sources of trouble'.[31] In the case of welfare economics, the goal is to ease allocation problems and therefore facilitate the smooth functioning of the economy. The strengths of this type of theory lie in its ability to achieve analytically precise solutions to particular problems. Furthermore, the moral subjectivism of welfare economics is often seen to be a strength. However, as Cox has argued, these strengths rest upon false premises. In particular, problem-solving theories assume that the social world is a fixed object that can fruitfully be studied without ideological bias. Indeed, as many commentators have noted, it is indeed possible to study the social world from a scientific, objective point of view, but the results may not be very fruitful, in terms of either understanding or emancipation.[32] Welfare economists may concede this point, but respond that problem-solving theory actually offers concrete solutions to problems which require imminent action. This is no doubt true, but it does not obviate the need for sustained consideration of the premises upon which problem-solving theory is based and the principles which it promotes.

In this regard, adopting a scientific approach to social science creates a very specific set of circumstances with regard to moral neutrality. In Cox's words, problem-solving theory 'is methodologically value-free insofar as it treats the variables it considers as objects; but it is value-bound by virtue of the fact that it implicitly accepts the prevailing order as its own framework'.[33] In other words, the practices of welfare economists *can* be considered morally neutral, but only *within* the context of a very particular framework of values and understandings. In unquestioningly accepting this as their framework of analysis, welfare economists betray their claims to moral neutrality.

In this regard, welfare economists clearly do not acknowledge that their analysis presupposes and perpetuates certain very particular values. Indeed, by not recognising that their position is actually a normative one, these approaches keep their moral agenda well buried, operating from the assumption that their values are generally acceptable. Indeed, as two renegade economists have noted, welfare economics is presumed to be a positivist discipline precisely because it rests on 'innocuous and uncontroversial moral premises'.[34] Denying that their premises are both normative and particular has several important effects.

First, because it assumes that it is morally neutral, welfare economics does not recognise that it is promoting a very particular conception of social justice. More importantly, however, welfare economists fail to recognise that their values ought to be justified vis-à-vis others. As a result, they fail to adequately justify their vision of social justice.[35]

Second, welfare economists also cannot understand that even their 'morally neutral' analysis promotes certain values and delegitimises others. Indeed, as we have seen in the previous chapter, market-based approaches consistently act to delegitimise the value claims of community-based approaches. They interpret the claims of community-based approaches from the context of their own moral paradigm, with the result that an impetus founded on cultural values is read exclusively as a protectionist and anti-competitive measure. Indeed, as will become even clearer below, welfare economics is ill-equipped to recognise that cultural particularity may go beyond a lifestyle choice, and may go to the heart of the principles of the system itself. In other words, the presumption of moral neutrality coupled with a particular underlying framework of values means that welfare economics cannot recognise culture as morally relevant in any way beyond individual choice.

It is clear from the above discussion that, far from being neutral, welfare economics is motivated by some very strong moral impulses. The claim that culture is only relevant in so far as people choose to consume it is buttressed by a significant and highly contestable moral foundation. It begins from an assumption about the relevance of culture for individual values that neglects significant aspects of our human and moral experience. Moreover, the fully developed picture generated by welfare economics is itself supported and legitimised by particular cultural values and practices. Bringing these two dimensions of culture to the fore requires us to acknowledge that welfare economics is not the neutral, 'scientific' paradigm that it claims to be. This is not to suggest that economic efficiency or utilitarian 'well-being' are irrelevant. Rather, they represent a very particular set of ends that are as contestable as any others. The unquestioning acceptance of these values creates some problems within the confines of pure economic theory.[36] However, when welfare economics is introduced through IPE as the legitimating standard for political action, as it is in the market-based approach to cultural policy, the issue becomes far more serious.

The prior moral premise: individual freedom

The concept of individual well-being set out above is clearly crucial to the concept of social justice espoused by welfare economics. However, the reader may have noted that it is not the only value at work in the claims of welfare economists. In particular, it is very difficult to make sense of and justify their explicit ethical vision (maximising individual well-being) without reference to the importance of individual freedom. Surprisingly, however, welfare economists make few direct references to freedom – they do not define what they mean by freedom, nor do they offer a justification of its central place in their work. This makes its role a particularly difficult one to understand. Nonetheless, the centrality of freedom, if not its precise content, can be highlighted by re-examining the treatment of individual preferences in welfare economics. Once the

importance of freedom has been demonstrated, we will discuss different means by which its precise content might be detected.

As the previous section discussed, welfare economists view individual preferences as having several characteristics. Most importantly, they are radically individual, they are morally subjective, and they are measurable along a single indexed scale of value. In other words, the individual is considered to be the best judge of his own interests, and no one else ought to be entitled to judge for him. Moreover, we can understand his preferences and the value of things to him by examining the choices he makes – what and how much he is willing to sacrifice of one thing in order to get more of another.

However, welfare economists consistently fail to explain and justify why we ought to view the individual as a radically separate unit and why his preferences must be treated as inalterable. Clearly, individualism and subjectivism are instrumentally important in achieving individual well-being. However, there is much more than this simple instrumental justification going on here. Indeed, the rhetorical power of individualism and subjectivism is hardly exhausted by the observation that they contribute to well-being. Without any greater sense of the importance of individualism and subjectivism, the argument remains a very weak one. Not only does it reveal very little about the substance of well-being but, alone, it gives us no firm reasons to desire it. To understand why well-being is valuable, we must be shown why individualism and subjectivism are themselves so important. This justification cannot come from their role in buttressing well-being; it must come from elsewhere.

The most obvious ethical source of these claims is individual freedom. Although this is not made explicit in welfare economics, it is clearly a value that must be accepted if we are to make sense of the normative bases of this branch of economics.[37] Ironically, the most obvious example of the role of freedom arises if one attempts to *disagree* with welfare economists' claims about individual preferences. As was noted in the discussion of merit goods in Chapter 2, any attempt to challenge the supremacy of the dictates of consumer sovereignty is met with great suspicion. Questioning whether the consumer is always right or querying the method of revealed preferences is tantamount to endorsing government coercion. If the individual is not free to choose, then who will be entitled to choose for him? After all, if one is not the judge of one's own interests, then someone else must be.[38] In this respect, the spectre of coercion, however ill-defined, provides much of the moral impetus behind the individualist, subjectivist claims espoused by welfare economists. Freedom, whatever its precise meaning, is clearly funda-mental in justifying the proposals of welfare economists.

In this respect, our intuitive sense of what freedom means and why it is important 'does the extra work' of substantiation and justification that welfare economics neglects to do. As a result, welfare economists gain great moral force from a premise that they consistently fail either to specify or to justify. Like well-being, freedom is a highly contested concept, whose use might invoke innumerable different meanings, each implying radically different conclusions. In this context, it is crucial to explore the meanings of freedom that could support the moral claims made by welfare economics. What does freedom mean for wel-fare economists? Is this a conception that we would want to endorse? Only in this way, and not through any intuitive sympathy with ill-defined claims, can the legitimacy of market-based approaches be fruitfully assessed.

The section that follows will focus on the work of Hayek. It will rely on his philosophy to draw out an understanding of freedom that accords with a market-based understanding of social relations. It will be careful to demonstrate the ways in which this particular view of freedom is central to the ethics of welfare economics, while being sensitive to important points of difference, where appropriate. In doing so, it is crucial to be sensitive to the fact that Hayek's thought may not always be an accurate reflection of the views of welfare economists. Indeed, we cannot be sure that what follows is a true and complete reflection of what welfare economists *would* say, if they were to address their norma-tive foundations. Nonetheless, we can be sure that it reflects important yet incomplete strands of thought within welfare economics, that it shares with them certain fundamental values, and that it provides important insights into the normative bases of the free market.

Hayek on freedom and the market

Hayek's substantial contributions to law and political economy may be read in many ways, as the diversity of secondary literature attests.[39] This chapter will focus only on the three main works in which he sets out his thoughts on the importance of the free market and its ideal nature, namely *The Road to Serfdom*, *The Constitution of Liberty*, and a short article entitled 'Individualism: True and False'.[40] The argument which follows will advance the claim that Hayek's work in this field, whatever its internal contradictions, can fruitfully be read as an attempt to define and defend a particular conception of liberalism – defined by the free market and the rule of law. To be clear, however, this liberal vision is not especially new. As Hayek himself admits, he is primarily seeking to update and reinvigorate the ideals of the nineteenth-century Whigs.[41] Indeed, it will soon become apparent that his vision of freedom owes much to their influence.

In particular, one of Hayek's main purposes is to illustrate the nature and value of freedom and the central importance of a market economy to the achievement of freedom. In this regard, he articulates the vision of freedom that market-based approaches take for granted. Further, he draws on the subjectivism within market-based approaches to develop a justification of freedom on seemingly non-universalist grounds. This approach not only provides a powerful argument for freedom, but it does so in a way that seems to leave room for culture.

Hayek's liberal ideal

Hayek devotes a great deal of attention to his conception of liberty. He defines it as 'that condition of men in which coercion of some by others is reduced as much as possible in society'.[42] Clearly, this is a negative conception of freedom, and, as Hayek acknowledges, it depends significantly on what is meant by coercion. In his view, '[c]oercion occurs when one man's actions are made to serve another man's will, not for his own but for the other's purpose'.[43] Coercion need not mean that a man is deprived of all choice, but merely that his choices have been manipulated to serve someone else's will. Crucially, in order for coercion to occur, the manipulation of a man's choices must entail both a threat of harm and an intention to bring about certain conduct. As a result, not every harm that befalls someone can be attributed to coercion. Where harm is not caused by coercion, society need not take responsibility for rectifying that harm. Hence the reverse claim about freedom – to be free is not necessarily to be protected from all harm, but only from those acts which aim to make one the instrument of someone else's will.[44]

For Hayek, freedom is best protected by a particular set of rules and institutions that he defines as liberal civilisation. The two main buttresses of liberal civilisation are the free market and the rule of law. Together, these institutions serve to protect freedom, while also ensuring the maximum rate of social progress. The relationship between freedom and the free market will be addressed immediately below. Subsequently, this chapter will discuss the way in which the rule of law provides the essential framework for the free market.

Liberty and the market

The free market and liberty are linked in Hayek's thought in two important ways. In both cases, the significance of liberty acts to legitimise the market, though in different ways. First, the free market gains normative force because it is essential to the *preservation* of liberty. Hayek builds his argument for liberty on the simple premise that '[t]he sum of the knowledge of all the individuals exists nowhere as an integrated whole'. As a result, 'the great problem is how we can all profit from this knowledge, which exists only dispersed as the separate, partial, and sometimes conflicting beliefs of all men'.[45] Liberal civilisation, and especially the free market, provides the solution to this problem. By allowing each individual to freely pursue his ends and act upon his particular knowledge, within a general agreement on the 'rules of the game', a free society can make the most of existing knowledge. This is so for two reasons. First, a free society allows individuals to make the most of their own individual and particular knowledges. Since no one else may have the same knowledge, no one else could be in a better position to decide on action. As Hayek comments, 'there can be no doubt that the discovery of a better use of things or of one's own capacities is one of the greatest contributions that an individual can make in our society'.[46] The free market is crucial in this regard. It is through the market's adjustment system that individuals receive knowledge crucial to their decision-making. Moreover, as a result of the market's adjustment mechanism all individuals can act on their own knowledge and yet society can remain orderly. As Hayek stresses, '[a] free system can adapt itself to almost any set of data, almost any general prohibition or regulation, so long as the adjustment mechanism is kept functioning'.[47]

Second, according to Hayek, the flow of new ideas springs from the sphere in which action and material events impinge upon each other. If free action were to be inhibited, then the flow of new ideas would be drastically reduced, leading, in turn, to a declining rate of progress and civilisational stagnation. For Hayek, new ideas are the driving force of progress and increasing wealth. In his words, '[i]t is through the free gift of knowledge acquired by the experiments of all that general progress is made possible, that the achievements of those who have gone before facilitate the advance of those who follow'.[48] Since we cannot know in advance which ones will be successful, nor which will appeal to future generations, it is crucial that the development of new ideas is unrestricted. According to Hayek, 'the advance and even the preservation of civilization are dependent upon a maximum of opportunity for accidents to happen.

These accidents occur in the combination of knowledge and attitudes, skills and habits, acquired by individual men.'[49] On the basis of these 'accidents', we achieve civilisational progress. This is because groups holding particular ideals compete for social survival. In Hayek's words,

> [w]ithin any given society, particular groups may rise or decline according to the ends they pursue and the standards of conduct that they observe. ... Though there is a presumption that any established social standard contributes in some manner to the preservation of civilization, our only way of confirming this is to ascertain whether it continues to prove itself in competition with other standards, observed by other individuals and groups.[50] Free competition, then, is a defining feature of Hayek's philosophy. Again, it is not difficult to see why the free market, with its competitive, self-adjusting structure, is such a central element of Hayek's work.

Liberty underpins the free market in a second way. In particular, the market is seen to be the *product* of liberty. In Hayek's view, the market arose spontaneously, as the result of free individual action. Unfortunately, he devotes little attention to a substantiation of this claim. On the two occasions where it is discussed in detail, Hayek merely asserts this claim and provides no historical evidence.[51] Nonetheless, for Hayek's argument to stand, the idea of a spontaneous market order *must* be true, regardless of the historical record. After all, according to Hayek, a social order that does not arise spontaneously must arise as the result of someone's rational design, and a planned order cannot but be coercive.[52] Furthermore, although Hayek claims that spontaneous order may erupt in any area of life,[53] the free market is the only sphere in which he can convincingly claim that spontaneous order has *actually* arisen. If the spontaneous development of the free market were to be challenged, then Hayek would have little basis upon which to argue that a spontaneous order would be possible at all. This would seriously limit the important normative claims established above. More importantly, however, the supposed spontaneous development of the free market provides a great deal of its normative force. The fact that the free market arose without planning or coercion provides a crucial element of its legitimacy. It also buttresses the claim that we should not presume to have enough knowledge to successfully amend or replace it. Thus, it is crucial to Hayek's argument that the free market developed as a result of free and spontaneous human action. The market is, for Hayek, the epitome of free social relations and its normative status is largely established on this basis.

The importance of the free market for freedom is further illustrated by Hayek's comments on the dangers of economic planning. According to him, competition is hindered by any attempt to control prices and quantities of particular commodities. He does admit that competition 'can bear some admixture of regulation', but argues that 'it cannot be combined with planning to any extent we like without ceasing to operate as an effective guide to production'.[54] Acceptable forms of planning include acquiring facts of general importance, providing a monetary system, setting weights and measures, surveying, census-taking, providing support for education, and in some limited circumstances, offering social security.[55] Hayek is also willing to support an extensive system of taxation, as long as it is proportional, rather than progressive.[56] Paralleling the claims of some welfare economists, Hayek argues that beyond these limits, however, government intervention is necessarily detrimental. More importantly, Hayek is convinced that a little planning always generates the need for more: 'the close interdependence of all economic phenomena makes it difficult to stop planning just where we wish. ... [O]nce the free working of the market is impeded beyond a certain degree, the planner will be forced to extend his controls until they become all-comprehensive.'[57] Finally, if economic activity is directed by government, then government will also be forced to decide on principles guiding its actions. Since no single principle will be agreeable to all, the powerful will be forced to use coercion and propaganda to stay on top. The details of how this breakdown is likely to occur are not especially relevant here. What is important is that, in Hayek's view, the consequences of departing from nearly free competition are nothing short of disastrous for freedom. There is no middle ground between Hayek's ideal of competitive capitalism and totalitarianism. Once we impair the free market in any way that Hayek does not condone, we are on the slippery slope to totalitarianism.

It is important to highlight the point that Hayek's justification of liberty does not rest on any assumed agreement about man's natural capacities or predispositions, nor does he require the type of social or pre-social agreement demanded by social contract theory. Instead, Hayek's case for freedom is grounded in an observation about the scope of man's knowledge and the limits of human reason. Hayek states this clearly: '[i]f we were omniscient men, if we could know not only all that affects the attainment of our present wishes but also our future wants and desires, there would be little case for liberty.'[58] The parallels between this claim and the comments made by welfare economists about individual preferences are striking. Indeed, for both Hayek and welfare economists, their final defence against critics is always the subjectivist one – that we cannot *know* what other people desire or what is good for society.

The argument above has shown the importance of the free market for Hayek's vision of freedom. Moreover, it has shown that Hayek has in mind a particular conception of the free market, with few deviations allowed. Hayek's free market is both the product and embodiment of freedom, and is the driving force of progress. In fact, so closely are freedom and the free market related that one must question whether a free society could continue to be free in any other form. This question and the implications it raises for the non-universality of Hayek's liberalism will be raised in due course. Immediately, however, we must turn our attention to the other pillar of Hayek's free society, the rule of law.

The rule of law

Hayek is careful to distinguish his liberalism from pure laissez-faire. While he clearly places great weight on the value of competition, he does not advocate a competitive free-for-all. As he claims, '[t]he liberal argument is in favor of making the best possible use of the forces of competition as a means of coordinating human efforts. ... It is based on the conviction that, where effective competition can be *created*, it is a better way of guiding individual efforts than any other.'[59] As a result, the liberal free market is meaningless without the rule of law. The rule of law both defines and embodies all the claims about freedom made above – it sets limits to coercion and thereby defines and protects the space for individual free action. Correspondingly, it provides the framework for the free market. As Hayek himself states, '[f]reedom of economic activity [means] freedom under the law, not the absence of all government action. ... [I]nterference or intervention ... [means] only the infringement of that private sphere which the general rules of law were intended to protect.'[60]

According to Hayek, the preservation of liberty entails that each person be assured of a delimited private sphere. Within this realm, the individual can be sure that his actions are safe from the coercive acts of others, including the government. But if the government may itself be tempted to coerce individuals, then how is the private sphere protected? According to Hayek, the private sphere can only be properly protected, and freedom assured, if government and all citizens are subject to a series of general rules. The first function of these rules is to set down 'the conditions under which objects or circumstances become part of the protected sphere of...persons'.[61] Here, Hayek is clearly referring to the establishment of private property, though there may be other relevant examples. More generally, however, these rules establish when and how the protected sphere of individuals may be breached.[62] In other words, general laws constitute a general doctrine on what particular laws are admissible. In order to achieve this, however, general rules must conform to three criteria. They must be general and abstract, in the sense that they set down general principles, rather than specific dictates. Second, they must be known and certain in the sense that they provide a predictable framework within which individuals may exercise choices. Third, laws must apply to all people equally, including lawmakers.[63] In this way, the rule of law provides a framework within which individual action may be free. In Hayek's words, '[i]n observing such rules, we do not serve another person's end. My action can hardly be regarded as subject to the will of another person if I use his rules for my own purposes as I might use my knowledge of a law of nature.'[64]

Hayek is aware that if the rule of law is to act as a safeguard against coercion by governments, it must be anchored securely beyond the easy reach of the lawmakers of the day. In this light, he sets out two related sources of the rule of law. The first, and most obvious, source is the constitution. Here, Hayek envisages that general rules will be set down by a representative 'constitutional convention'. Apart from conforming to the criteria set out above, these laws will be designed to endure for a very long period, and any modifications to them must require a very lengthy procedure.[65] But, according to Hayek, the principles behind any constitution do not merely come from the minds of the drafters. If a constitution is to be effective, it must recognise and embody the second source of general laws, namely the tacit rules which regulate conduct in any society. In Hayek's words, 'even constitutions are based on, or presuppose, an underlying agreement on more fundamental principles – principles which may never have been explicitly expressed, yet which make possible and precede the consent and the written fundamental laws'.[66] Moreover, the rule of law 'will be effective only in so far as the legislator feels bound by it. In a democracy this means that it will not prevail unless it forms part of the moral tradition of the community, a common ideal shared and unquestioningly accepted.'[67]

In this way, the rule of law provides the essential framework within which freedom can be guaranteed. Moreover, in making this claim, Hayek articulates the underlying assumption made by welfare economists that the free market be underpinned by 'rules of the game'. All agree that without minimal guarantees, such as those elucidated by Hayek, the free market could not provide spontaneous order, nor could it assure freedom. The rule of law therefore is an essential element of liberal civilisation. Without it, neither society nor the market could maintain any meaningful form of freedom.

The free market, liberty, and culture

As this chapter has already noted, one of the chief advantages of Hayek's interpretation of freedom is its basis in epistemological uncertainty.[68] Since Hayek avoids grounding his liberalism in universal values or a prior social contract, he seems to evade the charges of universalism that have been made against other liberal approaches.[69] If any liberal argument linking freedom and the free market can accommodate particularisms, Hayek's ought to have a very good chance. Nonetheless, it will become clear below that Hayek's non-universalist justification is not as open-ended as it seems. In order for freedom to legitimise the free market vis-à-vis other forms of social organisation, a very particular definition of freedom must be adopted. The particularities of this conception will first be drawn out. Second, it will be shown that Hayek refuses to see this as a particular, culturally imbued understanding of freedom. As a result, it will emerge that this concept of freedom is actually *incapable* of accommodating considerations of culture that might challenge the liberal ideal. Subsequently, Hayek's vision of social justice through the free market is fundamentally unable to conceptualise culture as morally relevant.

Freedom

Several observations must first be made about the very particular nature of Hayek's conception of freedom. First, it is a very strict negative conception. In other words, it focuses on eliminating unnecessary coercion and on the importance of non-interference in the individual's private sphere. In this context, it is rooted very firmly in equality before the law. Although Hayek acknowledges that formal equality may not imply material equality, he does not view material equality as necessary for freedom in any way. For Hayek, as was noted above, inequality is actually an essential force for progress. Not surprisingly, then, he understands formal equality to be incompatible with any government action towards material equality. In one sense, this conclusion is not altogether unreasonable. Indeed, it would strike most readers as reasonable that *full* material equality cannot consistently be the goal of a free society. However, for Hayek, *any* move to reduce inequality, however slight, is damaging to freedom.[70] Any non-market distribution would reward people who have failed to be productive on their own initiative. Further, in order to determine rewards, it would require that individuals be evaluated directly by their government. However, since no single schedule of values could ever be universally agreed upon, people's life chances would depend on their evaluation according to other peoples' standards. To understand the full significance of this for Hayek, we must be aware of his conviction that government involvement in people's lives can never be a matter of degree: '[t]he principle of distributive justice, once introduced, would not be fulfilled until the whole of society was organized in accordance with it'.[71] The result would be nothing short of a dictatorship. Negative liberty and equality before the law are therefore strict principles in Hayek's analysis – they cannot be applied partially.

Second, Hayek's conception of freedom is strictly individualist. According to him, the necessity of individualism emerges from the fact that no man can know the needs of all men. As a result, no single mind can comprehend a scale of value for a whole society, and scales of value will necessarily differ between individuals. The implications for freedom are profound. In Hayek's words, 'individuals should be allowed, within defined limits, to follow their own values and preferences rather than somebody else's; that within these spheres the individual's system of ends should be supreme and not subject to any dictation by others'.[72] Clearly, Hayek believes that some social limitations are necessary for individuals to be free. In particular, social organisation must be governed by some principles, but, according to Hayek, even these are by definition general and universally accepted, and so are unlikely to conflict with individual liberty.[73] In particular, a free society is defined, in individual terms, as one which maximises the results of free and spontaneous individual action. In this connection, Hayek does not rule out the possibility that some ends may be social, but defines these as nothing more than 'a coincidence of individual ends'.[74] In turn, '[c]ommon action is...limited to the fields where people agree on common ends'.[75] If common action, including state action, exceeds this sphere of agreement, then it is inevitable that those in power will 'impose their scale of preferences on the community for which they plan'.[76]

It is not difficult to establish that such a stringent conception of freedom is required by market-based approaches. To begin with, all of these approaches agree with Hayek's description of the free market located within the rule of law. Moreover, none of these approaches could consistently condone anything approaching a positive conception of freedom. Granted, they are all concerned that government should act to ensure equal and fair playing conditions for all market actors. Government may also be required to intervene to counteract market failures. This might entail sizeable interventions in some fields (as Hayek himself noted). However, only rarely may the government act to improve the lot of some at the expense of others. Hayek and market-based proponents agree that this would detrimentally alter the adjustment mechanism of the market. As Hayek has set out in detail, government intervention inevitably remunerates people according to criteria other than the value that their products have for their fellows. In so doing, it alters the incentives for socially productive work, encourages wastefulness and reduces men's sense of responsibility for their own actions.[77] Moreover, market-based approaches generally agree with Hayek that government intervention cannot be achieved without imposing a unified scale of values on society. Since, as was shown above, these approaches are also strongly individualist, any such imposition of values is necessarily seen to be coercive.

The important question, however, is how does such a view of freedom accommodate culture? According to Hayek, one of the chief advantages of this conception of freedom is precisely that it allows the individual to nurture and pursue whatever cultural impulses he should wish. In other words, culture remains clearly within the liberal private sphere. In the language of the market-based approaches, the individual can hold whatever values he chooses and can consume whatever cultural goods he wishes to. Indeed, like most negative conceptions of freedom, there is nothing in this theory that actively excludes cultural issues. However, once we acknowledge that such a view is not universal, but has a particular (negative and individualist) character, we can perceive how Hayek's vision of social justice reflects certain values and resists others.[78] Crucially, and contrary to what many liberals imply, the social rules at the heart of this arrangement are not impartial between different forms of life – they limit what is considered possible and valuable.[79] In particular, these rules are not impartial between cultures. They clearly bear the mark of an individualist, competitive, and self-reliant society, and leave little room for an understanding of non-quantifiable value, of common values, and truly social ends. In other words, this conception of freedom leaves little room for understandings of culture that view it as something deeper than an individual consumption choice.

It is clear that this conception of freedom is a very particular one. But, given Hayek's view that no one (including economists) can know what is good for society, it is important to assess whether we have grounds for claiming that he intends it to be understood as a universal. Clearly, if Hayek does understand his position as a morally particular one, then the force of the criticisms of this chapter will be reduced. Indeed, Hayek initially seems open to values other than his own. As he points out in the Preface to *The Constitution of Liberty*, his aim is not to put forward a scientific explanation of the world. Instead, he intends to 'picture an ideal, to show how it can be achieved, and to explain what its realization would mean in practice'.[80] In keeping with this approach, Hayek is quite willing to acknowledge that his work is political – that it is motivated by certain 'ultimate values' and that it is written in response to a very particular constellation of political and social forces after the Second World War.[81] Indeed, much of Hayek's argument reflects his sense that he is engaged in a political contest over the future of Western civilisation. His adversaries are not only committed communists and National Socialists, but also defenders of the extensive welfare state. In Hayek's own words, 'many who think themselves infinitely superior to the aberrations of nazism, and sincerely hate all its manifestations, work at the same time for ideals whose realization would lead straight to the abhorred tyranny'.[82]

Yet despite his formal acknowledgement that this is a political battle between contending views, there is little in the core of Hayek's argument to suggest that he recognises the possible validity of any values other than his own.[83] Clearly, people may prefer different things than Hayek and they may express these preferences in the market. However, at a deeper level, Hayek does not allow that people might fundamentally disagree with his understanding of the good life. In fact, the substance of Hayek's work demonstrates that he is completely convinced of the rightness of his position and the universality of his values. In one sense, this is what we should expect from someone engaged in such an important political battle. However, as we will see below, this universalism runs deeper than rhetoric and can be shown to have a detrimental effect on both the legitimacy and feasibility of his suggestions for social order.

Acknowledging the problems raised by a particularist conception posing as universal provides only part of the argument. And indeed, the discussion above has only hinted at the ways in which this manoeuvre acts to impede an understanding of the moral relevance of culture. The discussion which follows will shift the focus slightly to the free market. Within this context, it will demonstrate that the kind of freedom advocated by Hayek actually *requires* that cultural imperatives be limited within established procedural boundaries. In other words, despite his commitment to spontaneous development and limited knowledge, Hayek's vision of the free market and social justice is fundamentally unable to conceptualise culture as morally relevant.

Free market

Spontaneity is a crucial concept in Hayek's work. Once we have accepted that knowledge is limited, spontaneous innovation becomes the driving force of progress and both embodies and guarantees freedom. In this respect, much of the moral force behind the market emerges from its supposed spontaneity. Owing to this connection, the market is seen to be an order that both embodies freedom and that has been freely arrived at. In this sense, because it is spontaneous and, hence, fosters freedom, the market is especially valuable in the context of epistemological uncertainty.

However, it is not clear that Hayek would be so positive about any other arrangement that had arisen spontaneously. Indeed, as we will see, he is not so tolerant of any spontaneous development (no matter how freely arrived at) that might challenge his very particular conception of liberal civilisation.[84] This is most apparent in Hayek's discussion of two related subjects: the status of social norms and institutions, and the normative status of majority decisions.

One might assume that Hayek's treatment of the evolution of social norms and institutions would generally accord with his claims about competition. Indeed, he claims that the groups which espouse the most beneficial values will succeed and their values will be imitated by the rest of society. Other groups will destroy themselves by the moral beliefs to which they adhere. In keeping with his view of progress, he further claims that individuals should be able to transgress rules when it seems worthwhile.[85] After all, how could progress occur without innovation? Morally, too, the freedom to differ is important. According to Hayek, '[o]nly where we ourselves are responsible for our own interests and are free to sacrifice them [for what is right] has our decision any moral value'.[86] However, it soon becomes clear that Hayek is not willing to accept the possibility of general or unchannelled innovation. In particular, he argues that 'a successful free society will always in large measure be a tradition-bound society'.[87] In its more limited sense, this is an uncontroversial claim. As Hayek himself notes, existing institutions embody the experimentation of many generations.[88] However, Hayek takes the claim further, arguing that because our knowledge is limited, '[w]e ... have no choice but to submit to rules whose rationale we often do not know, and to do so whether or not we can see that anything important depends on their being observed in a particular instance'.[89] On another occasion, he repeats the claim, criticising his contemporaries for their 'new unwillingness to submit to any rule or necessity the rationale of which man does not understand'.[90] In this stronger form, it is difficult to see how this claim can avoid conflicting with the value that Hayek places on innovation and spontaneity. After all, an innovative spirit is unlikely to rest well with the blind acceptance of existing social rules. Hayek resolves this apparent tension by placing two qualifications on the exercise of spontaneity. Neither of these qualifications is explicit, but without them, Hayek's argument is untenable.

First, Hayek treats different types of rules and institutions differently. The first group comprises all those rules and institutions that define his vision of liberal civilisation, including the free market and the rule of law. The second group is made up of all other rules and institutions *within* a liberal civilisation. While innovation *within* liberal civilisation is crucial for progress, innovation which calls this civilisation into question is *never* endorsed. According to Hayek, freedom 'demands that it be accepted as a value in itself, as a principle that must be respected without our asking whether the consequences in the particular instance will be beneficial. We shall not achieve the results we want if we do not accept it as a creed or presumption so strong that no considerations of expediency can be allowed to limit it.'[91] The point is not necessarily whether one agrees or disagrees with Hayek about the value of freedom. What is important to note is that, for Hayek, certain rules and institutions are beyond question. In Hayek's own words, 'there is ample scope for experimentation and improvement *within* that permanent legal framework'.[92]

Viewed in this light, many of the tensions discussed above become clear. For example, Hayek can afford to neglect the possibility that spontaneous human relations might result in undesirable outcomes, since, by definition, spontaneity is only exercised *within* the context of liberal civilisation. As a result, it cannot do other than perpetuate the free market. In this respect, Hayek can afford to be so supportive of innovation precisely because his own values are never really in question. His liberal civilisation is both the existing framework and the goal of competition. It is more than a teleology – it is built directly into the system. How could conflicting values and cultures have a chance – the normative presumptions of liberal civilisation are brought in through the back door and are never defined or justified.

Second, Hayek qualifies his idea of spontaneity by limiting the types of people who can be trusted with the task of innovation. For example, in discussing majority rule, Hayek claims that 'the imposition of major-ity view ... is coercive, monopolistic, and exclusive and so destroys the self-correcting forces which, in a free society, ensure that mistaken efforts will be abandoned'. More specifically, he claims that 'it is always from a minority acting differently from what the majority would prescribe that the majority in the end learns to do better'.[93] Clearly, Hayek does not hold out much hope for the innovativeness of the majority.[94] However, given his vitriolic opposition to certain minority-governed systems, it is clear that he would not see the value in support-ing the innovativeness of just any minority. Not surprisingly, there is one particular minority group that Hayek believes is most likely to produce useful innovation, namely, 'men of independent means'.[95] According to him, if new ideas are to come forth, 'representatives of all divergent views and tastes should be in a position to support *with their means* ... ideals which are not yet shared by the majority'.[96] For Hayek, this does not mean that people with dissenting views ought to be *given* the means to promote their beliefs. Rather, it means that those who already have significant means are the principal ones who shall be trusted to represent new and innovative ideals. Using inheritance as a criterion will ensure that those 'who are given this opportunity are edu-cated for it and will have grown up in a material environment in which the material benefits of wealth are familiar and have ceased to become the main source of satisfaction'.[97] Moreover, the wealthy are perfectly placed for innovation. They 'are already living in a phase of evolution that the others have not yet reached'.[98] It seems to matter little to Hayek that men of independent means will not represent the full spectrum of ideas and are among the least likely to be truly socially innovative. In fact, it quite suits Hayek to limit spontaneity to that group which has most to lose from radical changes to the status quo. Innovation, in this context, may involve tinkering with the forms of life within liberal civil-isation, but it is never likely to call into question the basic structure of Hayek's liberal ideal.

The same paradox presents itself in other contexts. For example, on some occasions, Hayek exalts tradition, while on others, traditions are described contemptuously as 'relics of an earlier type of society', in com-petition with freedom.[99] Further, he notes that certain new policy aims have arisen that cannot be accommodated within his vision of the rule of law. Rather than acknowledge these as a potential source of social innovation, Hayek dismisses them as wrong and dangerous.[100] Similarly, in comparing the English and French visions of liberty, Hayek argues that 'the British philosophers laid the foundations of a profound and essentially valid theory, while the rationalist school was simply and completely wrong'.[101] These are harsh words for a social innovation that, two centuries later, is continuing to evolve.

It should be noted that welfare economists do not generally make claims as extreme as the ones above. They are generally supportive of democracy and political equality. However, the comments above are not wholly irrelevant. Similarly to Hayek, welfare economists begin from a position of limited knowledge and yet rely upon the claim that their vision of well-being and their particular model of market–society relations is the obviously right one. Indeed, what is actually a very particular understanding of the relation of people to society and the value of formal versus material equality is passed off as a universal and obvious model, requiring no elaboration or justification.

Several points are of relevance here. First, it should by now be clear that Hayek is not open to innovations simply by virtue of their spontaneous evolution, and hence their contribution to freedom. In fact, Hayek consistently and deliberately denigrates or excludes any values that do not support his vision of liberal civilisation, no matter how innovative or freely arrived at they may be. At best, such values are ignored. At worst, as much of *The Road to Serfdom* demonstrates, they are castigated as promoting totalitarianism.[102] Clearly, some uses of freedom are better than others. Unfortunately, because of the strength of his epistemological justification, Hayek gives no indication of what the additional ethical criteria may be and how they might be substantiated. In this respect, we can conclude that it is not solely the intrinsic value of freedom that justifies the form and substance of liberal civilisation, including the free market. With no further justification offered, Hayek's entire argument seems to rest on the simple claim that his view of freedom and the good society is better than others.

Second, however, we can only accept this latter claim if we accept that Hayek himself has the very knowledge of what is best that the epistemological uncertainty of his theory rules to be impossible. Indeed, the whole point of valuing spontaneity is that 'because every individual knows so little and, in particular, because we rarely know which of us knows best that we trust the individual and competitive efforts of many to induce the emergence of what we shall want when we see it'.[103] Yet the acceptance of Hayek's conclusions (including the naturalness of the free market) depends precisely on our acceptance that he has the very knowledge that he eschewed as impossible. In other words, believing

Hayek's conclusions about the universal legitimacy of liberal civilisation may actually require us to reject the very grounds upon which he justifies this civilisation. In this context, far from reflecting a victory for particularisms, Hayek's specific conception of freedom and the free market emerge as universalisms, bereft of any adequate justification whatsoever.[104]

To sum up, this engagement with Hayek's thought has illustrated the central role played by negative freedom in legitimising market-based approaches. Furthermore, it has shown how this conception of freedom is fundamentally unable to accommodate culture in any meaningful way. Even Hayek's innovative epistemological defence of freedom is ultimately grounded in his own very particular views on the form and substance of the good life. Because of its strong pretences to universality, such an approach fundamentally rules out a substantive pluralism. The appropriate nature of such a pluralism, and its attending justification, will be the subject of the remainder of this book.

Conclusion

This chapter has criticised welfare economics on several grounds. First, it has argued that welfare economists do not adequately acknowledge their own moral premises *as contestable moral premises*. Even the choice of individual well-being as the goal of economic theory is rarely seen by economists as a contestable normative claim. As a result, they are unable to recognise the particularity of their own approach, as well as the existence of other approaches based on other moral frameworks. Second, however, when the normative premises of welfare economics are examined in any detail, it becomes difficult to see how they are either 'innocuous' or 'uncontroversial'. In fact, they actively work to exclude considerations of culture as morally relevant. Their claims about individual well-being invoke a very strong individualism and a moral subjectivism. Moreover, their analysis is greatly strengthened by a reliance on implicit notions of individual freedom. When these notions are explored, they too invoke very particular claims about individualism, values, and the nature of human self-understandings. Combined, these arguments act to ensure that market-based approaches cannot understand culture as anything more meaningful than a consumption choice. In effect, they limit the legitimacy of other values and ways of life. In so doing, they foreclose the possibility of a genuine cultural pluralism.

In this regard, the success of this book does not depend on the strong claim that welfare economics is somehow obliterated by the rise of cultural concerns. Instead, it is motivated by the conviction that a greater sense of the relevance of culture can generate important insights into our self-understandings, our motivations, and our values. These insights are crucial to IPE and to public policy more generally, and yet, as this chapter has shown, they cannot adequately be captured by welfare economics. We need new approaches. In this spirit, the following chapters are dedicated to exploring the positive possibilities of cultural insight.

4
The Ethics of Culture and Community

Having discussed the legitimacy and universal applicability of welfare economics as a theory of the good life, this chapter will now address the question of whether and in what ways it is possible to provide a moral justification for community-based approaches to cultural policy. In other words, are there good ethical reasons why the state should intervene to support culture, and what might they be? This chapter will argue that, in considering community-based approaches, we can and ought to distinguish between those community-based approaches which are morally acceptable and those which are not. Having made this distinction, this chapter will focus on those community-based approaches which are *not* ethically justifiable, delineating the reasons why these approaches are unacceptable as a basis for cultural policy. This chapter will also indicate why a culturally sensitive liberal position is not endorsed. The subsequent chapter will build on this discussion, offering a detailed delineation of the ethics underlying acceptable forms of community-based approach. It will offer this analysis as a particular ethics to which cultural policy should aspire if it is to be justifiable.

Theorists of political morality raise this question of state support for the arts more often than one might expect. Ronald Dworkin, Joseph Raz, and Charles Taylor, for example, have all addressed the question specifically.[1] Their responses are quite illustrative within the context of their own theories, and also within the context of the liberal–communitarian debate. Relying on some of these ideas, this chapter will seek to ascertain what grounds there may be for asserting the moral status of culture, in the contexts in which it is framed by the various community-based approaches described in Chapter 2.

As the reader will recall, community-based approaches to cultural policy were defined earlier as those approaches which begin from the premise that cultural activity fulfils important social functions. They stress the benefits to the community of cultural production by, for, and representing that community. In turn, the good of the community, broadly defined, is the ultimate justification for cultural policy. Moving beyond the claims of Chapter 2, community-based approaches to cultural policy can be divided into two basic categories. The first type, comprising the majority of community-based approaches, can be labelled the *national survival* approach, while the second type can be titled the *cultural pluralism* approach. Importantly, both approaches share a broad view of the person as a moral agent that is inescapably culturally constituted. In other words, both approaches emphasise the central role of culture in defining our identities and shaping our conceptions of the good. Building from this, however, they differ radically in terms of the cultural influences that they prioritise and, consequently, in terms of the politics that they advocate. It is primarily in terms of the acceptability of their politics that both approaches will be evaluated.

National survival approaches focus exclusively on culture as it relates to the nation or the nationally defined political community. In this sense, they adopt a fairly singular view of identity. Factors other than the nation may contribute to identity, but these are perceived to be secondary allegiances. In this regard, they seek support for culture because this is instrumental to the achievement of other ends, such as national identity, national unity, state sovereignty, defence, and prosperity. However, these are not just any particular ends, but are goods that are perceived to be intimately bound to the survival of the national community. Indeed, as we noted in Chapter 2, the most common community-based themes are those that revolve around the very survival of the nation. State support for culture is very often presented as essential to the survival of the nation-state.

In contrast, cultural pluralism approaches take a much more plural view of culture and identity. They argue for the moral relevance of all cultural sources of identity, whether national or not, and they refuse to give priority to national cultures in the scheme of social justice. Building from the claim that culture is constitutive of identity, they argue for a conception of justice that can publicly recognise and embrace cultural difference. They seek to move beyond the shallow pluralism of liberal democracy towards a deeper, public pluralism characteristic of radical democracy.[2] Philosophically, these views are closest to the insights of those community-based approaches which emphasised democratic development and artistic fulfilment as the central contributions of culture to the community. However, even these latter approaches often revert to the idioms of national identity – a practice explicitly rejected by cultural pluralism approaches. As a result, cultural pluralists are less exclusivist in their understanding of the sources of identity, and less essentialist in their conceptualisation of national identities than most other community-based approaches.

This chapter will begin by discussing the national survival approach. The purpose of this discussion is to highlight the ways in which this particular type of community-based approach is an ethically unsatisfactory basis upon which to defend cultural policy. This discussion will raise important questions about the role of liberal theories in any ethical analysis of culture. The chapter will argue against the use of such approaches. This will create the basis upon which subsequent chapters, using the work of Taylor and Iris Marion Young, will delineate an ethically acceptable justification for community-based approaches.

National survival

The national survival approach has been exemplified repeatedly throughout this book, even though it has not previously been given this epithet. Indeed, it was dominant in the approaches described in Chapter 2. Further, as was fully demonstrated in that chapter, the claims being made are not only the simple ones that national identity or unity depend on cultural protection. Many commentators are quick to make the further claim that the very *survival* of the nation or polity is at stake. In Franklyn Griffiths' words, '[a]s we lose the ability to give voice to feelings, ideas, and purposes that unite us...we stand to lose control over our land.... The state of our cultural life becomes a key variable in our security, in our survival as a people.'[3] Survival of the nation is clearly a defining theme in these community-based approaches.

This is a variant of an essentially nationalist position. In the first place, it relies centrally on the claim that there *is* an identifiable and uncontested nation and that this nation is a good thing that ought to be continuously renewed. More importantly, however, proponents of this position understand culture in exclusively national terms. In a view that resonates with many theories of nationalism, culture is perceived as both a forum for, and a symbolic language of, national expression. It is, in this case, a defining element of the nation.[4]

Nationalism and ethics

The ethical problems with nationalist approaches such as this have already been repeatedly discussed in the so-called liberal–communitarian debate.[5] In fact, the claims made by national survival approaches represent some of the worst communitarian excesses, and the ones upon which liberal critiques most often focus. To briefly summarise, not all liberals take issue with the basic conception of the person posited by national survival approaches. Specifically, they do not contest that cultural influences may be a crucial element in the constitution of moral personhood. However, they charge that in a communitarian framework, the assumption of cultural embeddedness leads to a singular, group-based conception of the good. As Will Kymlicka argues, '[i]n a communitarian society ... the common good is conceived of as a substantive conception of the good which defines the community's "way of life" '.[6] Indeed, according to Kymlicka, 'the common good for communitarians is precisely the pursuit of these shared ends, which constrains the freedom of individuals to choose and pursue their own life-style'.[7] As a result, liberals perceive that, when applied within a communitarian framework, the assumption of cultural embeddedness can be used as a basis for 'the brutal oppression of individuals'.[8]

Given that both liberals and communitarians claim to accept some version of a culturally embedded view of the person, much of the debate between them actually centres on the extent to which the individual is able to revise his values and goals. In a liberal understanding, culture provides no more than a context of choice within which individuals make decisions about their lives. If individual freedom is to be respected, according to them, the individual must be considered able to reflect upon and revise his cultural and value commitments. Theorists identified as communitarians may accept the possibility of such revision, but contend that such revisions cannot necessarily be consciously or easily undertaken. Indeed, as was evidenced by Taylor's remarks in Chapter 3, they often try to highlight the ways in which the very idea of a free chooser, and hence the substance of the liberal project, is itself inescapably culturally embedded.

As we will see in Chapter 5, acknowledging culture as a way of life and granting it a corresponding ethical status does not in itself generate the stereotypical communitarianism that many liberals associate with it. In fact, the problem with the national survival arguments set out earlier is not their acknowledgement of the central relevance of culture in constituting individual identity. Instead, their failing lies in the distinctive politics that arise from their interpretation of cultural embeddedness. In particular, they essentialise the community and reify the relationship between culture and identity. They assume that the identity of an individual is a singular thing, that it exists in direct relation to a single, uncontested (national) culture which itself is manifest in a single well-defined (and usually political) community. These claims will be developed in the next few paragraphs.

First, and most importantly, this approach requires that the cultural basis of the community be understood in terms of the nation. Focusing as it does on the survival of the nation, such an approach leaves no room for the possibility that non-national cultural influences may constitute important moral sources. As Sylvia Bashevkin has noted, the national community may be only one of many plural and overlapping communities that together define (or compete for) the moral framework of the individual.[9] As a result, it is not a forgone conclusion that there is only one relevant moral community and that it is the national one. In this sense, focusing exclusively on the nation – its identity, unity, and sovereignty – generates an essentialist understanding of community that excludes the relevance of other cultural sources of value.

Second, the national survival view requires a fixed conception of the nation. In this sense, as we noted above, the nation is defined by certain values and goals. In one sense, this is required, if the idea of defending an entity defined as 'the nation' is to make any sense at all. However, it is still important to ask which values are being defended and to allow the possibility that the nation may change over time. To be fair, the question of which culture is being defended is hardly absent from the debate among community-based approaches to cultural policy. However, it is nonetheless clear that proponents of the national survival approach have defended *a particular* (i.e. national) culture on the grounds that it contributes to the good of *a particular* community. Within this type of approach, a view of who is in and who is out is unavoidable, however implicit it may be. Furthermore, and especially since the particularity of this vision is largely implicit, it is not clear that the nation is a concept open to substantive revision. It has boundaries, like any other concept, that are policed through the designation of what constitutes 'national culture', not least through government criteria for national content and ownership. In most states, such assertions about the basis of cultural value can be extremely damaging.

In this context, the potentially exclusionary politics of the national survivalist approach are evident. If this view is brought to bear on IPE, it creates the nationalist, protectionist, elitist, and rent-seeking state that economists have long decried. In contrast, and as a first step towards a more adequate ethic, the following two chapters will draw out another set of ethical claims arising out of the community-based approaches, namely the cultural pluralism approach. It will be argued that identities must be understood as plural and shifting and that these may be identified by many different (and often evolving and competing) cultures. In turn, these cultures may interact in very different ways and numbers to form communities. Moreover, and very importantly, none of these categories can be understood as fixed or given. The boundaries of membership as well as the substance of community are constantly the subject of political conflict. As a result, the claim that acknowledging culture in a deep way leads to totalitarianism must simply be rejected. However, this rejection need not neglect the constitutive significance of culture. It does mean that any adequate conception of social justice must more fluidly conceptualise the relationship between culture and identity. Such an approach will be set out in the following two chapters. First, however, it is necessary to deal with one further question.

Why not liberalism?

In the foregoing discussion of liberal and communitarian differences, it was noted that many liberals claim to accept the communitarian conception of the person as culturally embedded. Indeed, although liberals have often been criticised for adopting a view of the individual as completely unencumbered, much of this criticism has been unfair. In this context, although the previous chapter ruled out highly individualist forms of liberalism, it is reasonable to ask why this book does not adopt a moderate liberal approach, based on the constitutive relevance of culture, but seeking to accommodate it within a framework of liberal pluralism. In other words, why go to the bother of elucidating a communitarian-leaning framework, if culture is already adequately conceptualised by John Rawls, Raz, Yael Tamir, or Kymlicka? This is hardly a simple question, requiring as it does an elucidation of the finer points of certain liberal commitments. In this context, answering it is no easy task. Rather than taking issue with the already highly contested Rawlsian position or the uneasy middle ground of Raz[10] or Tamir, the argument which follows will take the harder road, focusing on the culturally oriented work of Kymlicka. Indeed, Kymlicka does offer the most detailed and consistent consideration of cultural themes of any modern liberal theorist. Taking the work of someone so intimately concerned with cultural themes will help us to avoid creating a liberal straw man. One drawback, however, is that in focusing our critique on Kymlicka's concerns, the book will not have space to critique the procedural dimension of some liberal theories. Fortunately, this criticism has been well developed elsewhere.[11]

More importantly, however, the book will not explore in any great detail the conception of cultural rights.[12] Nonetheless, most conceptions of cultural rights exhibit problematic ambiguities very similar to those which are drawn out and critiqued below. Once these key problems with the liberal conception of culture are realised, the basis for a rights position will consequently be seriously weakened. In this light, and taking the work of Kymlicka as an example, this section will argue that it is impossible to be a consistent liberal while maintaining that culture, defined broadly, is constitutive of people's ends.

Few theorists would now deny the basic point that culture is of fundamental importance to individuals. In this vein, Kymlicka concedes that '[p]eople *are* bound, in an important way, to their own cultural community. ... Someone's upbringing isn't something that can just be erased; it is, and will remain a constitutive part of who that person is.'[13] Moreover, he attributes similar ideas to both Rawls and Dworkin, though, at least for Rawls, such constitutive attachments should be confined to the private sphere.[14] However, while maintaining this as an 'ontological fact', many liberals would attach *ethical* significance to culture only in an instrumental and conditional way. Many of these are also theorists who would refer to our ordinary moral sense as the ultimate reference point for theories of justice. These claims, I will argue, cannot be reconciled. The attempt to make both of these claims – that culture is constitutive of individual identity, but that it is only instrumental in a moral theory – is inconsistent and represents an attempt to 'have the best of both worlds'. This will be illustrated below.

Throughout his work, Kymlicka seeks to show that liberalism can and, in fact, must accommodate 'the virtues and importance of our membership in a community and a culture'.[15] In this sense, his work is directed at communitarians who have criticised the liberal conception of the individual and its portrayal of the social context in which individual moral action takes place. Not surprisingly, he suggests that these critiques arise in large part due to a communitarian misreading of liberal ideas. However, his work is also directed at those liberals, such as Rawls and Dworkin, who, according to Kymlicka, are aware of the 'importance of the cultural context of choice', but do not recognise 'cultural membership as a primary good, or as a ground for legitimate claims'.[16] In this sense, Kymlicka's work can be read as a critique of liberals for what they have failed to say about culture, rather than for what they are unable to say. This section will address Kymlicka's work with particular attention to three questions: (1) what is Kymlicka's definition of culture; (2) how does culture relate to identity; and (3) what is the moral status of culture? Taking culture as constitutive of identity, but valuing it only instrumentally, I will argue, leads to a disjuncture between the answers to questions 2 and 3.

Kymlicka is quite keenly attuned to the myriad uses of the term 'culture' in contemporary theory. Within this range of ideas, he locates himself by focusing on 'societal culture', 'that is, a culture which provides its members with meaningful ways of life across the full range of human activities, including social, educational, religious, recreational, and economic life, encompassing both public and private spheres. These cultures tend to be territorially concentrated, and based on a shared language.'[17] This is synonymous with 'a nation' or 'a people', and includes shared memories and values as well as common institutions and practices. Although Kymlicka claims that he does not wish to dismiss the importance of claims made by non-national minorities,[18] he never adequately explains why he prioritises this national understanding of culture over others. Moreover, as we will see, his theory requires that he prioritise the claims of national minorities over immigrant groups. Both of these issues create problems for him when he later wishes to accord a moral status to culture.

In any discussion of the moral status of culture, the relationship of culture and identity must be a central issue. Here, Kymlicka's position is not as clear. It is essential for his ethical theory that he subscribe to the vision of the individual as able to question and revise his chosen ends and projects. But what is the role of the community and communal attachments in this process? According to Kymlicka, cultural attachments cannot be dismissed. However, '[l]iberals ... insist that we have an ability to detach ourselves from any particular communal practice. No particular task is set for us by society. ... Nothing is authoritative before our judgement of its value.'[19] More specifically, for Kymlicka, '[w]hat is central to the liberal view is not that we can *perceive* a self prior to its ends, but that we understand our selves to be prior to our ends, *in the sense that no end or goal is exempt from possible re-examination*'.[20]

There are two arguments at work here. First, Kymlicka seems to be saying that it is a matter of common agreement that the self is encumbered and that a liberal theory can only make sense in this context. For example, he claims that 'Taylor is right to emphasize the importance of his social book, and hence the importance of a secure social context, of public principles of justice, and of civic participation. All these are of unquestionable importance. But that is just the problem. No one does question their importance.'[21] However, in making that very point, Kymlicka relies on a second argument that threatens to contradict the first. While he clearly thinks that it is impossible for someone to choose to have no culture at all, it is feasible for someone to choose between two cultures as if they were discrete products with no relation to the identity of the person concerned. For example, with regard to immigrant groups, Kymlicka claims that '[a]fter all, most immigrants choose to leave their own culture'.[22] Elsewhere, he argues that 'the process of ethical reasoning is always one of comparing one "encumbered" potential self with another "encumbered" potential self'.[23] As will be argued below, Kymlicka is quite determined to preserve this element of choice and to resist the full implications of adopting a view of ends as constitutive, even when this does serious damage to his own understandings. In so doing, he is endorsing a view of identity that suggests that, while culture is important, one can choose to replace any particular culture by another. I will argue that this is based on a fundamental misunderstanding of the implications of describing ends as constitutive.

In this context, Kymlicka is quite clear about the moral status of culture. Similarly to Raz, he argues that '[c]ultures are valuable, not in and of themselves, but because it is only through having access to a societal culture that people have access to a range of meaningful options'.[24] Within a liberal framework, this range of meaningful options is itself relevant in so far as and because it contributes to the freedom to hold and question our own beliefs: '[l]iberals should be concerned with the fate of cultural structures, not because they have some moral status of their own, but because it's only through having a rich and secure cultural structure that people can become aware, in a vivid way, of the options available to them, and intelligently examine their value'.[25] Thus, culture (and cultural membership) is instrumentally and conditionally valuable; it is valuable in so far as it contributes to the value of freedom, defined in terms of certain civil and personal liberties.[26]

The problem for Kymlicka is that in order to successfully defend this point, he relies on an understanding of meaning and especially its social construction that cannot make sense without a conception of culture as constitutive of identity. For example, Kymlicka argues that

> freedom involves making choices amongst various options, and our societal culture not only provides these options, but also makes them meaningful to us. People make choices about the social practices around them, based on their beliefs about the value of these practices. And to have a belief about the value of a practice is, in the first instance, a matter of understanding the meanings attached to it by

our culture.... To understand the meaning of a social practice, therefore, requires understanding this 'shared vocabulary' – that is, understanding the language and history which constitute that vocabulary.[27]

This understanding of language and meaning is crucial for Kymlicka to be able to defend the value of cultural membership. However, this interpretive conception of meaning cannot easily be reconciled with an instrumental conception of culture.

The same difficulty manifests itself again in a second sense. The fact that Kymlicka lacks an idea of constitutive culture means that he cannot satisfactorily account for several important dimensions of our conceptions of what it means to be human. First, he is unable to provide an explanation for why people need access to their own societal culture. His answer is fundamentally an empirical one – that culture is important to people. He draws an analogy with the choice to take a vow of perpetual poverty: '[i]t is not impossible to live in poverty. But it does not follow that a liberal theory of justice should therefore view the desire for a level of material resources above bare subsistence simply as "something that particular people like and enjoy" but which "they no longer can claim is something that they need".'[28] Not only does this reiterate the idea that culture is something, though important, which can be *chosen*, it begs the question of why culture should be so important to people.

This is the second question which Kymlicka's theory only inadequately explains. For, if culture is as important to people as Kymlicka suggests, then this must be accounted for in a way that does not conflict with his view of it as instrumentally valuable. Faced with the empirical commitment of individuals to their culture, but with no deep theory of human interaction, Kymlicka can only reply that '[i]t is an interesting question why the bonds of language and culture are so strong for most people'.[29] Nonetheless, he claims, as above, that '[p]eople *are* bound, in an important way, to their own cultural community.... Someone's upbringing isn't something that can just be erased; it is, and will remain, a constitutive part of who that person is. Cultural membership affects our very sense of personal identity and capacity.'[30] Clearly, however, Kymlicka cannot afford to entertain the possibility that such a conception of the value of culture might undermine his earlier claims that the individual must be seen as prior to his ends. In other words, Kymlicka is keen to partake of the theoretical advantages provided by a view of culture as constitutive of identity, but he is not willing to accommodate the implications of this for his universalist foundations.

Kymlicka does, however, admit that to revise one's ends is a difficult task. He comments that '[i]t is not easy or enjoyable to revise one's deepest ends, but it is possible, and sometimes a regrettable necessity'.[31] Moreover, he claims that in making judgements about the value of ends, 'we must take something as a "given". ... But liberals believe that what we put in the given in order to make meaningful judgements can not only be different between individuals but can also change within one individual's life.'[32] Neither of these points would be contested by some (although not all) communitarians. Taylor, for example, makes precisely these points.[33] The difference is that Taylor's deep theory of identity is able to show precisely why a revision of one's deepest ends is such a tortuous process. He can account for the 'how', 'why', and 'with what effects' questions that are obscured by Kymlicka's reliance on the idea of a free choosing individual whose culture is important, but nonetheless instrumental. In other words, without a deeper theory of identity, Kymlicka is unable to adequately explain why cultural membership is, in fact, important. Clearly, culture may have moral significance in terms of its contribution to the promotion of other liberal values. However, this does not provide any substance to our intrinsic sense that culture is of value to us. Moreover, it threatens to conflict with his later assertion that non-liberal societal cultures should not be coerced into adopting liberal values.[34]

This latter point raises a very interesting question about the broader context in which something can be described as instrumental or constitutive. It is possible to make two distinct claims in this regard. First, one could argue that culture is instrumental or constitutive in relation to the ends of the individual concerned. Second, culture may be instrumental or constitutive vis-à-vis the moral values of the perspective from which culture is discussed. For example, it might be possible for someone like Kymlicka to argue that while culture is constitutive of individual ends, it should not be accorded value in itself by a moral theory. This is not an uncommon perspective – it is reflected, for example, in the desire to separate atavistic from civic nationalism.[35] However, this position relies on a separation between the value attributed to culture by agents and the judgement of this value by cultural outsiders. While this allows us to attribute moral standing to culture only in so far as it serves 'good' purposes, it fundamentally does not do justice to the value that non-liberal cultures may have for those who belong to them. More broadly, it does not adequately make sense of the human feeling that culture is foundational.

So, despite his discussion of culture, Kymlicka is fundamentally committed to the idea of the free chooser. However, in an interesting twist, this assumption is not in fact necessary to make the claims that he wishes to make. Instead, his insistence on holding to the idea that ends cannot be constitutive rests, I will argue, on a fundamental misreading of the communitarian position. In one passage, Kymlicka claims that

> [c]ommunitarians deny that we can 'stand apart' from (some of) our ends. According to Michael Sandel, ... some of our ends are 'constitutive' ends in the sense that they define our sense of personal identity. ... Whereas Rawls claims that individuals 'do not regard themselves as inevitably bound to, or identical with, the pursuit of any particular complex of fundamental interests that we may have at any given moment', Sandel responds that we are in fact 'identical with' at least some of our final ends. Since these ends are constitutive of people's identity, there is no reason why the state should not reinforce people's allegiance to these ends, and limit their ability to question and revise these ends.[36]

This may be an accurate reading of Sandel, but it is fundamentally misleading to apply these conclusions to all those who might perceive ends as constitutive. There is no necessary reason why having constitutive ends should mean that these could not be revised. It only means that we are required to give a fuller account of the ways in which this occurs and the implications that it produces. At one point, Kymlicka addresses the possibility that communitarians do not mean to suggest that ends cannot be revised. He claims that in this case,

> the advertised contrast with the liberal view is a deception, for the sense in which communitarians view us as embedded in communal roles incorporates the sense in which liberals view us as independent of them, and the sense in which communitarians view practical reasoning as a process of self-discovery incorporates the sense in which liberals view practical reasoning as a process of judgement and choice. The differences would be merely semantic.[37]

Apart from a short footnote asserting that liberals and communitarians have achieved their positions in different ways, this is the end of Kymlicka's discussion of what should have been a crucial point. Although this book would not agree that the differences between liberals and communitarians are semantic, Kymlicka ought to have given greater consideration to the possibility of a more moderate communitarianism. However, despite the allusion above, he soon reverts to the assertion that acknowledging ends as constitutive requires that these be unrevisable. This (false) assertion is one major factor in explaining his reluctance to explicitly acknowledge the constitutive value of culture, despite the fact that his theory implicitly relies on a much deeper conception of the moral value of culture than he acknowledges.

Acknowledging that culture is constitutive, whether implicitly or explicitly, has fundamental implications for any theory of political morality. Most importantly, it raises the question of how this can be reconciled with another fundamental human (or liberal) commitment, namely that to basic universal rights. Few among us would wish to argue that culture should be accorded moral status no matter how unfavourably *we* judged the ends to which it was addressed. More importantly, the status of cultural dissenters within our own and other communities cannot be ignored. Nonetheless, it is not clear that these problems can be dealt with as easily as liberals sometimes assert.

There is a strong tendency among liberals to judge the merit of communitarian positions according to how their positions deal with such extreme cases. In this regard, it is crucial to recall that liberalism has its own series of extreme cases. As Kymlicka asks in a section entitled 'Is Liberalism Sectarian?', if all people do not value autonomy or believe that we can stand back from and evaluate our ends, then how can liberal institutions be defended? His own answer is to affirm the value of autonomy, although this time it emerges less as a matter of fact and more one of belief. In Kymlicka's words, 'I believe that the most defensible liberal theory is based on the value of autonomy, and that any form of group-differentiated rights which restricts the civil rights of group members is therefore inconsistent with liberal principles of freedom and equality.'[38] Admitting culture to be constitutive necessarily raises the question of cultural and moral relativism. In response to this, Kymlicka's reduction of liberalism to a question of his own beliefs hardly accounts for his moral prioritisation of autonomy over culture in cases of conflict. We must resolve the question of competing values in a different way.

What is clear from the above discussion is that it is inconsistent to claim that culture is ontologically constitutive and yet morally instrumental. If we are to take seriously the fact that people value their cultural attachments as essential to their self-understandings, then we must be willing to admit that these attachments have value, even when they lead to ends which we might not appreciate. In this context, the liberal approach to culture must be rejected. Nonetheless, in developing an alternative ethic for cultural policy, we must be attuned to the criticisms that liberals have raised. Indeed, we must strive to avoid the essentialisation of the community that has consistently raised the spectre of totalitarian politics.

Conclusion

This chapter has assessed the various claims surrounding community-based approaches. It has argued that several different ethical visions can be drawn from the same starting assumptions about the cultural constitution of the moral agent. Indeed, this chapter has assessed two such ethical visions, judging them both inadequate as a basis for cultural policy. First, national survival community-based approaches were rejected on the grounds that they rely upon an essentialist understanding of the nation and the community, and that they thereby act to exclude non-national moral sources. Second, this chapter considered the claims made by some liberal political theorists that their approach could recognise the fundamental relevance of culture in the constitution of moral personality. The chapter argued that the success of such a claim depends fundamentally on our acceptance that liberals can consistently uphold two inconsistent claims. This is not to suggest that there is no middle ground in this debate, but only that it must be approached from a different point of view. Indeed, finding an adequate middle ground is precisely the task of the next two chapters. The ethics that is developed in this discussion will underscore the relevance of the second community-based approach – that of the cultural pluralists. Finally, it will provide grounds for a sympathetic critique of Canadian and European cultural policy. It will suggest ways in which cultural policies can be made more ethically sound and, therefore, more defensible on an international stage.

5
Towards an Ethics for Cultural Policy: Charles Taylor Considered

The argument of the past few chapters has claimed, first, that economic efficiency cannot be considered of value in itself. This led us to argue that theories of welfare economics cannot provide a satisfactory account of the good life; they must be located within other moral theories. Second, the book sought to assess the moral claims of community-based approaches to cultural policy. So far, we have found market-based and some (national survival) community-based approaches to be inadequate and distorting.

In an attempt to move beyond these arguments and to generate a basis for new insights, this chapter will discuss the work of Charles Taylor. He understands culture as integral to identity, as an ontological fact and gives moral value to culture for this reason. Crucially, however, he does not neglect the important ways in which people *do* revise their ends. As a result, his work is ideally placed to further our conceptions of culture and identity and to suggest ways of understanding cultural policy that are substantively located within the liberal–communitarian 'debate'.

The first part of this chapter will set out Charles Taylor's ontology and especially the main points of his understanding of culture and its relationship to identity. The second part of the chapter will focus on the cultural ethics which is generated by Taylor's work. It will also address several criticisms of Taylor which are the most relevant for the argument of this book. In this regard, this chapter establishes the value of Taylor's ontology, even though it argues that his ethical and political positions contain serious difficulties and are inappropriate for this project. In this light, the chapter which follows will show how Taylor's ontology can be developed to produce a different and more useful ethics for cultural policy.

Taylor's position

Taylor's philosophical writings are extensive and yet they are relatively cohesive. As Taylor himself describes the collected articles in his *Philosophical Papers*: 'they are the work of a monomaniac. ... [A] single rather tightly related agenda underlines all of them.'[1] His target, in this collection, as well as in his broader works, is naturalism and its related concepts (atomism, proceduralism, disengaged reason). Taylor himself describes these approaches as a family, and defines them by 'the ambition to model the study of man on the natural sciences'.[2] According to Taylor, it is crucial to ask what conception of the person underlies these theories and what moral sources inform this conception. These questions lead him across a broad terrain of philosophical argument and, ultimately, require him to present a full development of his own views. Elements of Taylor's critique of welfare economics were set out in Chapter 3. Here, the remaining details of his critique will be set aside so that the focus can rest on Taylor's own philosophical position.

Culture and identity

Taylor begins from the premise that the influences of culture are an inescapable fact of human existence. However, this point is not simply stated, but is illustrated with a complex theory of language and identity. According to Taylor, humans are distinguished from other beings by their ability to make qualitative distinctions of worth. This means that they not only have desires, but that they can pass judgement on these desires. For example, one may want something, but also be able to judge that such a desire is base.[3] This ability to discriminate is uniquely human. Moreover, the evaluations that result are inseparable from identity. In Taylor's words,

> the concept of identity is bound up with that of certain strong evaluations which are inseparable from myself. This either because I identify myself by my strong evaluations, as someone who essentially has these convictions; or else because I see certain of my other properties as admitting of only one kind of strong evaluation by myself, because these properties so centrally touch what I am as an agent, that is, as a strong evaluator, that I cannot really repudiate them in the full sense.[4]

In other words, it is impossible to imagine a human agent who was not defined by some orientation in moral space. However, as Taylor is careful to point out, '[o]ur evaluations are not chosen. On the contrary they are articulations of our sense of what is worthy.'[5] Nonetheless, change is possible: '[t][hat description and experience are bound together in this constitutive relation admits of causal influences in both directions: it can sometimes allow us to alter experience by coming to fresh insight; but more fundamentally it circumscribes insight through the deeply embedded shape of experience for us'.[6] In this sense, '[t]here are more or less adequate, more or less truthful, more self-clairvoyant or self-deluding interpretations'.[7]

More importantly, these commitments and identifications cannot be understood apart from an understanding of the language within which certain terms are distinguished from others and within which meaning is constructed.[8] In his words, '[t]here is no way we could be inducted into personhood except by being initiated into a language. ... I can only learn what anger, love, anxiety ... are through my and others' experience of these being objects for *us*, in some common space.'[9] For Taylor, however, language is not merely designative or descriptive, but is also irreducibly expressive. Moreover, language 'is fashioned and grows not principally in monologue, but in dialogue'.[10] In other words, the question of meaning is inescapably social. The implications of these two points are profound. For Taylor, ideas cannot exist prior to their expression in language; nor can man articulate his own ideas and values in the absence of language. Thus, language is not an instrument under the control of any speaker: '[t]o speak is to touch a bit of the web, and this is to make the whole resonate. Because the words we use now only have sense through their place in the whole web, we can never in principle have a clear oversight of the implications of what we say at any moment.'[11] As a result, one cannot 'have' an identity without having first been inducted as an interlocutor in a language community. Identity is inherently social. Moreover, language is essential to the condition of being reflectively aware, which is crucial to the human capacity to make qualitative distinctions of worth.

It is important to note that although language is not manipulable by any single person, it is not static and unchangeable. Language can be altered, but only within certain limits. Since language is developed in dialogue, it is constantly evolving through the articulations and rearticulations of the speech community. More importantly, however, individuals may break away from the language community. Taylor is nonetheless somewhat dismissive of the possibilities of detaching oneself completely: 'is [such detachment] not always in view of a fuller, more profound and authentic communication, which provides the criterion for what I now recognize as an adequate expression?'[12] This is because alterations of language 'are never quite autonomous, quite uncontrolled by the rest of language. They can only be introduced and make sense because they already have a place within the web.'[13] This is quite a deep point, and one that should not be taken lightly. For any innovation to make sense and have meaning within a particular context, it cannot exist completely outside of the language in which it is deployed. Thus, while one can and is constantly making alterations to language, one can never be completely in control of the language, nor can one simply choose to define oneself outside of this language. One's identity, then, as a complex of different goals and ends, cannot arise except in the context of a language in which one is an interlocutor. It is an inherently social process. But what is the relationship of culture to identity?

Taylor defines culture as 'the background of practices, institutions, and understandings which form the langue-analogue for our action in a given society'.[14] Culture, then, is the framework which provides the background for identity. What Taylor presents, then, is a view whereby culture is the inescapable premise, the ontology, upon which all other goals, values, and conceptions of the person must be based. In this sense, there is no question of establishing the value of culture itself in relation to other values. In other words, culture is not something that one can choose to dispense with when universal morality dictates otherwise. Culture, moreover, is constitutive, but there is nothing to prevent the individual from seeking to re-evaluate his own life projects, or elements of the culture of which he is a part. However, this is a deep process of self-examination, articulation, and rearticulation.[15] It is by no means a simple choice. In this way, Taylor acknowledges culture as constitutive, but contests the liberal criticism that this 'communitarian' claim provides grounds for the state to intervene to preserve a singular view of the good life.

Intercultural understanding

Although Taylor places great importance on culture as the framework in which we can locate our identities, he is radically opposed to any kind of subjectivism or cultural relativism. In fact, he is determined to show that there can be a middle ground between value subjectivism and universalism. This middle path is grounded in Taylor's theory of language.

Taylor is clearly not willing to endorse the universalist position and thereby assume that there are some values which may be appealed to universally. Even more importantly, he is not willing to suggest that his own, culturally informed values be applied to everyone else – either in everyday or in extreme cases. There is no bedrock of universal values to which Taylor appeals. However, he also rejects the notion that there can be no judgement whatsoever in the absence of universals. In his own words, '[t]he interpretive view, I want to argue, avoids the two equal and opposite mistakes: on the one hand, of ignoring self-descriptions altogether, and attempting to operate in some neutral "scientific" language; on the other hand, of taking these descriptions with ultimate seriousness, so that they become incorrigible'.[16]

But, on what grounds should such judgements be made; or, to rephrase the question to better suit Taylor's terms, in what language can these judgements be made? According to Taylor, making a judgement about another culture using our own language and our own distinctions of qualitative worth would be ethnocentric.[17] However, 'the type of understanding needed when we have to grasp the articulating–constitutive uses of words is not available from the stance of a fully disengaged observer'.[18] In other words, once it is accepted that language is not merely designative, nor is it monological, it becomes clear that 'it is plainly impossible to learn a language as a detached observer'.[19] This is crucial for Taylor, since it implies that it is impossible for an outsider to understand another culture without actively engaging with it. In this sense,

> we only arrive at this understanding by some exchange of mutual clarification between ourselves, or some other member of our culture, and members of the target culture. ... [I]n a kind of language negotiated between the anthropologist and his informants. There has to take place a kind of 'fusion of horizons' if understanding is to take place.[20]

For Taylor, this is not merely a fusion of languages, nor is it the imposition of one language upon the other. It is, instead, a 'language of perspicuous contrast' in which both our way of life and theirs might be formulated.

However, this active engagement with another culture does not leave either party unchanged. As Taylor contends, '[b]y challenging their language of self-interpretation, we may also be challenging ours. ... Understanding is inseparable from criticism, but this in turn in inseparable from self-criticism.'[21] Thus, in approaching other cultures, we should begin from a 'presumption of equal worth', which would allow us to be open to a comparative cultural study of the kind that might displace our original horizons.[22] Judgements could then be made about the merits of different cultures on the grounds of the relative merits of the interpretations that they offer. According to Taylor, 'the ultimate basis for accepting any of these theories [of identity] is precisely that they make better sense of us than do their rivals'.[23]

These few premises ground most of Taylor's extensive writings. In fact, the relationship that he sets out between identity and culture has proven to be a very powerful weapon in his debates with naturalism and procedural liberalism. It also has successfully grounded a crucial new way of understanding and accommodating demands for cultural recognition. Because it treats culture as constitutive of identity and gives it moral value for that reason (and not for any instrumental reasons) and because Taylor deliberately argues against the method which informs welfare economics, this theory promises to contribute a great deal towards a normatively adequate approach to cultural policy.

Taylor's ethics

Taylor's work is not directed at producing a thoroughgoing statement of cultural ethics. In fact, this is one of the primary drawbacks of using Taylor's work to inform a book on cultural policy. Nonetheless, a careful reading of his writings suggests that he does have a coherent sense of what constitutes the cultural good and, more specifically, what the goal of cultural politics should be. This section will first set out Taylor's main claims in relation to the cultural good. It will argue that Taylor's ethics is based on a conception of cultural freedom, best described as 'freedom to be'. Although Taylor does not often use either of these terms, this section will argue that cultural freedom acts as the ethical core which grounds his two main ideas about intercultural ethics: understanding and recognition. Each of these ideas will be discussed before conclusions about Taylor's ethics can be drawn.

For Taylor, understanding is the goal of intercultural communication. It is the good, in cultural terms, that we should strive for in our dealings with other cultures: it is only through a 'fusion of horizons' that it is possible to ethically engage with cultures other than our own. Without this fusion of horizons, a judgement of the worth of other cultures would either be ethnocentric (it would praise the other for being like us) or it would be condescending (it would give a positive judgement on demand).[24] But why is it important for us to treat cultures in this way? What is the ethic which underlies the goal of understanding? Taylor is very quiet on this point. However, on several occasions, he employs the language of 'letting people be' as the ultimate justification for understanding. In Taylor's words, 'the goal is to reach a common language, common human understanding, which would allow both us and them undistortively to be'.[25] In similar language, he also argues elsewhere that 'we only liberate others and "let them be" when we can identify and articulate a contrast between their understanding and ours, thereby ceasing...to read them through our home understanding'.[26] It should be noted that Taylor does not intend to advocate any form of passivity or disengagement towards other cultures. Being, in this context, is connected to the dialogical and social nature of identity and so the only ethical way of letting someone be is through the active achievement of a language of perspicuous contrast.

The suggestion that 'letting them be' plays a pivotal role in Taylor's ethics is reinforced by the second strand of his cultural ethics – the concept of recognition. The importance of recognition in Taylor's thought cannot be understood outside of the centrality he accords to language in the constitution of identity. In particular, it should be remembered that it would be impossible to have an identity without being an interlocutor in a language community. Identity is dialogical. Moreover, our self-understandings, which very much shape what we feel, cannot be understood outside of the context of the language community.[27] As a result, Taylor argues, 'our identity is partly shaped by recognition or its absence, often by the *mis*recognition of others, and so a person or group of people can suffer real damage...if the people or society around them mirror back to them a confining or demeaning or contemptible picture of themselves'.[28] This is particularly true since, according to Taylor, people cannot simply or easily renounce their identities just because it would be instrumentally advantageous to do so.

Just as with understanding, recognition is a central element of the good in intercultural relations. However, recognition cannot be separated from understanding: authentic recognition is impossible in the absence of a fusion of horizons in which the worth of the other culture could be appreciated. Moreover, recognition adds a new dimension to Taylor's 'freedom to be'. For if '[n]on-recognition or misrecognition can inflict harm, can be a form of oppression, imprisoning someone in a false, distorted and reduced mode of being',[29] then the recognition of people 'for what they are' is a crucial element of letting them be.

The discussion above has suggested that Taylor's cultural ethics can be described as an ethics of freedom. Taylor's two cultural goals are both valuable because they serve the higher goal of letting people be. This is an important starting point. However, the specific nature of Taylor's conception of freedom can be drawn out in more detail. His discussion of freedom is sparse, but Taylor does make a few direct comments which can provide us with some insight into his thinking on this question.

In a clear contrast to market-based approaches, Taylor is clear in his rejection of freedom as the independence of the subject from external interference.[30] Specifically, he claims that true freedom is not simply a matter of available opportunities, but must also entail an element of self-understanding. In Taylor's words,

> [f]reedom cannot just be the absence of external obstacles, for there may also be internal ones. And nor may the internal obstacles be just confined to those that the subject identifies as such, so that he is the final arbiter; for he may be profoundly mistaken about his purposes and about what he wants to repudiate. ... For freedom now involves my being able to recognize adequately my more important purposes, and my being able to overcome or at least neutralize my motivational fetters, as well as my way of being free of external obstacles. ... I must be actually exercising self-understanding in order to be truly or fully free. I can no longer understand freedom just as an opportunity-concept.[31]

If freedom requires self-understanding, and self-understanding can only make sense within the language community, then freedom must be incomprehensible in terms which do not relate to this community. Freedom, then, involves a certain self-realisation that is not achieved by denying one's identity. Instead, for Taylor, freedom is achieved by recognising that identity is constitutive of who people are and what they value. Freedom means allowing people to be who they are – in a deep, culturally informed sense.

This view of freedom also emerges in Taylor's discussion of Hegel's relevance for modern society. Taylor argues that the difficulty in defining modern freedom arises from the problem of relating freedom to a situation. In other words, what is needed is the recovery of

> a conception of free activity which is ours in virtue of our condition as natural and social beings. ... The struggle to be free ... is powered by an affirmation of this defining situation as ours. *This* cannot be seen as ... a mere occasion to carry out some freely chosen project, which is all that a situation can be within the conception of freedom as self-dependence.[32]

Situation, in this sense, is who we are and where we are located in moral space. This is not to say that this situation can never be altered. As was discussed in the opening paragraphs of this chapter, our cultural position may change, but this entails a deep personal upheaval. In this sense, freedom cannot be seen as the denial or refusal of our situatedness, but instead embraces that situation. In Taylor's words, 'the philosophical attempt to situate freedom is the attempt to gain a conception of man in which free action is the response to what we are'.[33]

This conception of freedom could be criticised on the grounds that its emphasis on culture and community provides an easy gateway to totalitarian politics. In fact, Taylor acknowledges this possibility.[34] However, he does not see that his ethics necessarily commits us to endorsing such a politics. Moreover, he sees that his ethics has the potential to ground another, more productive form of politics that cannot arise from a procedural ethics. This is a civic humanist republicanism. The delineation of what is entailed by such a politics adds detail to Taylor's concept of freedom and, moreover, highlights how Taylor's ethics might work in practice. According to Taylor, the civic humanist thesis 'is that the essential condition of a free (nondespotic) regime is that the citizens have a deeper patriotic identification'.[35] Freedom, in this understanding, is not noninterference, but 'citizen liberty, that of the active participant in public affairs'.[36] In other words, civic humanism entails a citizen identification with the polis. This is a common good, but not one that is the sum of instrumental individual purposes. According to Taylor, 'the very definition of a republican regime as classically understood requires an ontology very different from atomism'.[37] It requires that we examine the 'possible place of we-identities as against merely convergent I-identities'.[38]

In the context of Taylor's ontology, the above discussion clearly leaves open the question of how cultural 'we-identities' might be reconciled with civic 'we-identities'. In arguing against procedural liberalism, Taylor does address this question, showing how identification with society might arise out of identity politics. He claims that if liberals value certain human capabilities, then they should also accept that 'any proof that these capacities can only develop in society or in a society of a certain kind is a proof that we ought to belong to or sustain society or this kind of society'.[39] Of course, this necessarily raises the question of when, how, and by whom any interference is justified, as well as whose freedom is being promoted. These are difficult questions which, as will be shown below, Taylor has difficulty answering. Nonetheless, it is clear that Taylor's political ideals reinforce his view that freedom can only be achieved through the linguistic community.

This section has aimed to show that Taylor's conception of the cultural good can usefully be characterised as an ethics focused on the freedom to be. This ultimately underlies the value that he places on understanding and recognition – the two central concepts in his intercultural relations. Moreover, Taylor's vision of 'freedom to be' is reinforced by his political vision and his critique of procedural liberalism.

Taylor's ethics reconsidered

The discussion of the previous few pages has aimed to extract the most important elements of Taylor's ethical position. Most importantly, it has aimed to provide a sketch of the cultural good in Taylor's work. However, Taylor's ethics is not without its difficulties. The remainder of this chapter will argue that although Taylor's claims provide a useful starting point, they leave several crucial difficulties unresolved. The most important of these for this book concern the paradigm of understanding, the conception of culture, and the status of Taylor's conception of the good. It will be argued that Taylor's cultural ethics provides few workable insights for cultural policy. Nonetheless, as this chapter will conclude, his ontology can be built upon in different ways to produce a more workable cultural ethics.

Paradigm of understanding

The main difficulties with Taylor's ethics stem directly from his ideas about intercultural communication and his paradigm of understanding. As described above, Taylor believes that understanding can come about through a language of perspicuous contrast, or a fusion of horizons. At first glance, this formulation seems as though it can facilitate mutual understanding without misunderstanding or misrecognition of the 'other'. However, by asking how this understanding is supposed to come about and the conditions under which it is possible, some important qualifications to the paradigm become apparent.

Taylor is not especially clear on the details of how this understanding is supposed to come about. At some points, he argues that the first step towards understanding a completely foreign culture is the ability to articulate a contrast between their practices and ours so that we no longer read them entirely from our own frameworks. In other words, understanding is a comparative exercise. At other times, Taylor argues that understanding entails having a sense of why particular things are meaningful for people of other cultures.[40] Finally, and most comprehensively,

Taylor argues that practical reason is the best route to understanding. The task of practical reason is to convince someone of the rightness of a certain position, to reach agreement, by showing that the *transition* between two points of view is an error-reducing one. But how can we be sure that we agree on what constitutes an error? Taylor is remarkably brief on this point, stating that our proof should be 'the direct sense of the transition as an error-reducing one'.[41] However, other comments offer some insight into what is necessary to achieve a common understanding on what constitutes an error. In several places, Taylor comments that overcoming an error may entail 'rescuing from (usually motivated) neglect a consideration whose significance they cannot contest'.[42] In this sense, then, reaching intercultural agreement requires at least a small number of values whose significance is commonly recognised. Without shared values, there would be no grounds for convincing someone of the advantages of the transition to a new position. Taylor admits this point, stating that '[t]he notion that we might have to convince people of an ultimate value premise that they undividedly and unconfusedly reject is, indeed, a ground for despair. ... [I]n this case, practical reason is certainly powerless.'[43] This claim seems to remove the greatest force of Taylor's argument. After all, if his paradigm of understanding is of no use between cultures which share no values, then it can hardly been seen as a great new model for ethical intercultural communication.

However, Taylor is quick to qualify his claims, asking, '[d]o we really face people who quite lucidly reject the very principle of the inviolability of human life? In fact, this doesn't seem to be the case.'[44] This is quite a remarkable claim. Not only does Taylor suppose that there is a significant degree of shared values throughout all cultures of the world, he is suggesting that this convergence occurs around the respect for human life. As an empirical claim, this is clearly contestable, especially as Taylor's understanding of culture is intended to apply back in time as well as around the entire globe. However, as a justification for a philosophical position, it is unacceptable. The difficulties of intercultural communication can hardly be assuaged by the assertion that cultures simply do not disagree on the 'universal' value of respect for human life.

Taylor further complicates the argument by suggesting that '[i]t is not just cases where we can explicitly identify the common premise from the outset that allow of rational debate'.[45] Because debate rarely takes place between two completely firm and discrete positions, 'a great deal of moral argument involves the articulation of the implicit, and this extends the range of the ad hominem far beyond the easy cases where the opponent offers us purchase in one explicit premise'.[46] This raises two crucial epistemological questions. First, how can we know that we have accurately represented the position of the opponent? In other words, how can we be sure that we have not read our own values into their position? This is particularly important in conversations where power plays a significant role and in those where one of the 'conversing' parties has already passed away and is communicating through a written legacy. The second epistemological question concerns how we can tell whether and why this method is not working. For example, if we are arguing with someone and they are not coming over to our position, is it because they ultimately do not share any of our value premises or is it because our method is flawed? As with most epistemological questions, Taylor is loath to provide an answer. However, he does claim at one point that 'there is no way to go except forward, to apply further doses of the same medicine'.[47] Taylor eludes the epistemological question by reaffirming a faith in his method, possibly at the expense of great cultural misunderstanding.

There is still another question outstanding in this analysis. How does the language of perspicuous contrast relate to the grounds for arguing discussed above? Is this language anything more than winning someone over to our point of view? If premises are often implicit, in what language can we carry out the debate that will establish whether we have shared premises or not? Taylor clearly wishes that the language of perspicuous contrast will be one that can do justice to all interlocutors. In his words, 'the goal is to reach a common language, common human understanding, which would allow both us and them undistortively to be'.[48] However, in trying to address the criticism that it is always we who are devising the language in which the other is understood, he finally admits what has seemed obvious in the few paragraphs above, namely that 'the contrast is in a language of our devising'.[49] In other words, we still judge other cultures in light of reality, but our reality has (hopefully) expanded as we have tried to make sense of the contrasts with other cultures. This premise might aid us in understanding how we might be less ethnocentric, but it is not strong enough to support the claim that a fusion of horizons has taken place and that a language of *mutual* understanding has been developed.

Nonetheless, Taylor does not account for how interaction might move from 'our' attempt to highlight errors in 'their' position (the transcendence argument) to an attempt to create a language in which a more egalitarian conversation might take place (the common language argument). These two elements of Taylor's paradigm of understanding seem to be in tension with one another. For example, Taylor wants a common language that respects all cultures, but he also wants to maintain the integrity of judgements about what constitutes an 'error-reducing move'.[50] He argues that whatever we make of the differences between cultures, we cannot reduce reason to the status of a cultural myth. Specifically, 'whatever it is that has pushed modern western culture to study others, at least nominally in the spirit of equality ... is missing in many other cultures. Our very valuing of this equality seems to mark a superiority of our culture over some others.'[51] What Taylor is discussing here is the idea that as members of modern Western culture, we cannot be true to ourselves and still reject the hierarchy of rational over not-yet-rational. This, however, seems to be precisely the difficulty with the aspiration to a language of perspicuous contrast.

Much more can be read into Taylor's paradigm of understanding if it is located in the context of his politics. In particular, the paradigm of understanding must be understood in part as Taylor's contribution to resolving the constitutional conflict between Quebec and Canada. Clearly, Taylor believes that a great deal of progress can be made in this context if a greater degree of mutual understanding could be reached. His goal is to stimulate both parties towards that understanding. For example, in his 1970 article, 'A Canadian Future?', Taylor claims that he will defer the problem of incompatible perspectives 'by speaking first in one perspective and then in the other. Let me try to draw out of both some understanding of the common predicament and common goals.'[52] Taylor achieves this by carefully and sensitively elucidating the positions of both parties. He shows that English Canada's reticence to accept a special status for Quebec stems from a misunderstanding of the demands of nationalism. In particular, English Canadians do not see that French Canadians simply need to be recognised for who they are. Instead, they view Québecois national identification as an antechamber to separatism and therefore deny the recognition that Quebec needs. In turn, French Canadians need to understand English Canada's anxiety about unity. In this way, Taylor attempts to show each side why the other is responding in a particular way and thereby break the pattern of destructive relations and mutual misunderstanding that has characterised relations between French and English in Canada for so long. Moreover, he claims that Canada and Quebec can be brought together by common purposes: 'the continuance of Canada may ... depend on our giving a more meaningful content to the positive sense of being part of a bigger country'.[53] These common purposes include building a bicultural society, focusing on Canada's role in the world, and the creation of a more egalitarian society. In this article, it is clear that Taylor is struggling to define a common language for Canada and Quebec. He is hoping to contribute to the achievement of intercultural understanding and therefore to the resolution of Canada's constitutional woes.

Although the discussion above clearly demonstrates the high place that understanding holds in Taylor's ethics, it nonetheless highlights certain problems with his approach. First, it is difficult to see where Taylor himself stands. It is clear that he sees great value in intercultural understanding. However, it is not clear whether he views himself as belonging to the French Canadian group, the English Canadian group, or both. In the context of his theoretical claims about our ability to understand people who are culturally different from us, one would suspect that Taylor sees himself as having a dual allegiance and therefore as uniquely placed to achieve understanding between the parties. However, Taylor never discusses these issues and in this sense, vital questions about the nature of a common language and how precisely understanding might arise are left unanswered.

By 1991, these questions have been answered at a specific level in Taylor's work on Quebec. In 'Shared and Divergent Values', Taylor again approaches the question of understanding and delineates in greater detail the cultural background to French and English misunderstandings. The English Canadian position is defined by its existential questions about unity and identity. These doubts have largely been answered for 'Canada outside Québec' (COQ) by a common agreement on and pride in the rule of law, collective provision, the equalisation of life chances, multiculturalism, and, most recently, the Charter of Rights and Freedoms.[54] French Canada, on the other hand, has no uncertainty over identity. Thus, the above 'rallying points' are less important to them than is Canada's contribution to the defence and promotion of the French Canadian nation. In turn, the latter would require not only a commitment to French language rights, but also a formal recognition of the autonomy of Quebec.

However, this particular resolution of Taylor's difficulties serves only to highlight even greater difficulties with his ethics. In this later article, however, the problem is one of serious incompatibility between Canadian and Québecois visions of the good life. In fact, the special treatment entailed by the recognition of Quebec would challenge the procedural equality enshrined in the Charter. In other words, the cultural values upon which Canadian unity is presently based are actually incompatible with the needs of Quebec. The procedural liberalism of the Charter actually reinforces the existing denial of recognition to Quebec. This framing of the problem is much more consistent with those situations in which the paradigm of understanding is most needed, i.e. where there is no pre-existing common language. However, in this case, Taylor is unable to show how his paradigm might lead to a resolution of differences. He does refer to the need for 'common ground' between Canada and Quebec, but in his view 'the possible common ground is obvious. Procedural liberals in English Canada just have to acknowledge, first, that there are other possible models of liberal society and, second, that their francophone compatriots wish to live by one such alternative.'[55] Here, Taylor provides a much more definite statement of what needs to be done if the Canadian federation is to stay together. However, Taylor's own starting language is now acutely obvious and his ability to facilitate understanding is circumscribed. In fact, the understanding which Taylor now suggests seems very one-sided. Moreover, the cultural engagement and fusion of horizons so necessary to intercultural understanding have disappeared entirely from Taylor's analysis.

Despite these difficulties, it is not hard to see that the paradigm of understanding provides a very ready explanation of, and solution to, Canada's constitutional situation. In fact, it is tempting to suggest that Taylor had Canada in mind when he was developing the paradigm. Canada is already a liberal democracy with a significant amount of decentralisation and a precedent of respecting cultural rights. Within this hospitable framework, a dialogue between Canada and Quebec about the terms of their cultural coexistence is already under way. The problem in this case is how to achieve a resolution that entails understanding and recognition of the cultural other. However, this is less true of the issues surrounding other cultural conflicts. In most cases, the cultural others are more obviously multiple, both within and between states. Moreover, the achievement of understanding between all of these parties, even if it could be achieved, does not provide a very adequate guide to cultural policy. How could a dialogue be initiated if some (perhaps the most powerful) parties did not feel the need to talk? What if an understanding was reached between the many different groups within one state alone – how could this inform external cultural policy towards another state? The paradigm of understanding can be helpful in showing how two different cultures can learn to peacefully coexist. Beyond this, however, it gives little direction as to the appropriate goals of policy or the means by which these should be pursued. In short, it is difficult to fruitfully apply Taylor's paradigm in this form to the case under study in this book.

To sum up, Taylor argues that intercultural understanding can come about through the application of practical reason. In turn, this relies upon the existence of some shared values. These 'shared values' could, in principle, be composed of anything that those cultures held dear. However, Taylor clearly does not wish to endorse the cultural relativism implicit in the idea that any value which attracted agreement was good. To support his position, Taylor introduces his own standard of the good. But, he does so in a backhanded way. He avoids tackling the ethical question of what the good is and how it is constituted by making an empirical claim about the widespread acceptance of the value of human life. This has two advantages for Taylor. First, it widens the potential scope of his paradigm of understanding to include nearly all cultures and so sidelines the question of how to engage with 'non-liberal' societies. Second, it allows him to evade an ethical justification for his standard of the good. Where does it come from and how does it get its legitimacy? This latter point will be addressed in greater detail below. First, however, it is necessary to address the second point of critique: Taylor's conception of culture.

Conception of culture

The second difficulty with Taylor's ethics concerns his conception of culture. In an insightful article, Amelie Oksenberg Rorty makes several important points about Taylor's usage of the term 'culture'. One of her main criticisms is that Taylor sometimes slips from one usage of the term to another without explaining or justifying the shift.[56] She is clearly right that there is some shifting in Taylor's discussions of culture. In *Sources of the Self* alone, Taylor employs the term 'culture' in no less than 39 distinct ways. However to characterise these different usages as slippage would be to fundamentally misunderstand Taylor's conceptualisation. At the very least, Taylor's usages of culture can be grouped into families. For example, it would not be too far-fetched to argue that 'our culture', 'national culture', and 'German culture' might be used interchangeably with very little slippage. The same might be true of 'modern culture', 'scientific culture', and 'contemporary culture'. The fact that Taylor does indeed use some of these terms interchangeably indicates that his terms could use greater definition. However, it also indicates that Taylor does not view these terms as mutually exclusive. It is quite possible that 'national culture', 'scientific culture', and 'family culture' are all contexts of experience and frameworks of meaning that vie for our moral attention. As Taylor remarks, 'our identities, as defined by whatever gives us fundamental orientation, are in fact complex and many-tiered'.[57] Moreover, it is clear from his discussion of Enlightenment rationalism that a complex of values such as 'scientific culture' can generate meaning just as easily as 'national culture'. So, Taylor's conception of culture is a fluid one, but it does not justify the criticism levelled at it by Rorty.

Nonetheless, such a fluid conception of culture does raise the question of where one culture ends and another begins. Taylor does not address this issue, preferring instead to use the label 'culture' wherever it fits the situation. For example, his treatment of Canada and Quebec focuses on several cultures: Canadian, Québecois, and those of the unnamed minorities. However, his discussion would become significantly more complicated if he also wished to include religious, scientific, political, modern, Western, intellectual, or capitalist cultures. In fact, the question of what was cultural might become so clouded as to preclude any useful comment at all. It might be possible to argue that language or national sentiment are so prominent in meaning creation for Quebec that special attention to these factors is justified. However, it is still not clear why these factors should be singled out as defining of cultures in this case. Why not the cultural ties which place Canada and Quebec as part of the same culture (say, modern culture), or those which command allegiance among some people on both sides of the provincial boundary (say, Muslim culture)? By ignoring these cultural ties, it seems as though Taylor is prioritising certain types of culture, at least in this case. Without further explanation or justification, this prioritisation has the effect of glossing over the difficulties of Taylor's fluid conception of culture. As Rorty has noted, Taylor's 'argument occasionally exploits the ambiguity of his usage'.[58]

More importantly, this criticism points to the fact that the very definition of a culture and the identification of who its members are is often the site of serious political contestation. To take terms such as 'us' or 'Quebec culture' as given implies that these debates are settled. This may seem like an oversensitive claim. After all, if we wish to undertake empirical studies, then we must at some point refer to recognisable entities, even if these cannot be precisely defined. However, as the Canadian constitutional case has shown, the characterisation of the debate as 'Quebec versus Canada' grossly underestimates the variety of cultural claims involved and could lead to a solution which ignores the needs of many people. The most notable group in this regard are probably the non-French-speaking Québecois, although French speakers outside Quebec are also an obvious example, as are aboriginal peoples. Making claims about Quebec, as though the question of who is Québecois is already settled, threatens to neglect the claims being made on behalf of these groups, among many others. This is perhaps an overly politicised example. However, the debates about what is modern, Western, or scientific are no less affected by the politics of setting boundaries. Taylor's approach to culture is unable to address some of these crucial questions.

A further question arises out of Taylor's fluid understanding of culture. If it is the case that culture is a very broad concept and if we all may be influenced by many different cultures in the composition of our identities, then it must be asked how this affects the relationship between culture and identity that was set out above. Clearly, it is still possible that cultural frameworks provide the background understanding upon which identity relies. However, if these frameworks are plural and competing, then there is no reason why any identity will rely on cultures in the same combination as any other. In other words, unless Taylor is willing to essentialise identities and to fix the relationship between culture and identity, then his argument is forced back to the individualisation of identity. The frameworks may be common, but each identity is individual. This forces a gap between culture and identity and suggests the possibility that even culturally informed identities may entail greater subjectivity than Taylor would appreciate. This point is reinforced by the discussion of culture in the previous paragraph. The idea of a multicultural society already implies such a great deal of cross-cultural interchange that it becomes impossible to discuss the 'cultures' involved as anything like identifiable, separate entities. For example, in the case of the daughter of Chinese immigrants to Montreal, one must ask how easily her identity could be understood in terms of two distinct cultures operating on and against one another. Nonetheless, it is also not the case that her identity can be 'read' directly from a single particular culture. In other words, there is no doubt that her identity is impacted upon by plural cultural forces and yet this does not mean that these cultures can be separated and identified. Taylor's theory of intercultural understanding, as much as his conception of culture, relies upon pre-existing, identifiable, fixed cultural entities.[59] His paradigm can accommodate cultural evolution, but only in so far as this generates a new cultural entity. The first difficulty with this understanding is that it provides an inadequate account of cultural evolution and intercultural interpenetration. This is particularly problematic for a theory attempting to cope with multicultural societies. Second, the concept of plural identities tends towards a subjectivity that Taylor would reject. This can only be avoided by an implicit essentialisation of identity and a fixing of the relationship between identity and culture more firmly than Taylor acknowledges.

The necessity of a tight relationship between culture and identity emerges again in an article where Taylor discusses how the public sphere relates to policy-making. He defines the public sphere as 'a common space in which the members of society meet ... to discuss matters of common interest; and thus to be able to form a common mind about those matters'.[60] According to Taylor, the public sphere is crucial for democratic decision-making in that it enables 'the society to reach a common mind, without the mediation of the political sphere'.[61] But what role does culture play in the ability of a society to reach a common mind? This becomes clear when Taylor sets out the conditions for genuine democratic decision-making. According to Taylor,

> they include (a) that the people concerned understand themselves as belonging to a community that shares some common purposes ...; (b) that the various groups, types, and classes of citizens have been given a genuine hearing and were able to have an impact on the debate; and (c) that the decision emerging from this is really the majority preference.[62]

In a sense, Taylor is setting out how it is possible to be sure that any public policy decision embodies a respect for cultural difference. Taylor does admit that his description of the public sphere is an ideal type. Nonetheless, his suggestion that a 'common mind' is both desirable and possible, and his predication of democracy upon community presuppose a greater degree of cultural homogeneity than is likely. In other words, they reinforce the idea that people in a certain area can be expected to subscribe to the same culture. Not only does this presuppose a very tight relationship between a single culture and identity, it leaves very few resources for policy-making in situations where cultures are diffuse or where there is no common mind or sense of community.

In sum, then, Taylor wishes both to give moral value to culture as constitutive and to avoid the possibility of relativism or radical subjectivity. In order to tread this middle course, he is required to firmly fix the relationship between culture and identity. This is not achieved in the unnuanced way that many communitarians are often accused of adopting.[63] Nonetheless, it produces a similar essentialisation. As the next section will show, this view of identity is itself energised by a very powerful but also very subtle conception of the good. The following section will argue that this conception is not adequately defended, thereby creating problems for Taylor's argument. The final section will show how Taylor's theory could adequately defend a narrower conception of the good, without relying exclusively on culturally specific norms or on universals.

Conception of the good

The final aspect of Taylor's cultural ethics that requires critical examination involves his conception of the good. Much of Taylor's work is devoted to negotiating a middle way between complete moral subjectivism and moral universalism. As was shown above, this attempt to chart a middle course created some difficulties for his paradigm of understanding. The difficulties for his conception of the good are even more serious. In *Sources of the Self*, Taylor is concerned to retrieve and elaborate the moral sources which underpin the modern self. As his theory of culture and identity would suggest, Taylor is critical of approaches which locate moral sources within each individual. According to Taylor, thoughts, goods, and values can only be the thoughts, goods, and values that they are against the social background of meaning.[64] Equally, however, Taylor resists the opposite notion, namely that moral sources are external to people. In particular, he argues that '[u]nderlying our modern talk of identity is the notion that questions of moral orientation cannot all be solved in simply universal terms'.[65] But where, then, do our moral sources originate? More importantly, what is the 'good' for the modern self?

Taylor's discussion of these questions is rarely direct and the reader is often left grasping at short comments and unexplained references. For example, Taylor seems highly sympathetic to the Romantic notion of nature as an external source that can only be realised within. According to Taylor, 'these modern views give a crucial place to our own inner powers of constructing or transfiguring or interpreting the world, as essential to the efficacy of the external sources. Our powers must be deployed if these are to empower us.'[66] Moreover, he often remarks how a moral source is one which moves us or resonates within us. For example, Taylor claims that '[w]e sense in the very experience of being moved by some higher good that we are moved by what is good in it rather than that it is valuable because of our reaction'.[67] Later, he argues that our concern should be with 'the search for moral sources *outside* the subject through languages which resonate *within* him or her, the grasping of an order which is inseparably indexed to a personal vision'.[68] In other words, the standard of the good is not purely subjective. Nonetheless, we recognise the good by our subjective reaction to it. This is a very delicate position to maintain successfully, and Taylor does not offer enough detail to be convincing. Most importantly, he does not provide an explanation of what motivates our moral reactions. For example, he often refers to being motivated by 'the higher' but does not adequately explain what this might consist of or why it has legitimacy as a moral source. These are crucial questions if Taylor is to successfully negotiate the middle course between subjectivism and universalism.

There are several things which might fill this criterion of 'the higher'. In Taylor's view, one clear possibility is God. Many critics have discussed Taylor's theistic references and especially the place given to the Augustinian thread in *Sources of the Self*.[69] Indeed, Taylor's frequent references to epiphany as an unveiling of moral sources and his interest in the question of grace are suggestive. Moreover, no reader can fail to note his comment in the closing pages of the book that his hope for the future 'is a hope that I see implicit in Judaeo-Christian theism (however terrible the record of its adherents in history), and in its central promise of a divine affirmation of the human, more total than humans can ever attain unaided'.[70] Indeed, Taylor fully intends to depict God as a moral source in the modern Western world. However, as Michael Morgan has convincingly argued, 'opponents of religion have to distort what he says in order to mount an attack on him'.[71] There are two reasons for this. The first is that Taylor is exceedingly fair both to the believers and the non-believers. In fact, far from overstating the claims of Christianity, it seems more that he overstates the degree of non-belief in the modern world. Second, as Morgan notes, '[h]e does not argue directly that God and religion *should* play a central role in our moral lives; he does show how, subject to detailed clarification, they *could* do so'.[72] Moreover, while religion seems to be Taylor's personal favourite, he is equally aware of two other modern moral sources: nature and reason. The former derives its force from the remnants of Romantic expressivism, while the latter is handed down to us from the Enlightenment.

The more important question, perhaps, is why these particular sources have legitimacy. Clearly, Taylor believes that they are unavoidable terms of reference for the modern identity. He is probably correct that the legacy of these sources permeates our identity, at least in the modern West. However, it is not clear that the very existence of these as sources of meaning makes them legitimate. As Ronald Beiner has argued in relation to another value, that of ordinary life,

> if it is the case that the basic justification for the prominence that domestic life has in the lives of modern individuals is simply that this is in fact how individuals inhabiting the modern dispensation have

come to understand themselves and articulate their self-identity, then what objection could be posed if individuals within some new dispensation come to understand themselves and define their identity in a way that requires radical liberation from the moral constraints and social obligations of family life?[73]

Beiner goes on to argue that Taylor would be uncomfortable with such an outcome. This is probably an ungenerous representation of Taylor's views on the family. Nonetheless, several broader points are highly relevant.

Most importantly, Taylor makes it seem that a practice or an idea is morally valuable simply by virtue of it having evolved as part of human experience. As Beiner comments, 'the standard of theoretical judgement is simply the historically contingent evolution of identity'.[74] In other words, the conception of the self which triumphed just happens to be judged by Taylor to be a good one. This coincidence will be discussed in greater detail below. However, the important point for this discussion is that Taylor is not willing to accept as valuable any practice that might arise out of or be affirmed by human experience. For example, some practices, such as family life, are clearly valuable, while others, such as Nazism and nationalism, are bad.[75] What are the criteria which distinguish some meaningful practices from others? Taylor's own comments give no indication. This is hardly surprising given that any such principle would almost certainly lend significant support to the liberal universalism that Taylor critiqued so vehemently. Nonetheless, there are strong grounds for suspecting that an unacknowledged and undefended standard of the good operates in Taylor's work.

The value of Taylor's approach

The difficulties described above are serious enough to prevent this book from advocating that Taylor's ethics should underscore policy for culture. Nonetheless, Taylor's ontology is highly insightful and will provide the necessary theoretical grounding of the position developed in the next chapter. Taylor's ontology is important because of the strong challenge it provides to the atomist preconditions of much scientific endeavour (be it natural or social). He does not simply state his own disagreement with atomism, but sets out in great detail and depth what an alternative social ontology entails. It is a forceful concept that demonstrates the possibility of seeing culture as constitutive of identity and yet allowing for a plurality of cultural frameworks.

Nonetheless, the ethical position which Taylor himself draws from this ontology is beset with difficulties. The three most important ones for cultural policy were set out above. Despite the seriousness of these criticisms, they do not present a large impediment to the development of a different and more adequate cultural ethics. In fact, as the next chapter will show, it is even possible to develop such an ethics without betraying Taylor's powerful ontology. The following chapter will draw on the work of Iris Marion Young to show how, starting from Taylor's ontology, it is possible to develop a radical democratic ethics that can empower a useful and ethical policy for culture.

6
Social Justice in a
Multicultural Context

The previous chapter set out the foundations of the approach that this book will take towards cultural policy. It established the value of Charles Taylor's ontology, even though it argued that his ethical and political positions contained serious difficulties and were inappropriate for this project. The tasks of this chapter are twofold. First, it will show how Taylor's ontology can be developed to produce a different and more useful ethics for cultural policy. This will be achieved by drawing on the work of Iris Marion Young. Second, this chapter will briefly suggest the ways in which this ethics can inform cultural policy. The details of these suggestions will be drawn out in the next two chapters.

Ontology

Like Taylor, Young's work is rooted in her firm opposition to the atomist ontology which grounds much social and political theory. However, in contrast to Taylor's focus on culture, Young's foundation is her conception of the social group.

Young begins her discussion of the social group by rejecting two common models of social association. These are the aggregate model and the associationist model. In the aggregate model, groups are defined by a certain attribute which all group members are thought to possess. For example, a group might equally be composed of people who are women, just as easily as it might be composed of people who own red cars. According to Young, however, '[a] social group is defined not primarily by a set of shared attributes, but by a sense of identity'.[1] Although the members of a group might share certain attributes, these are not the basis of their identification with the group. Instead, '[g]roup meanings partially constitute people's identities in terms of the cultural forms, social situation, and history that group members know as theirs'.[2] Groups are forms of social relations, rather than combinations of people. This means that the ongoing processes of engagement and identification are crucial to the identity formation of both the group and its members.

The second common model of social organisation is the associationist model. Social contract theories are one prominent example of this model. Unlike the model of aggregates, associationism understands that practices and processes may be pivotal in group formation. However, according to Young, both models still understand that the individual is constituted prior to his affiliation with the group. In Young's words, 'the person's identity and sense of self are usually regarded as prior to and relatively independent of association membership'.[3]

Instead, Young defines a social group as 'a collective of persons differentiated from at least one other group by cultural forms, practices, or way of life',[4] and argues that the individual cannot be understood outside of her group affiliations. According to Young, '[a] person's sense of history, affinity, and separateness, even the person's mode of reasoning, evaluating, and expressing feeling, are constituted partly by her or his group affinities'.[5] Young maintains that the self must be considered as a product of social and linguistic processes and that identity is constituted relationally.[6] In order to give some idea of what it might actually mean for identity to be constituted relationally, Young highlights the work of several recent philosophers. She refers to post-structuralist philosophies which challenge the assumption that consciousness develops prior to language. Instead, they claim that 'the self is an achievement in linguistic positioning that is always contextualized in concrete relations with other persons'.[7] She also describes Jürgen Habermas' claim that 'group categorization and norms are major constituents of individual identity'.[8] Finally, Young takes on Martin Heidegger's notion of 'thrownness' to explain how 'one *finds oneself* as a member of a group, which one experiences as always already having been'.[9] This is perhaps to overstate the case, as it ignores the processes by which groups may form and by which they evolve to assume identity proportions. However, Young does temper Heidegger by suggesting that we come to be members of a group not by 'satisfying some objective criteria, but [by] a subjective affirmation of identity with that group, the affirmation of that affinity by other members of the group, and the attribution of membership in that group by persons identifying with other groups'.[10] In other words, the group, in general, exists as ontologically prior to any individual. Group affiliations may change or that some may be overcome and replaced by others. However, according to Young, 'changes in group affinity are experienced as transformations in one's identity'.[11]

Unfortunately, Young does not develop her conception of group identification in any greater detail. In fact, apart from these few references to Jacques Lacan, Habermas, and Heidegger, she gives very little indication of what it might actually mean for identity to be social and relational. Nor, as we noted, does she indicate how groups develop or lose their capacity for fostering identities. Nonetheless, much of what she describes as her social ontology can very comfortably be grounded in Taylor's ontology. Like Taylor, Young denies the ontological priority of the isolated individual. Also like Taylor, she seeks to show that individual identity is inescapably group-based and yet wishes to avoid giving licence to the community to determine what is good for the individual. Not surprisingly, in grappling with this problem, Young also turns to post-structuralist theories of language in order to ground her conception of the self and its relation to society.[12] The result is that both theorists lay great importance on the need for social recognition of, and respect for, people's different identities. Neither can conceive of a meaningful freedom in the absence of this. Moreover, they both stress the importance of conceiving of society dialogically and relationally. In short, both Young's arguments against atomism and her positive comments about how the self should be understood mirror Taylor's very closely. There is clearly no contradiction in taking Taylor's ontology as the basis for an ethics of culture that draws heavily on Young. In fact, since Young devotes so little attention to the philosophical underpinnings of her ethics, a connection to Taylor's ontology adds greater depth to her work and underscores its normative significance.

Nonetheless, one important point of divergence must be dealt with. As was mentioned above, where Taylor emphasises the centrality of culture for identity, Young focuses on the social group. As will be shown below, such a shift in emphasis need not affect the utility of Taylor's ontology in this context. In fact, in the context of this book, Young's conception of the social group is able to fulfil the most important functions of Taylor's theory of culture while avoiding many of its difficulties. As a result, it provides a much more useful basis for the development of a satisfactory cultural ethics.

The particular features of Young's conception of the social group which make it especially useful arise in her discussion of social groups and oppression. Young is careful to claim that while certain particular groups have been oppressive, there is nothing inherently oppressive in recognising the primacy of the social group. This is only true, however, if one adopts a conception of group identification that is 'much more relational and fluid' than many commentators, including Taylor, are willing to acknowledge.[13] It should be recalled that Young argues that groups are not defined according to the specific attributes of their members and that they are essentially the product of dialogical and relational social engagement. Following from these claims, Young argues that '[t]here is no common nature that members of a group share. As aspects of a process, moreover, groups are fluid; they come into being and may fade away.'[14] In this way, Young is able to give primacy to social groups without thereby assuming an essentialised group, externally and arbitrarily fixing what is entailed by group membership, or predefining what the good for the group might be.

Young is also attuned to the multiple nature of modern group attachments in a way that Taylor is not. She recognises that 'every social group has group differences cutting across it, which are potential sources of wisdom, excitement, conflict, and oppression'.[15] These cross-cutting group differences serve to create multiple affiliations and allegiances within society, but also within individuals. As a result, although the social group remains the central category of human relations, it is no longer possible to assume a homogeneity of values or interests within smaller groups, never mind within nations or classes as a whole. Nonetheless, this lack of homogeneity does not rule out the utility of the social group as a concept. In fact, it is the very fluidity of it that can capture our modern sense of multiple and sometimes conflicting poles of identification.

Young's focus on the social group can very easily be substituted for Taylor's conception of culture. Once culture is understood broadly to incorporate people's values and ways of life, it is imperative that we also broaden our understanding of 'cultural groups' to include the many different affiliations that comprise a 'way of life' for any particular person. That these are not easily definable or homogeneous does not make them any less constitutive of our identities. It may create difficulties for social theory, but, as Taylor's ethics showed, without such a fluid and cross-cutting conceptualisation, the pluralistic type of freedom envisaged by both Taylor and Young would be an impossibility.

In this way, the strengths of Taylor's ontology can be retained and used as the foundation for a different ethics of culture. This ethics is the subject of the next section.

Ethics

The problems with Taylor's ethics were discussed at length in the previous chapter. Any attempt to build on his ontology in order to develop a workable ethics will have to remedy those problems and avoid generating any new and serious difficulties. The section above set out Young's conception of the social group as an important substitution in Taylor's ontology. This section will show that the ontology developed above can spawn an ethics that is much more useful and culturally sensitive than Taylor's.

Unlike Taylor, Young's ethics are clearly stated and occupy the forefront of her work. She begins by locating her position in contrast to what she terms the distributive paradigm. According to Young, this paradigm dominates much of contemporary thinking about justice. It is characterised by an understanding of social justice in terms of 'the morally proper distribution of social benefits and burdens among society's members'.[16] Young sees this approach as problematic for two reasons. First, she claims that it ignores and often presupposes the institutional context that underlies particular patterns of distribution. As a result, these institutional structures are never brought forward for normative evaluation. Second, she claims that when distributive approaches do deal with non-material issues, they do so by treating any social value 'as some thing or aggregate of things that some specific agents possess in certain amounts'.[17] This provides a misleading account of the issues of justice entailed, since '[i]t reifies aspects of social life that are better understood as a function of rules and relations than as things. And it conceptualizes social justice primarily in terms of end-state patterns, rather than focusing on social processes.'[18]

Instead, Young argues for a conception of social justice that she describes as 'enabling'. In other words, our conception of justice should be broadened beyond distribution to include an examination of institutional conditions. More specifically, we should expect institutional conditions to 'make it possible for all to learn and use satisfying skills in socially recognized settings, to participate in decision-making, and to express their feelings, experience, and perspective on social life in contexts where others can listen'.[19] Young is very open about the values that underlie this position. In particular, she highlights two values that are especially important for social justice: '(1) developing and exercising one's capacities and expressing one's experience, and (2) participating in determining one's action and the conditions of one's action'.[20] These values are central to Young's ethics. They reappear throughout her work, though often in different formulations. For the purposes of the discussion below, the first value will be referred to as enablement and the second as participation. These will each be discussed before their relationship to democracy will be drawn out.

Enablement

The idea of enablement appears throughout *Justice and the Politics of Difference*. Although Young uses it only in the context of social justice, it nevertheless has several meanings. First, enablement is used to refer to expression. Justice, for Young, entails that people are enabled to express themselves in a variety of ways. They must be able to express their experiences, their needs, their feelings and perspective on social life, their desires, and the particularities of themselves.[21] At the most basic level, expression is crucial for people to be able to communicate with one another, and to meet their needs. According to Young's ontology, people cannot simply or easily change who they are, even if such a change might bring social or material benefits. As a result, ensuring that people have both the freedom and the capacity to express themselves is crucial to the achievement of social justice based on an appreciation of diversity. Moreover, as will become clear below, participatory democracy would be meaningless in the absence of the freedom for people to express themselves and publicly discuss their needs and desires.

Second, enablement refers to the capacity to perform certain actions. More specifically, Young discusses the importance of people being enabled to develop and exercise their capacities, to meet their needs, and, ultimately, to exercise their freedom and realise their choices.[22] Young does not detail why this second type of enablement is important, although she clearly assumes that the ability to exercise one's capacities is central to human fulfilment. This is evident in her discussion of the need to reform the hierarchical division of labour. In particular, she criticises the distinction between 'those who plan their own or other's work routines ... and those who follow routines that have been planned for them'.[23] This distinction, she claims, fosters the notion that some types of work are better or more important than others and therefore 'tends to ignore intelligence and skill that have different and in some ways incomparable forms'.[24] This reproduces the oppression of these groups, since it 'condemns a large proportion of the population to a situation in which they cannot develop and exercise their capacities'.[25]

The precise requirements of enablement can further be drawn out by examining Young's approach to injustice and specifically her conception of oppression. Paralleling her description of social justice according to two values, Young defines two types of injustice, namely oppression and domination. Domination is the opposite of participation and so will be dealt with in the subsection on participation below. Oppression, however,

> consists in systematic institutional processes which prevent some people from learning and using satisfying and expansive skills in socially recognized settings, or institutionalized social processes which inhibit people's ability to play and communicate with others or to express their feelings and perspective on social life in contexts where others can listen.[26]

In this sense, oppression names the conditions that enablement must overcome. According to Young, oppression is a 'family of concepts and conditions'.[27] No group is oppressed in the same way or to the same extent as any other. In an effort to avoid the reduction of oppression to a single indicator, Young discusses it according to its 'five faces'. These are exploitation, marginalisation, powerlessness, cultural imperialism, and violence.[28] In this context, we can gain some insight into the specific demands of enablement by briefly delineating the injustices that it is expected to rectify.

First, *exploitation* describes the type of oppression in which the results of the labour of one social group are transferred to benefit another. The injustice in this case consists not just in the unequal distribution of income, but also in the structural relations that 'are produced and reproduced through a systemic process in which the energies of the have-nots are continuously expended to maintain and augment the power, status, and wealth of the haves'.[29] Rectifying this situation, therefore, entails not just a redistribution of incomes, but also requires a restructuring of decision-making and a reorganisation of the division of labour. Second, *marginalisation* describes the situation of people that 'the system of labour cannot or will not use'.[30] As a result, '[a] whole category of people is expelled from useful participation in social life and thus potentially subjected to severe material deprivation and even extermination'.[31] Third, *powerlessness* describes those people 'who lack authority or power even in [a] mediated sense, those over whom power is exercised without their exercising it; the powerless are situated so that they must take orders and rarely have the right to give them'.[32] The injustice occurs because people are prevented from exercising their capacities, they have no decision-making power, and they are subjected to disrespectful treatment. These first three types of oppression are all linked quite closely to the division of labour. In this context, several demands of enablement are highlighted. These include a reorganisation of the institutions of decision-making power, a restructuring of the division of labour, and a recognition of the value of all social groups. In this way, people can be enabled to express their needs in a context where others can listen, exercise their capacities, and exercise some power over their actions and the conditions of their actions.

The fourth type of oppression, *cultural imperialism*, refers to the process by which 'the dominant meanings of society render the particular perspective of one's own group invisible at the same time as they stereotype one's group and mark it out as the Other'.[33] Unlike the previous three types of oppression, cultural imperialism does not refer mainly to the division of labour. Instead, it relates to social processes of cultural representation and recognition. The injustice consists precisely in the fact that 'dominant cultural expressions often simply have little place for the experience of other groups'.[34] Not only is the experience of subordinate groups not recognised as valuable, but the dominant group often universalises its own way of looking at the world and imposes it on other groups. In this context, enablement must entail a recognition of and respect for the plurality of cultural experiences. It should allow people to express their particularities in a context of social recognition and respect.

The final type of oppression is *violence*. This refers not simply to specific violent acts, but more importantly to its existence and reproduction as a social practice. Young is concerned to show that certain types of violence against particular social groups are not random, but instead are 'rule-bound, social, and often premeditated'.[35] Moreover, according to Young, it results from the threat to dominant identities that is posed by subordinate groups. The particular details of Young's theory that difference is threatening to identity will be drawn out further below. It is sufficient here to note that, for Young, enablement must entail a change in 'cultural images, stereotypes, and the mundane reproduction of relations of dominance and aversion in the gestures of everyday life'.[36] Only in this way can the identity-based violence be overcome.

Participation

After enablement, the second value that dominates Young's work is participation. Most commonly, Young refers to participation in deliberation and decision-making.[37] The importance of this type of participation is that it allows people to have the power over their actions and the conditions of their actions that was described as a condition of social justice. However, she also refers to the value of participation in social and political institutions, in dialogue, and in moral and social life.[38] Specifically, Young's conception of social justice demands participation that is universal – in terms of the people who participate *and* the institutions subject to democratisation – but also immediate, local, and accessible.[39] It must give people a chance to discuss and decide on issues concerning the institutions and rules that affect them. Moreover, in keeping with her social ontology, Young requires forms of participation that adequately take account of group difference. As will be discussed in the following section, this view of participation itself requires that group representation be guaranteed in certain decision-making institutions.

Mirroring the relationship described above between oppression and enablement, the illustrative flip-side of participation is domination. Specifically, domination is an injustice created by the absence or denial of participation. According to Young, it 'consists in institutional conditions which inhibit or prevent people from participating in determining their actions or the conditions of their actions'.[40] In this sense, social justice demands that decision-making structures and institutions of all types be made more participatory. Moreover, it entails that many institutions become more democratic. The details of Young's concept of democracy give substance to the minimal claims about participation made in the preceding paragraphs.

Democracy

Enablement and participation are the two values that define Young's conception of social justice. They detail the meaning of social justice as a goal towards which our action and policy should be oriented. However, they also explain and justify Young's commitment to democracy as a normative and political principle. This section will set out Young's idea of democracy, focusing particularly on her conceptions of the heterogeneous public and the need for group conscious policies.

According to Young, '[s]ocial justice entails democracy'.[41] In other words, the values of enablement and participation are best achieved in a democratic society. Specifically, Young claims that democracy has value on two grounds. First, instrumentally, 'participatory processes are the best way for citizens to ensure that their own needs and interests will be voiced and not dominated by other interests'.[42] Second, 'democratic participation has an intrinsic value over and above the protection of interests, in providing an important means for the development and exercise of capacities'.[43] Here, Young relies on the work of many theorists before her who argue that participatory democracy fosters certain capacities of consideration and action that would otherwise remain underdeveloped.[44] In particular, she claims that democracy urges people to consider their needs in relation to those of others and gives them an active relationship with social processes and institutions. Moreover, it should be clear that democracy is an essential means by which the demands of enablement and participation can be met.

Young never explicitly defines her conception of democracy. However, it is evident that she has in mind something far more radical than most theorists would advocate. Specifically, she argues that '[a]ll persons should have the right and opportunity to participate in the deliberation and decisionmaking of the institutions to which their actions contribute or which directly affect their actions'.[45] Accordingly, democratisation should not be restricted to institutions of government, but must be extended to 'all institutions of collective life'.[46] The implications of this claim are drawn out in Young's criticism of impartial moral reasoning and in her development of the ideal of the civic public.

Young is an adamant opponent of the ideal of impartiality which dominates much modern moral reasoning. She claims that most moral theories are based on the assumption that 'in order for the agent to escape egoism, and attain objectivity, he or she must adopt a universal point of view that is the same for all rational agents'.[47] In turn, this impartial point of view is attained by abstracting from the particularities of the agent's position and situation. So, an impartial reasoner must be detached, dispassionate, and universal.[48] He presents the point of view that any rational person could adopt, regardless of their situation, experience, or feelings. Given her ontology, it is not surprising that Young takes issue with this picture of moral reasoning. She argues that it attempts to deny existing difference in order to create a singular, transcendental subject.

Specifically, the attempt to achieve disengaged moral reasoning actually forces difference out of the moral and political realm altogether: 'the concrete interests, needs, and desires of persons and the feelings that differentiate them from one another become merely private, subjective'.[49] What results is an ideal of the civic public which is itself impartial and expresses a general will. It is a homogeneous public, since all difference has been removed to the private sphere. In the first place, this acts to exclude from public life all those who cannot or do not wish to distance themselves from feeling and experience. However, if Young is correct that it is impossible to achieve the disengaged stance, then the ideal of impartiality actually serves to mask 'the inevitable partiality of perspective from which moral deliberation...takes place'.[50] The ideal of impartiality, then, aids in the universalisation of a particular, usually dominant perspective. The universal standpoint itself cannot but be imbued with the particularity of experience and feeling. As a result, the desire to limit all particularities to the private realm actually functions to limit the public participation of groups whose own experience and subjectivity do not mirror that presented as universal by the ideal of impartiality.

Instead, Young argues that the public sphere and the democratic ideal should embrace difference, allowing the feelings, experiences, and desires of all to become part of public discussion. It should be recalled that Young's idea of enablement repeatedly referred to feelings, experiences, and desires – these are the elements of who we are and where we are coming from which must be expressed in a context of recognition for social justice to be achieved. Moreover, this need for recognition explains why existing civil rights are insufficient to promote Young's social justice. According to Young, civil rights may offer participation, but not on a basis which affirms the different experiences and perspectives of the groups involved. Civil rights do allow for a great variety of different ways of behaving, but these are considered private choices. Instead, Young's politics of difference takes as an example gay pride which 'asserts that sexual identity is a matter of culture and politics, and not merely "behaviour" to be tolerated or forbidden'.[51] So, '[i]nstead of a fictional contract, we require real participatory structures in which actual people, with their geographical, ethnic, gender, and occupational differences, assert their perspectives on social issues within institutions that encourage the representation of their distinct voices'.[52] This, in turn, explains why social justice requires a radical form of participatory democracy. In Young's words, '[r]adical democratic pluralism acknowledges and affirms the public and political significance of social group differences *as a means of* ensuring the participation and inclusion of everyone in social and political institutions'.[53]

Social justice also requires a particular type of public sphere, namely one characterised by heterogeneity. Somewhat unusually, Young defines the public as 'what is open and accessible'.[54] Ideally, 'persons should stand forward with their differences acknowledged and respected, though perhaps not completely understood, by others'.[55] In contrast to theories which present a homogeneous public sphere, according to Young, 'the perception of anything like a common good can only be an outcome of public interaction that expresses rather than submerges particularities'.[56] The private, in this context, is not what the public sphere excludes, but instead what the individual chooses to withdraw from the public. Both spheres exist, but the boundary between them is fluid and often itself becomes a public issue.[57] Within this context, the achievement of a heterogeneous public sphere has two preconditions: '(a) no persons, actions, or aspects of a person's life should be forced into privacy; and (b) no social institutions or practices should be excluded a priori [*sic*] from being a proper subject for public discussion and expression'.[58]

Thus, social justice requires not that group differences be overcome or assimilated but that they be acknowledged and affirmed. Equality, in this context, refers not to equal treatment, but to the principle that differential treatment may be justified to ensure the 'participation and inclusion of all groups' in society's main institutions and practices.[59] Moreover, because of the centrality of the social group for identity, 'a politics that asserts the positivity of group difference is liberating and empowering', most particularly for those who have not been recognised or valued by the dominant culture.[60] For Young, what this means is that group conscious policies, including affirmative action, are an intrinsic part of social equality. According to Young, groups cannot be socially equal without recognition of and respect for who they are. Clearly this applies to all groups. However, groups that are oppressed or disadvantaged also require additional mechanisms to ensure representation, such as public aid to help them organise, obligations on decision-makers to take group-generated proposals into account, and group veto power regarding decisions that affect them directly.[61] Young does hint at the fact that this principle of representation is a broad one, but, she argues, '[s]ocial justice would be enhanced in many American cities ... if a citywide school committee formally and explicitly represented Blacks, Hispanics, women, gay men and lesbians, poor and working-class people, disabled people, and students'.[62] She also acknowledges that such a degree of representation may increase conflict but argues that such conflict is more just in that differences are brought out into the open and are discussed, even if this makes decision-making more difficult.[63] As will be argued below, there are logistical and ethical complications created by this principle of representation. These must be mitigated if Young's approach is to be useful.

There is one aspect of Young's ethics that remains to be discussed. Specifically, it should be recalled that Young's conception of oppression described cultural imperialism as an injustice that is often symbolic and rarely expressed through society's formal structures. In setting out why this is so, she refers to Anthony Giddens' three levels of subjectivity – discursive consciousness, practical consciousness, and basic security system.[64] She argues that while aversion at the level of articulated, discursive consciousness is rare, such aversion often manifests itself through unconscious or unintended reactions stemming from the practical consciousness or basic security system. More specifically, Young argues that cultural imperialism arises from a threat to identity caused by that which is different. She claims that we feel aversion in this context, not because that which is different is in fact foreign, but rather because it is so close to our own identities that we must constantly push it away. Our identities are not fixed and so the possibility that we too might be 'other' is ever-present. As a result, we are constantly policing the borders of our identity and reacting to difference with aversion.[65]

Since cultural imperialism does not manifest itself at the level of discursive consciousness, it is impossible to remedy it through changes to the formal structures of society. The achievement of more democratic decision-making or structures of representation will be of little help in overcoming this type of oppression. In order to eradicate cultural imperialism, Young argues that we must initiate a cultural revolution, whereby 'we who are the subjects of this plural and complex society should affirm the otherness within ourselves, acknowledging that as subjects we are heterogeneous and multiple in our affiliations and desires'.[66] What this entails is illustrated in Young's discussion of homophobia. Specifically, Young claims that we must accept 'the possibility that one might become different, be different, in sexual orientation'.[67] This is more than a simple demand for empathy with oppressed groups. It requires people to see that their own identities are not completely secure, to acknowledge the sites of difference within themselves, and to recognise the value of such a fluid subjectivity. Without this type of revolution in attitudes, cultural imperialism will never be completely overcome. This is one of Young's most radical claims and it is also one of her most problematic. Some important criticisms of it will be raised in the final section of this chapter. First, however, it is necessary to delineate the particular political institutions that Young argues will best promote her ethics.

Political institutions

Although Young clearly enjoys critique, she is also determined that normative political theory must have a more active political role to play. This role takes two forms. In the first place, normative theory must engage with existing social and political conflicts, to look 'for the unrealized possibilities of emancipation latent in institutions and aimed at by social movements in those conflicts'.[68] Second, and in this context, normative theory has an obligation to set out its alternative view of social and political relations and institutions. This is not to suggest that normative theory must aim to control political processes. As Young makes clear, normative theory can offer 'proposals in the ongoing political discussion and means of envisaging alternative institutional forms, but they cannot found a polity. In actual political situations application of any normative principle will always be rough and ready, and always subject to challenge and revision.'[69] It is in this specific way that Young intends normative theory to engage with and hopefully also motivate political action. Indeed, this is also the spirit in which the conclusions of this book are offered.

Young begins by explicitly rejecting the vision of social life as community that she attributes to her fellow critics of atomism. In particular, she claims that the ideal of community presents subjects as 'understanding one another as they understand themselves, fused'.[70] This can only serve to reinforce the desire for homogeneity in social life and 'denies the ontological difference within and between subjects'.[71] Instead, Young offers an alternative political vision centred around the ideal of city life. According to her, city life is defined by the fact that very different people live side by side and often share public spaces. In contrast to visions of community, this ideal exemplifies the affirmation of group difference. This is so for four reasons. First, city life demonstrates how group differences may coexist without necessary exclusion. It allows for 'a side-by-side particularity neither reducible to identity nor completely other ... groups do not stand in relations of inclusion and exclusion, but overlap and intermingle without becoming homogeneous'.[72] Second, city life fosters variety. Social spaces are often multiuse and have multiple and coexisting meanings for the people who use them. Third, city life encourages people to view that which is different as exciting and interesting: '[o]ne takes pleasure in being drawn out of oneself to understand that there are other meanings, practices, perspectives on the city'.[73] Finally, cities exemplify the heterogeneous public sphere. According to Young, '[c]ities provide important public spaces ... where people stand and sit together, interact and mingle, or simply witness one another, without becoming identified in a community of "shared final ends"'.[74] They provide exceptional opportunities for enablement and participation while affirming group differences. The complexity of politics, then, is not assumed away through positing a common identity or subjective understanding between participants. Instead, it is affirmed and realised through the heterogeneous public of city life. This is why city life defines Young's political vision.

In keeping with her views on the role of normative theory, Young is quite clear that city life represents an *ideal*. She acknowledges that modern cities do not often display the positive characteristics that she describes. However, she does see that there is an unrealised potential within cities to become more just. Decision-making structures may be made more just, people may be given more power over their lives, and existing patterns of segregation and exclusion may be overcome. In order for this to be achieved, Young recommends that participation should be broadened and reinforced at the local level. She suggests that the basic unit of democracy should be the neighbourhood assembly, a local institution, 'right where people live and work, through which they participate in the making of regulations'.[75] The goal of such assemblies, however, is not to make decisions, but to 'determine local priorities and policy options'.[76] Young argues that if decision-making authority is too concentrated at the local level, then the bigger picture will be ignored and more serious inequities will result. Instead, the lowest level of decision-making government should be regional. Regional bodies should have extensive power to make decisions concerning tax, regulation, investment, land use, and the design and implementation of public services.[77] Neighbourhood assemblies would be represented at the regional bodies, and representation for oppressed groups would be guaranteed. Above the regional level, several other tiers of government would be necessary, although Young does not detail how these might be organised or what powers they might have.

The few sections above have set out the most important elements of Young's ethics. They have argued that this ethics can best be understood through Young's two central values – enablement and participation. Moreover, these two values combined provide the foundation for Young's commitment to radical pluralistic democracy. In other words, for Young, social justice can only be realised through an enabling, participatory democracy. A renewed city life is the ideal which exemplifies these values.

Critiques

The discussion of the previous few sections focused on setting out Young's ethics and her vision of ideal political institutions. Throughout this elaboration, several problems were highlighted and then deferred.

Before Young's ethics can be extended to provide suggestions for cultural policy, these criticisms must be addressed.

The problems with Young's ethics do not arise from her general call for enablement, participation, and a democratisation of decision-making structures. Instead, they occur mainly in some of her specific proposals for overcoming oppression. Nonetheless, these problems bring to the fore some less obvious and less useful elements of Young's conception of the good. The two main problems – limitless affirmative action and ontological insecurity – will first be discussed before the implications for our understanding of Young's underlying conception of the good are detailed. Finally, some ways of mitigating these problems will be suggested.

Limitless affirmative action?

From the starting point that group-based differences are relevant in the political sphere, it does not require a big leap to argue that equality and positive freedom may actually require differential treatment. Young and many philosophers preceding her have made exactly this connection. However, in Young's formulation, the particular demands of equality produce some very difficult issues. This is because according to Young's definition, oppression defines a huge variety of social processes. In fact, it would not be unfair to argue that, in one way or another, nearly all members of society are exploited or marginalised by the world economy, are made powerless by elephantine bureaucratic machinery, or are un- or under-recognised within the dominant set of social meanings. Perhaps this is simply a feature of modern life. Nonetheless, it creates several problems for a system of affirmative action based on extra representation for oppressed groups: a problem of identification, a logistical problem, a representation problem, and an ethical problem.

The problem of *identification* is twofold. First, we must be able to identify which groups are actually constitutive of identity as opposed to those associations based merely on common interest. Young is aware of this difficulty and attempts to resolve it by distinguishing between group memberships based on the type of identification entailed. Social groups involve 'a social process of interaction and differentiation in which some people come to have a particular *affinity* for others'.[78] Mere interest groups, on the other hand, are primarily defined by shared interests or ends and do not share certain cultural forms. According to Young, social groups may have shared interests, but these do not constitute the primary reason for group identification. This distinction is somewhat helpful. Nonetheless, one is still left wondering whether and under what circumstances an interest group may become a social group or vice versa. Young does not address this point directly. However, since groups are themselves aspects of a social process, it is clearly possible that common interests may, over time, produce a deeper kind of group identification and also vice versa, that groups may wither away.[79] Understanding groups in this way, however, highlights the importance of subjective identification in group constitution. In this context, an answer to the question of which groups are social groups cannot avoid placing great importance on the sense of identification that group members convey. Empirical study may contribute to our understanding of a particular group, but it ultimately cannot do justice to the sense of identification which defines the group as a social group.

The second aspect of the problem of identification is that we must identify cases in which groups are actually oppressed. As with the first problem of identification, the subjective element of feeling oppressed is an important element in identifying which groups may be oppressed. However, unlike the case above, the identification of oppression is much more conducive to empirical study. In this context, Young's 'five faces of oppression' can be understood as an attempt to describe very broadly what can be considered oppression. Her aim is to capture the wide variety of forms that oppression can take, while still setting a standard by which we can judge which groups are oppressed. This method is certainly not precise, and nor is it empirically foolproof, but it does do some justice to the subjective claims involved while preserving a general standard of judgement.

However, Young's 'five faces of oppression' also produce a *logistical* problem. The standard set by the 'five faces' is so broad that almost everyone could legitimately claim to be oppressed. Moreover, Young is adamant that we should recognise all claims to oppression without judging which are more fundamental or more urgent.[80] In this context, it is difficult to see how affirmative action can mean anything at all. Nonetheless, as will be discussed below, Young cannot consistently sustain the claim that we should abandon all standards of judgement about which groups are socially acceptable. However, even if we focus exclusively on the groups which Young most often cites – blacks, ethnic minorities (immigrants and First Nations), women, and homosexuals – then there is still a logistical problem. Specifically, if people have many different group affiliations, then the permutations of types of people requiring representation multiply dramatically. For example, taking Young's school council example that was cited above, would it be enough that blacks, hispanics, women, gay men and lesbians, poor people, disabled people and students were represented? What about black, professional men or hispanic lesbian students? The representation problems highlighted here will be discussed below. Disregarding the issue of representation, however, there is still a significant logistical problem relating to the numbers of people requiring representation. There is a very real danger that the demands of representation might make the decision-making process so cumbersome as to impede the achievement of any kind of decision at all. These difficulties are clearly important for the achievement of social justice. Unfortunately, however, it is not clear that logistical problems such as these can or should be addressed by moral theory. The question, perhaps, is not whether a suggestion is perfectly implementable, but whether it expresses values that the people concerned wish to endorse. If the values are acceptable, then a more sensitive and just solution to these logistical problems can be better achieved through negotiation and debate at the political level, by the groups concerned in their particular social contexts.

More importantly for this book, the problem of logistics also rebounds into a problem of *representativeness*. For example, if professional men are considered to be a dominant group, can a black professional man still represent black people more generally? These are huge problems of group politics which are played out every day. However, it is not clear that this struggle undermines the need for a group-based understanding of subjectivity and, by extension, ethics and politics. In fact, in some ways, the fact that these types of political conflict are so common in so many different societies lends support to the claim that group identities matter. In this context, it is clearly important to ensure that the structures exist for adequate discussion within a group and that the question of representativeness is brought to the fore. Beyond allowing representativeness to be raised as a political issue for all the groups in question, it is not clear that there is any role for formal political theory. In terms of generating opportunities for group discussion and deliberation, Young's ethics cannot be faulted.

The final difficulty with Young's concept of affirmative action is an *ethical* one, although it does relate generally to the problem of identification discussed above. Specifically, is it the case that we would want to offer additional assistance to all oppressed groups? This question raises directly the issue of Young's conception of the good and will be addressed in the penultimate section of this chapter.

Ontological insecurity

It was suggested earlier in this chapter that Young's conception of the social group is useful precisely because it introduces a fluidity and pluralism to the study of identity. Indeed, her full avoidance of cultural essentialisation is crucial to the ethics being developed in this book. However, when suggesting that a cultural revolution is necessary to overcome cultural imperialism, Young creates a few major problems. Specifically, the extension of fluidity and pluralism to the very core of identity through a revolution in subjectivity is both unrealistic and undesirable. In particular, in her rush to condemn the vilification of difference, it seems that Young has completely ignored the psychological function of the basic security system. In Giddens' original depiction, the basic security system represents the unconscious. It differs from practical consciousness in that the agent is psychologically barred from accessing what is contained there.[81] Young hints at this when she discusses 'aspects of subjectivity one refuses to face'.[82] However, where Giddens sees that the bar acts as a necessary protection mechanism against overwhelming ontological anxiety, Young treats it as though it exists only in order to differentiate and therefore alienate others. It may well be that our identities are fluid. However, this does not diminish people's need for a certain degree of ontological security, or, in Giddens' words, 'trust that the natural and social worlds are as they appear to be, including the basic existential parameters of the self and social identity'.[83] In this sense, it is unrealistic to expect the cultural revolution that Young describes. Moreover, precisely because ontological security is so crucial to our ability to function normally and to cope with anxiety and self-questioning at the conscious level, a society which denied this security to its members would itself be in a permanent state of crisis. It is important for people to think that they know who they are, even though this may place limits on our ability to accept those who are different from us. After all, without ontological security, we could not express our desires, exercise our capacities, or realise our freedom. In short, we could not hope to achieve any kind of social justice at all. In this sense, it may be possible to accept that identity necessarily entails difference *without* accepting the goal of eliminating difference altogether. However, if this is to be possible within the ethical framework described here, we must be able to show how the demands of enablement and participation *themselves* require that the goal of eliminating difference must often be overridden. These issues are worked out more fully in the section which follows.

'Difference' and the limits of the good

Young's conception of the good is not easy to ascertain. She clearly sees value in her conception of social justice not just for its own sake, but also because it creates the conditions for a culturally sensitive and therefore more authentic human emancipation and fulfilment. This is also why diversity is important. However, Young avoids the question of whether there are or should be moral limits to diversity. In discussing oppressed groups, she always refers to those that Western society has already formally accepted, such as blacks and homosexuals. The implication is that all oppressed groups are good and that they all deserve recognition and adequate representation. Oppression is bad wherever it occurs. This might be an acceptable claim if social justice entailed only a minimal requirement – the universal right to have one's views heard and considered. However, the demands of Young's ethics are much greater. In this case, what should we do about groups that we might not find acceptable? To take extreme examples, does Young anticipate that paedophiles or Nazis should also be recognised and granted representation? Naziism might be dismissed on the grounds that it does not constitute a true social group, but that is not necessarily true for all groups that we might find reprehensible. Some, even paedophiles perhaps, might be able to make a strong subjective claim to status as an oppressed social group.

The question of the good also arises in the context of Young's calls for a revolution in subjectivity. Should we be aiming for a cultural revolution which acknowledges our own unconscious tendencies towards paedophilia? This is not a spurious question, and nor is it meant to equate Young's example, homosexuality, with paedophilia. Instead, it is meant to highlight the fact that even if we should struggle to normalise some oppressed groups, we must nevertheless draw boundaries around what is tolerable in society. Not only does this entail that some people must necessarily and rightfully be considered 'other', but it forces us to consider what conception of the good we should promote. By advocating diversity for its own sake and by focusing solely on oppressed groups that we already consider acceptable, Young effectively avoids the important question of precisely where and how to draw the boundaries of the normal. In short, there are elements of her standard of the good that cannot be adopted by this book in their current form.

Nonetheless, there are elements within Young's work that may fruitfully be developed to provide the kind of boundary of acceptability described above. Most importantly, it is crucial that diversity be properly limited within the context of Young's focus on social justice as enablement and participation. Thus, no group conscious policy can be supported if it conflicts with the realisation of social justice for other groups. Fortunately, Young herself sets out a non-interference principle of this sort. Although Young develops this principle to describe the limits of autonomy for regional governments, it can very easily be applied in this context. Young describes it as a modified Millian test which entails the following:

> [a]gents, whether individual or collective, have the right to sole authority over their own actions only if the actions and their consequences (a) do not harm others, (b) do not inhibit the ability of individuals to develop and exercise their capacities within the limits of mutual respect and cooperation, and (c) do not determine conditions under which other agents are compelled to act.[84]

Although this is usually seen as a basically liberal condition of noninterference, it necessarily takes on new dimensions when incorporated into a society based on a deeper pluralism. In particular, since the development of capacities is an intrinsically social process, it is highly unlikely that the Millian test described above would, in fact, require a return to an individualist, procedural liberalism. It is impossible to say in advance exactly how these conditions would be implemented in any given society, but this does not make them any less important. In fact, they are required if the conception of the good endorsed by Young's ethics is actually to be upheld.

Clearly, Young's work has both ethical and practical difficulties. In ethical terms, the most important problems arise not in terms of Young's basic ethical commitments, but in her suggestions for eliminating oppression through affirmative action and a revolution in subjectivity. As the section above demonstrated, the first principles of Young's ethics are sound. Moreover, these principles provide a very good basis from which to rework some of her more problematic claims. In other words, the issues that created the greatest problems can easily be accommodated while reinforcing Young's basic ethical commitment to social justice.

In terms of practical problems, moreover, it is not clear that the question of logistic feasibility is within the scope of this, or any, academic exercise. Of course, any ethics should not be completely implausible. However, the question of whether, to what extent, and in what form an ethics is taken up is always a political issue, subject to the competing efforts of many social agents. As Young herself has noted, the role of normative theory is to develop an ethics that is as fair and just as possible, to detail the alternative vision created by this ethics, and to highlight political opportunities for steps to be taken towards this vision. It must be workable, but it cannot solve in advance the many institutional and political problems that may arise. To do so would be to undermine the political agency of the society in question.

In terms of the concerns of this book, Young's ethics clearly has value. It builds upon the many attributes of Taylor's ontology, developing a sound and useful statement of how culture should be accommodated in social theory and practice. Her conception of social justice and its manifestation in radical democracy will be taken up by this book as the ethical basis for its claims about cultural policy. The next two chapters will detail the specific, practical implications of Young's ethics for European and Canadian cultural policy.

7
Cultural Industries and Cross-Border Trade: Canadian Periodicals Examined

Previous chapters have set out the main approaches to cultural policy, paying particular attention to their respective conceptions of culture, their understandings of 'good' policy, and their views about the appropriateness of free trade in cultural goods. Earlier chapters have also offered some critiques of these positions and suggested ways in which an ethical cultural policy should be considered. However, these chapters have indicated only briefly the ways in which these ideas have influenced policy. This chapter and the next will seek to show the relevance of the arguments developed earlier by examining two case studies. This chapter will discuss Canadian magazines policy and some recent disputes between Canada and the US regarding trade in magazines. The chapter following this one will discuss European cultural policy, enquiring whether it is possible to make further ethical gains with a non-national approach to cultural policy. Each chapter will begin with an elaboration of the policies under consideration, showing the relevance of the market- and community-based approaches as a lens for understanding cultural policy. This analysis will provide the basis for a constructive critique of these policies and a discussion of ways in which the policies could be improved.

Periodicals in Canada: an overview

Periodicals make an interesting and useful case study for several reasons. First, periodicals have very recently been a high profile issue in both Canada and the United States. At the time of writing, they are the most recent cultural sector to be the subject of a Canada–United States trade dispute. Moreover, Canadian policy pertaining to periodicals is the first Canadian cultural policy to be challenged by the United States before a dispute resolution panel of the World Trade Organisation (WTO). As a result, a study of periodicals can provide important insights into very recent trade developments in the cultural sector. Finally, there has been no detailed study of Canadian periodicals since the 1974 publication of Isaiah Litvak and Christopher Maule's *Cultural Sovereignty: the Time and Reader's Digest Case in Canada*.

The state of the industry

Magazines generally have two main revenue sources – advertising revenue and circulation revenue. Throughout the 1990s, circulation revenues in Canada remained fairly constant at about 30 per cent of total revenues. Advertising revenues accounted for about 60–65 per cent of the total, with the difference being accounted for by back issue sales, grants, and donations.[1] These revenue streams are highly interdependent, however, since circulation figures are an important determinant of the amount of advertising a magazine can attract and the rates that it can charge to advertisers. As the 1994 Task Force on Periodicals noted, this interdependency can lead to a spiralling action – either upwards or downwards.[2]

Tied to these two revenue sources are two different types of foreign competition in the Canadian market and, in essence, two different categories of Canada–United States trade in magazines. In the Canadian market, the main competition for circulation revenues comes from 'overflow' circulation of American magazines. These are magazines that are exported to Canada in exactly the same form as they are sold in the United States – no new editorial or advertising content is added. Trade in these magazines has never been limited by the Canadian government. As a result, the main effect of these magazines has been to compete with Canadian magazines for circulation and subscription revenues.

Primarily, however, competition for advertising revenues takes on a different form. In this case, the main foreign competitors are split-run or 'Canadian' editions of US magazines. These are editions of US magazines sold in Canada with little or no new editorial content, but with ads solicited from Canadian advertisers. These types of magazine have been considered dangerous to the Canadian magazine industry because they largely recoup their editorial costs in the US market and can afford to undercut the ad rates of Canadian magazines. This type of competition is seen to be particularly threatening because of the high degree of dependence of Canadian magazines on advertising revenue and the small size of the overall advertising market in Canada. As a result, limiting trade in foreign split-run magazines, or at least limiting their access to the Canadian advertising market, has been a goal of Canadian policy for several decades.

(i) Circulation

In the 1996–97 reporting year, 1137 Canadian publishers produced 1552 periodicals. Both periodicals and publishers have suffered a small but steady decline in numbers at least since 1991–92, when 1733 periodicals were published by 1282 publishers.[3] Overall industry revenues, however, remained fairly constant, at around C$1billion (US$850 million). To put this in perspective, in 1993, the US magazine industry published more than 11,000 periodicals and earned US$22.7 billion in revenues. US periodical exports in 1992–93 alone exceeded US$800 million, 78 per cent of which went to Canada. More importantly, however, in 1992, Canadian magazines accounted for 67.6 per cent of total circulation in Canada. This remains one of the lowest figures in the industrialised world, although it nonetheless marks a significant improvement over the 1959 figure of 23.3 per cent. This jump is usually attributed to Canadian cultural policies in effect through the 1970s and 1980s.[4]

(ii) Advertising

In terms of advertising, the situation is somewhat different. As noted above, advertising revenues provide by far the largest share of magazine revenues in Canada. In this way, advertising not only supports the creation of original editorial content, but it allows magazines to be provided to readers at competitive rates. In 1992, the pool of total advertising dollars in Canada was estimated at C$8.295 billion, with 6.8 per cent (C$569 million) allocated to magazines. Owing to several key policy decisions which are outlined below, no foreign split-run magazines were allowed to compete for this advertising revenue from 1965 until early 1999. However, it should be noted that the Canadian advertising market was not completely without competition, as magazines are constantly competing among each other and with other media for advertising revenue.

The basis of public policy

The goals of Canadian policy for periodicals have remained virtually unchanged since the 1960s. Most importantly, successive Canadian governments have prioritised the need to create the conditions in which a distinctly Canadian periodicals industry could flourish. As the 1961 Royal Commission on Publications (the O'Leary Commission) put it, 'the Commission has no desire to create a protected haven or storm shelter for Canadian periodicals. ... Its sole aim is to secure a climate of competition in which Canadian publications ... shall have a chance to survive.'[5] The framing of this question in terms of the very survival of the industry has continued to the present day, just as the survival and flourishing of Canadian magazines have remained the central goals of policy.

Nonetheless, there has been some change in the subtle remarks that serve to indicate precisely *why* such an indigenous magazine industry should be important. In this regard, the history of Canadian magazine policy reveals two key themes. The theme that recurs most often builds upon notions of national identity, though it often appears under the guise of political culture. Indeed, the Canadian government has often claimed that magazines are essential for the spread of information and, hence, national values. The report of the O'Leary Commission exemplifies this argument and so is worth quoting at length:

[C]ommunications are the thread which binds together the fibers of a nation. They can protect a nation's values and encourage their practice. They can make a democratic government possible and better government probable. They can soften sectional asperities [*sic*] and bring honorable compromises. They can inform and educate.... In these functions it may be claimed – claimed without much challenge – that the communications of a nation are as vital to its life as its defences, and should receive at least a great measure of national protection.[6]

Several years later, in supporting legislation to protect magazines, then Prime Minister John Diefenbaker made the similar claim that 'this legislation is necessary in the interest of the Canadian identity and as an assurance that Canada's destiny will be preserved. ... [U]nless action is taken we shall ... be dependent entirely or almost entirely on the viewpoint of another nation.'[7] Similarly, in 1994, the Canadian Task Force on Magazines asserted that '[f]ree speech would lose much of its potency if there were no Canadian magazines. Without the means to express a distinctive voice, speaking to a Canadian audience, cultural expression, social cohesion and a sense of national destiny would be impaired.'[8] Most clearly, Canada's International Trade Minister claimed that 'what we're trying to do here is preserve our cultural identity through our magazine industry'.[9] In this sense, it is clear that national identity is a central driving force behind the protection of magazines.

It is important to note here that this strand of reasoning clearly exemplifies the community-based approach to trade and culture. Indeed, national identity was a central theme of the community-based approaches discussed in Chapter 2. Nonetheless, even in the arguments above, several separate community-based claims are intertwined. For example, national identity, national values, national defence, democratic participation, citizen education, free speech, the need to hear distinctive voices, and social cohesiveness all appear as reasons why indigenous magazines should be protected. Although this combination clearly provides rhetorical force, the separate ideas expressed may not actually be consistent with one another.

In particular, the comments quoted above rely on the assumption that increased communications and the transmittal of particularly Canadian information will necessarily lead to a strengthening of national identity. This might be true if the Canadian nation was understood only as a civic association rather than an ethnic or cultural one, since knowledge about other Canadians and particularly about Canadian political and social conditions could be crucial for the continuance of an independent and democratically active polity. Unfortunately, however, it is clear that in considering culture and national identity, most of the ideas expressed above *require* something that includes but goes well beyond a narrow idea of political culture. They require, in other words, a sense in which Canadian people can be understood as a group with greater coherence and value than a simple political association. Indeed, in most cases, their claims are underlain by a very particular (though often unarticulated) sense of what is meant by 'Canadian'. The problem is, however, that even if it were possible to articulate this vision, Canadian policymakers are agreed that they should not dictate what constitutes legitimately 'Canadian' culture. The resulting gap has often been bridged by introducing criteria of ownership or production, assuming that Canadian culture is that which is produced by Canadians. However, these criteria can hardly support the strong associated claims being made about national identity.

The second, and much more minor theme that appears as a justification for magazine protection is the idea of freedom of choice. As the statistics presented above demonstrate, even without split-run magazines, Canadians are presented with a great variety of periodicals, both

Canadian and foreign. Indeed, as the Canadian government stressed in a 1987 report, 'Canadians are keen internationalists, a vocation implying a depth and breadth of choice'.[10] However, as the report went on to say, 'the concern is not with ease of access to the products of other cultures, it is rather with the difficulty of access to our own products. ... The effects are economic, to be sure, but our concerns are cultural – the need to sustain for Canadians an adequate choice.'[11] Indeed, as successive Canadian governments have consistently maintained, blocking trade in split-run magazines is not really about preventing freedom of information or a lack of Canadian openness to foreign influences. It is about maintaining a reasonable number of Canadian magazines among the choices available to Canadians.

Supported by these assumptions, the preservation of a distinctly Canadian magazine industry has consistently been the central goal of Canada's policy for trade and periodicals. In turn, the importance of an independent magazine industry has been explained with reference to national identity and freedom of choice. In pursuing these goals, Canadian policy has consisted of four main instruments. All of these policies have been in place since the 1960s and 1970s and provided the policy context of trade in magazines until the WTO challenge of the late 1990s.

(i) Section 19 and Tariff Item 9958

The two most important legislative measures in support of magazines are Section 19 of the Income Tax Act and Customs Tariff Code 9958. Both were first applied to magazines in 1965 and both were primarily directed at preserving Canadian advertising revenue for Canadian magazines by preventing competition from split-run editions. First, Section 19 of the Income Tax Act was amended in 1965 to remove the tax deduction on advertisements directed at the Canadian market in non-Canadian publications. Notably, in order for a magazine to be Canadian, it would have to be directed by 'a partnership of which at least 3/4 of the members are Canadian citizens' and in which Canadian citizens own at least 3/4 of the total value of the partnership property.[12] However, this legislation excluded special 'Canadian' editions of foreign magazines already printing in Canada, namely *Time* and *Reader's Digest* – the two magazines whose Canadian presence had sparked the need for protectionism.[13]

The second policy instrument, Customs Tariff Code 9958, took a slightly different tack and was more directly protectionist. It prohibited the following magazines from entering Canada:

(i)   special editions, i.e., split-run or regional editions, of a periodical that contain an advertisement that is primarily directed to a market in Canada and that did not appear in identical form in all editions of that issue of that periodical distributed in the country of origin; and

(ii) issues of a periodical in which more than 5 per cent of the advertising space is used for advertisements primarily directed at Canadians.[14]

When these two measures were introduced, Canadian publishers were clearly pleased to be offered protective measures. However, there was frustration among publishers and politicians that *Time* and *Reader's Digest*, the most dangerous competitors in the Canadian market, would remain unchallenged and, in fact, would also be protected from any further American competition. The Canadian Finance Minister, for example, was later to admit that 'the passage of the automotive agreement through the U.S. Congress had run into difficulties, and it was felt the agreement might not be approved if a full-scale row developed with Mr. Luce [Editor of *Time*]'.[15] In this context, it seems certain that key government ministers, including the Finance Minister, actually had wanted stronger legislation and did not wish to support the exemption of already existing special Canadian editions.

By 1975, the Canadian government was willing to take a more defiant stance. Through the introduction of legislation known as Bill C-58, Section 19 of the Income Tax Act was again altered. Bill C-58 directed that magazine advertisements purchased by Canadian advertisers would not be tax deductible unless they were placed in a magazine that was at least 75 per cent Canadian-owned and had editorial content at least 80 per cent different from that of other magazines.[16] *Time* and *Reader's Digest* were not excluded. These terms were stringent and they gave *Time* and *Reader's Digest* the choice between giving up their Canadian operations completely or significantly restructuring these operations so as to 'Canadianise' the company. This legislation did not significantly affect magazines already operating outside of Canada, since they were still subject to Tariff Item 9958 which restricted entry into Canada of magazines containing more than 5 per cent advertising directed at the Canadian market. In practice, it was reasonably effective, although *Time* magazine was able to lower its ad rates sufficiently to compensate advertisers for the lost deduction.

Together, Section 19 and Tariff Item 9958 diverted ad revenues away from US magazines and towards their Canadian competitors. This led to a vast increase in the overall health of the magazine industry in Canada and has been directly credited with the emergence of Canada's first weekly newsmagazine.[17] For the 30 years they were in place, these legislative items were highly successful in meeting Canadian policy goals. They secured advertising revenues for Canadian magazines, without interfering with the inflow of 'overflow' circulation. Importantly, these policies had no effect on the importation of American magazines that did not seek Canadian ad revenues.

(ii) Postal subsidy

The third element of Canadian policy was the postal subsidy. This measure dated back to the early twentieth century and was designed to contain the costs to readers of delivering magazines in a country as large and thinly populated as Canada. It should be noted that the subsidy did not cover all postage costs, but offered concessionary second-class postage rates for publishers. Initially, the subsidy was granted to all forms of magazine produced in Canada, including free circulation-controlled copies and foreign split-run editions (for the time from 1943 to 1965 in which they flourished in the Canadian market). Foreign magazines mailed from outside of Canada would pay their mailing rates directly to their own post offices. However, many American magazines are shipped in bulk to Canada and then mailed to Canadian subscribers through the Canadian postal system. Rates for these magazines were initially kept low to encourage publishers to use the Canadian rather than American postal system. However, by 1990, for example, made-in-Canada magazines were charged an average of 6.6 cents per copy, while foreign magazines shipped in bulk to Canada were charged an average of 42.3 cents per copy.[18] As a result, the postal subsidy became one of the main grounds upon which foreign magazines protested that they were being discriminated against. Further, in 1991, the Canadian government began phasing out the subsidy for all magazines except paid-circulation, Canadian-owned magazines.[19] Since *Reader's Digest* had decided to become a full Canadian magazine under C-58, this change actually affected only *Time* magazine, but it nonetheless strengthened the general grounds for complaint by American, mailed-in-Canada magazines.

(iii) Grants

The final policy means for protecting magazines in Canada (and the only one not to be challenged by the United States at some time) came in the form of grants. Since its inception in 1957, the Canada Council has acted as an arm's length body allocating government grants to numerous cultural endeavours. Each year, it provides about C$2 million in direct grants to magazine publishers for the purposes of publication, translation, and promotion of their periodicals.[20] More limited financial assistance is also provided by other federal government departments, as well as provincial and municipal governments.[21]

In this context, several themes can be drawn out before the discussion moves on to consider key recent events in Canada–United States trading relations. First, it is important to remember that what is at issue between Canada and the United States is not the trade in US magazines produced for the US market. Instead, the disputes centre on editions of US magazines which are identical in content to their US counterparts, but which contain advertisements directed at the Canadian market and so compete for advertising revenues. In other words, the disputes deal only with a very particular subcategory of US magazines. Trade in magazines between the two countries is inhibited only in this category.

Second, the disputes are not only about physical limitations to cross-border trade. In important respects, they are also complaints about the discriminatory nature of particular Canadian domestic periodicals policies. Some of these policies, such as Tariff 9958, are discriminatory trade measures, while others, such as the postal subsidy, were developed with specific domestic conditions in mind. In this way, these disputes reflect the increasing tendency for domestic regulations to be evaluated by the extent to which they inhibit or facilitate trade, even when traditional protectionism is not the aim of legislation. Using the expressions of neo-liberal IPE, Canadian policies are exemplary of the 'new protectionism'.[22]

Third, for at least four decades, the Canadian government (and much of the Canadian public) has perceived the issue in terms of the very *survival* of the Canadian magazine industry. Further, they view a domestic magazine industry as important because they accept the legitimacy of arguments linking cultural industries to national identity. In contrast, the American government and American publishers have perceived the issue as a simple case of fair market access. They do not accept the legitimacy of a connection between magazines and national identity, preferring to see this claim as paternalistic towards consumers and as a guise for protection of vested interests in the Canadian magazine industry.

These three points provide the initial framework within which the details of Canada–United States trade in periodicals can be understood. The following section will highlight examples of tension between Canada and the United States. It will reinforce the claims made above, while also demonstrating how the market-based and community-based approaches have played out in actual disagreements surrounding periodicals and trade.

Canada–US trade disputes over periodicals

This section will highlight an instance in which Canadian attempts to implement a policy protecting periodicals resulted in disputes between the two governments. An examination of the positions taken by the governments, opposition groups, publishers, and advertisers demonstrates the precise ways in which the market- and community-based approaches have played out in practice. The section will show that US publishers and policy-makers rely very heavily upon market-based assertions, even when their actions are not consistent with free market logic. Similarly, the Canadian government has trumpeted the rhetoric of community-based positions (national identity, in particular), even when, in practice, it has sometimes balanced these concerns against economic or other policy interests. This section will attempt to do justice to the variety of positions in Canada, while showing how the majority of Canadian opinion has nonetheless converged around a broad community-based position. The conclusion of this chapter will address the ethical implications of the policy issues laid out below.

Sports Illustrated and the WTO challenge

Section 19 of the Income Tax Act (amended in 1975) and Tariff Item 9958 remained Canada's main instruments of support for magazines until 1995. They were not perfect pieces of legislation, but together they ensured a stable and supportive policy context for Canada's magazine industry. However, by 1993, technological advances gave American magazine publishers the means to circumvent the law. The Canadian government attempted to develop new means to reinforce the intent of C-58 and Tariff Item 9958 and in so doing, reawakened the magazine dispute with the United States.

The issue came to public attention in early 1993 when Time Inc. announced its intention to publish a split-run edition of *Sports Illustrated* in Canada. As will be recalled, Tariff Item 9958 virtually prohibited split-run editions by stopping at the border any magazine with more than 5 per cent advertising intended for the Canadian market. C-58, in turn, made it difficult for an American magazine based in Canada to secure Canadian advertising. With *Sports Illustrated*, Time Inc. proposed to circumvent these difficulties by sending the split-run issue electronically from their editorial offices in the United States to a printing plant near Toronto. As the magazines never technically crossed through a border point, the applicability and enforceability of Tariff Item 9958 were seriously in question.

The first issue of *Sports Illustrated* (Canada) appeared on 6 April 1993. Predictably, it caused an uproar among Canadian magazine publishers. Their fear was not so much about *Sports Illustrated* (Canada) – as Time Inc. had rightly pointed out, there was no Canadian general interest sports magazine that would be losing ad revenues as a result of the Canadian *Sports Illustrated*. Primarily, Canada's magazine publishers were concerned that *Sports Illustrated* would set a precedent for other American magazines, eventually eroding the entire policy structure which they credited with creating a vital Canadian magazine industry in the first place.

Within a month of the first issue of *Sports Illustrated* (Canada), the Canadian government announced the creation of a special Task Force on the Canadian Magazine Industry. The Task Force was to 'propose measures that will enable the Government to effectively carry through on its policy objective of ensuring that Canadians have access to Canadian ideas and information through genuinely Canadian magazines'.[23] It was clear that the Canadian government did not want to re-evaluate its long-standing policy objectives and the community-based reasoning behind them. Instead, its aim in setting up the Task Force was to ascertain how to continue the policy status quo in the face of new technological developments.

In its final report, the Task Force reiterated the importance of Canadian magazines to national identity, stressing all the familiar community-based themes. It reaffirmed the findings of all previous commissions and committees with regard to the poor economic health of the magazine industry and the centrality of public policy measures to ensure a level playing field for Canadian magazines.[24] It asserted that 'there is nothing in our research that would lead us to believe that policy measures currently in place have made the Canadian industry any less efficient or profit-conscious than its foreign counterparts'.[25] Moreover, as described above, it estimated the potential results of allowing split-runs to freely enter the Canadian advertising market. On this they were clear: 'some Canadian magazines would simply stop publishing altogether and others, in attempting to stay competitive, would reduce the budget for quality editorial content. The number of pages of editorial (non-advertising) content would decrease, and circulation would decline.... The end result would soon be evident: a downward spiral.'[26] The viability of the Canadian periodical industry was perceived to be at great risk. In this light, the Task Force asserted that strong measures must be taken to maintain the support necessary for the government's policy objectives to continue to be met. Moreover, they claimed that '[i]t is possible to strike a balance between Canada's international trade commitments and our legitimate concerns about cultural development'.[27]

In this spirit, the Task Force made 11 recommendations.[28] By far the most important recommendation, however, suggested levying an excise tax on any 'periodical distributed in Canada that contains advertisements primarily directed at Canadians and editorial content which is substantially the same as the editorial content of one or more issues... of periodicals that contain advertisements that... are not directed at Canadians'.[29] The tax would be levied at 80 per cent of the amount charged for all advertising in the offending issue and would be paid by the printer or distributor of the magazine. Furthermore, the Task Force recommended that split-run magazines already publishing in Canada (i.e. *Sports Illustrated*) should be exempt, but only for the number of issues that they distributed in Canada in 1993.

Almost as an aside to the main recommendations, the Task Force made one additional, very important suggestion. They argued that the government should remove the concept of Canadian content from its pivotal role in defining Canadian cultural policy. They suggested that the government should replace this with the concept of 'original content', or editorial content that has not previously been published elsewhere and is not simultaneously being published elsewhere.[30] In justifying this shift, they stated that 'it is better to aim wide and comply with Canada's trade obligations... than to target a narrow field and end up in protracted disputes with Canada's principal trading partners'.[31] Although the Task Force did not touch on any further justifications for this suggestion, it is clear that a shift to original content would avoid the considerable difficulties that the Canadian government has had in adequately and fairly defining what constitutes Canadian content. As we will see below, this suggestion was not seriously considered by the government until 1997. However, as will be argued below, the shift towards original content is a crucial one in assuring the democratic and pluralist development of Canadian cultural policy.

The reaction to the recommendations was overwhelming. *Sports Illustrated* claimed that they were about to publish more than their exempted seven issues and warning that if the government imposed an excise tax, they would consider it 'impairment and confiscation of our business'.[32] Reinforcing this view of the issue as purely commercial, Time Inc. claimed that '[t]he new tax ... is not really a tax, but a thinly disguised means of driving us out of business'.[33] The Canadian magazine industry expressed its frustration that the Task Force had not made bolder recommendations. The Task Force chair replied, stating that they had deliberately chosen a 'pragmatic' approach in order to respect Canada's trade commitments, and in the hopes that the government would be more likely to effect their recommendations.[34]

Within several months, it was rumoured that the government was preparing legislation to effect the 80 per cent excise tax and that it was not preparing an exemption for *Sports Illustrated*. When news of these measures leaked, United States Trade Representative (USTR) Mickey Kantor lobbied the Canadian government to delay the legislation. He described the tax in pure market-based terms, as 'concrete evidence of an increasing and disturbing trend in Canada toward the implementation of policies which are intended to protect Canadian industry by discriminating against legitimate US broadcasting, publishing and copyright interests in Canada'.[35] At the same time, he threatened retaliation in the cultural sector, and rumours abounded that a specific hit list of targets for retaliation was being drawn up.[36] Nonetheless, Canada's Heritage Minister announced that the tax would be implemented as soon as legislation to support it was drawn up.[37] Predictably, Washington was outraged, but claimed that they needed time to study the issue. Indeed, the Canadian government, too, needed time to draft the legislation, and so the issue was quiet again for the first few months of 1995.[38]

In September 1995, the Canadian government formally introduced the promised legislation into the House of Commons. In the debate that followed, Canada's Liberal government, as well as the Conservative and New Democratic parties, supported the legislation. Reform Party MPs took the opposing position. Always more inclined towards market-based arguments, they argued that the tax was unfair and unnecessary and that Canada should not enact legislation that would lead to a trade war with the United States.[39] If Canada was serious about helping magazines, one Reform Party MP stated, it should reduce taxes that hurt the profitability of all magazines.[40] When Canadian magazine publishers were invited to present to the House Committee, they reasserted the dire predictions made by the Task Force should split-runs be allowed.[41]

Officials from Time Inc. were invited to make a presentation to the House Committee, in which they repeated their market-based claim that the proposed law was 'unfair, discriminatory and represents the effective

confiscation of a commercial enterprise that was legitimately established in Canada'.[42] Moreover, they threatened that the US government
would retaliate under the 'notwithstanding' clause in NAFTA's cultural
provisions. Finally, Time Inc. suggested that the law would violate
Canadian Constitutional guarantees on freedom of expression for
Canadian advertisers. Again, the arguments against Canadian policy
relied mainly on market-based reasoning.

Indeed, just as Time Inc. promised, the US government began to make
serious threats of retaliation. In a December statement, USTR Kantor
again referred exclusively to commercial considerations, claiming that
the Canadian action was 'directly contrary to the open trade and investment relationship we have worked so hard to establish'. *Sports Illustrated*
discontinued its Canadian edition. In March of 1996, pursuant to Time
Inc.'s complaint to the USTR, the US government announced that it
would lodge a formal complaint against the Canadian tax with the
WTO. At the request of Time Inc., the complaint also included Tariff
Item 9958, and two postal subsidy measures. A WTO dispute resolution
panel was convened in late 1996.

Before discussing the arguments presented by both parties, it is revealing to question the logic behind the United States decision to use the
WTO dispute-settlement mechanism. United States thinking on this
matter seems to have been twofold. First, the United States clearly felt
that their case was strong enough to withstand WTO scrutiny. Success at
the WTO would give them firmer grounds for retaliation than the use
of the 'notwithstanding' clause of NAFTA. Second, the United States
very much wanted this case to set a very public and universally applica-
ble precedent. In the words of Kantor, '[w]e want to say to the world that
this is not to be tolerated. ... [T]he US is prepared to act on so-called cultural issues.'[43] Since the 1970s, cultural goods have remained among the
most profitable US exports. In the 1990s, for example, cultural exports
were the second-largest revenue earners, after the aerospace industry.
Nonetheless, cultural exports have been (and still are) consistently
under threat from culturally protectionist policies throughout the
world. In this context, it is clear why the United States was so eager to
set a market-based precedent in its response to the Canadian actions.

Clearly, the argument could also be made that presenting a cultural
dispute before the WTO is itself indicative of a market-based approach to
trade and culture. During the Uruguay Round, the United States had not
succeeded in convincing its trading partners that culture ought to be
treated commercially and therefore included in the agreement. Bringing
a cultural case before the WTO would establish a market-based precedent

for the treatment of culture and so, as Keith Acheson and Christopher Maule note, 'would be a chance to ... win a partial victory'.[44] Even if one does not accept that bringing an issue before the rules-based system of trade constitutes a market-based strategy, some American comments in this regard shed light on their particular view, which was clearly market-based. In particular, in announcing the WTO action, Kantor made an important claim which clearly betrayed the market-based approach of the United States. He repeated his dim view of Canadian policies, claiming '[w]hat they're trying to do is protect the financial and economic viability of a Canadian industry, not the cultural identity of a people'.[45] Most obviously, this statement focuses on commercial concerns and dismisses cultural ones. More importantly, however, in an effort to delegitimise Canadian policies, it characterises industry protection and the promotion of national identity as mutually exclusive activities. This is highly typical of market-based approaches, and, notably, it is in direct contrast to the Canadian community-based policy which has consistently viewed these activities as inseparable, at least vis-à-vis magazines.

To return to the WTO dispute resolution panel, the grounds of the US complaint involved the simple market-based argument that the Canadian policies were discriminatory against US magazines and therefore were inconsistent with General Agreement on Tariffs and Trade (GATT) obligations. According to the United States, Canadian measures 'effectively prevent US and foreign-produced magazines either from entering the Canadian market or from competing on an equal footing with their Canadian rivals when they do'.[46] Specifically, the United States claimed that Tariff Code 9958 violated Article XI of GATT 1994, which prohibits quantitative import quotas. Regarding the excise tax, the United States argued that Article III of GATT 1994 (national treatment) could be applied to advertising in magazines, and therefore, that the tax could be seen to discriminate between like products, namely foreign split-run and domestic periodicals. Finally, the United States claimed that differential postal rates were applied to Canadian and foreign publications, and that the funding for the lower rates could be constituted a subsidy. If proven, these measures were also in violation of Article III.[47]

The Canadian government made several general points. First, they reasserted the community-based claim that Canadian measures should not be considered protectionism. Instead, they should be seen as 'a legitimate response to an anti-competitive abuse in the advertising field, with the ultimate object of ensuring the survival of a distinct Canadian culture'.[48] Moreover, they claimed that the measures did not prevent foreign magazines from entering the Canadian market, so long as these did not contain Canadian advertising. Far from discouraging readership of foreign magazines, the Canadian government argued, their measures were designed to maintain an environment in which Canadian magazines could exist alongside foreign ones.

In March 1997, the WTO panel's report was published. It ruled in favour of the United States regarding the excise tax, Tariff Item 9958 and one aspect of Canada's publication mail system. The legitimacy of postal subsidies for Canadian periodicals was to be upheld.[49]

Canada's Heritage and Trade ministers were stunned and vowed to appeal as soon as the final ruling was issued.[50] Importantly, the United States also appealed the findings of the WTO on postal subsidies. In July 1997, the WTO appeals panel ruled to uphold the initial rulings on the excise tax and 9958, and judged in favour of the American appeal with regard to postal subsidies.[51] The former ruling had largely been expected, but the latter was a complete surprise.[52] Paradoxically, Canada's appeal had resulted in an even greater loss than in the first judgement. Canada was given 15 months to adjust to the decisions, if it wished to avoid US retaliation. During this time existing policies could remain in force.

The Canadian government's reaction was surprisingly muted. The Trade and Heritage ministers expressed their disappointment, but did not criticise the WTO directly. True to their community-based logic, they were also anxious to point out that the WTO ruling did not challenge the ability of any member to take measures to protect its cultural identity.[53] Instead, the Canadian ministers interpreted the ruling as a judgement against the particular *means* that Canada had used to achieve its cultural policy objective.

On 29 July 1998, the Heritage and Trade ministers outlined their proposal for new legislation to protect magazines. The legislation would repeal Tariff Item 9958 and suspend the excise tax and would harmonise postal rates for foreign and Canadian magazines at the lower domestic rate. To replace the excise tax, the ministers proposed to ban Canadian companies from advertising in American split-run or 'Canadian' editions, with the exception of *Time* and *Reader's Digest*. The ban would be backed up with a court order to cease publication of the ad, followed by a hefty fine (up to C$250,000). But, in a strange twist designed to avoid a Charter of Rights challenge from advertisers, the proposed legislation would be directed against the foreign publishers who had 'solicited' Canadian advertising, rather than against the advertisers. Clearly, the intent of the legislation was to deter foreign publications from accepting Canadian ads. However, it is not clear how the legislation would act as a deterrent, since the fine could not legitimately be collected unless the publisher had assets in Canada. Nonetheless, enforcement of this bill never became an issue.

The United States derided the new policy as 'protectionist and discriminatory', 'anti-competitive', and 'every bit as inconsistent with Canada's international trade obligations as its current discriminatory practices'.[54] The new USTR, Charlene Barshefsky, had already established her market-based credentials, claiming at her confirmation hearing, 'we do object to the use of culture as an excuse to take commercial advantage of the United States, or as an excuse to evict American companies from the Canadian market'.[55] Despite the US protestations, the Canadian government introduced legislation (Bill C-55, otherwise known as the Foreign Publishers Advertising Services Act) in October 1998. As the Bill moved through the House, the United States continued to accuse Canada of ignoring international trade rules. Furthermore, rumours again circulated that the United States was exploring areas of retaliation.[56]

By December, the US government was preparing for a diplomatic assault designed to prevent the Bill from passing into law. According to former Presidential Trade Advisor Bill Merkin, the US government was planning across-the-board retaliation, including key sectors such as steel and finance. These broad retaliatory threats were meant to create division within Canadian society, forcing other business sectors to oppose the cultural legislation.[57] Although the potential damage caused by retaliation was serious, many Canadian commentators felt that the United States was merely rattling its sabres. In response, the Canadian government postponed its consideration of C-55.

Just as consideration of the Bill was about to resume, the Deputy USTR gave notice that if the Bill was passed, the United States would target Canada's steel, wood, and textile industries.[58] As threats of US retaliation against the legislation became stronger, it emerged that they intended to act under the terms of the NAFTA rather than the WTO. In particular, it was argued that they wished to do so not only because it would be quicker, but because it would largely be unilateral – the onus would then be on Canada to justify a reversal of US action.[59] Moreover, the United States maintained that Canada's new policy was the 'same old thing' and so did not merit a new consideration of it by the WTO.[60] As it turned out, Canada asserted that it had prepared the legislation carefully to withstand a WTO challenge, but they were not prepared for a possible $3–4 billion retaliation under the NAFTA 'notwithstanding' clause.

The US threats and Canadian declarations of confidence continued through the early months of 1999. A senior US official claimed that C-55 was about nothing more than protecting Canada's two biggest media companies (Maclean-Hunter and Télémedia),[61] and *Time*'s editor in Canada argued that Canadian policy had enabled Canada to 'wrap itself in the flag of culture with what is essentially a bankrupt economic argument'.[62] The USTR also put forward an interesting theory of cultural diversity, arguing that 'competition is the best way to achieve cultural diversity. ...The objective here is to enhance freedom of speech, freedom of choice, multiculturalism, and diversity within Canada. I think that's what the Canadian government would like too.'[63]

Canadian officials claimed that '[i]f the only standard is market competition, obviously the stories that are uniquely ours will be swamped in a larger market. So you have to say that, for culture, it isn't simply a market issue, it's also an issue of cultural choice and cultural space for our own country.'[64] In a more abrasive tone, Canada's Minister for International Trade charged that Americans either 'don't want to understand or ... can't understand what we mean by the word culture'.[65] Indeed, if there were any doubts about the commitment of the two governments to market- and community-based positions respectively, a Canadian negotiator summed it up neatly, stating that 'our bottom line is all about [Canadian] content and storytelling. And their bottom line is all about access to the Canadian market.'[66]

Yet, behind the scenes, representatives of both governments were working all-out to negotiate a workable solution. At the end of May, negotiators announced that they had reached a final-hour deal on C-55. Under the agreement, American magazines in Canada can have as much as 18 per cent of their advertising directed at a Canadian audience. Foreign magazines can claim a greater percentage if the Canadian edition contains greater than 51 per cent original content. Furthermore, the Canadian government agreed to allow up to 100 per cent foreign ownership of periodical publishing businesses, provided that these periodicals contained a 'substantial' level of original content. Full tax deductibility on advertisements will be allowed for publications that contain at least 80 per cent original content. The amended legislation was quickly passed through the Senate and approved by Cabinet.

Although this was not a central policy issue, it should be noted that the revised C-55 was the first Canadian cultural policy to rely on the idea of original content rather than Canadian content. In keeping with this, C-55 also removed ownership criteria from the definition of a 'Canadian' magazine. Although foreign takeovers of Canadian magazines will not be allowed, new magazines may be 100 per cent foreign owned and still be considered 'Canadian' as long as they meet original content requirements. It seems that this was a long-delayed reaction to the recommendation of the 1994 Task Force. Furthermore, Canadian content issues were a big sticking point in the negotiations surrounding Bill C-55. In this context, it is possible that the idea of 'original content' was part of the compromise reached by Canadian and American negotiators. Whatever the reasoning, this shift has important implications for the ethics of cultural policy. These implications will be addressed in the conclusion of the book.

Despite this final policy compromise, it is clear that there has been no real 'meeting of minds' between the community- and market-based approaches. Indeed, Canada continues to assert that it has a right to ensure the survival of its cultural industries, and US interests continue to press for increasing liberalisation in the cultural sphere. The periodicals issue may now go through another quiet phase, but the question of market vs community is far from solved. As Acheson and Maule noted in early 1999, '[f]urther rounds of the same unproductive engagement appear inevitable'.[67]

This historical discussion has aimed to show how different ideas about the relationship between trade and culture have been manifest in Canadian cultural policy and American responses to it. In this context, several summary observations can be made.

The past 25 years has been a time of broad agreement within Canada about the need to protect Canadian ad revenues from split-run or nominally 'Canadian' editions. This is not to suggest that there has been agreement about the means by which this protection should be assured, nor about the reasons why periodicals should be protected. Nonetheless, the rhetoric of Canadian magazine publishers and most Canadian policy-makers has relied upon a strong connection between ad revenues, the survival of an independent magazine industry, and the health of the national community. In essence, the Canadian position has broadly exemplified the community-based approach, in its many strands. Indeed, the Canadian government's many references to national identity, unity, and the importance of civic debate suggest that at least several strands of the community-based approach are relevant to understanding their stated position.

Moreover, even though Canadian protectionist rhetoric can often be shameless, there is definitely more than simple economic self-interest underlying the Canadian position. Indeed, Canada has very few cultural exports and the magazine industry makes only a small contribution to the Canadian economy. Even the two biggest publishers in Canada have relatively little influence with the government, compared to the large US lobbies.[68] However, questions of cultural sovereignty are highly emotive issues in the Canadian polity and few governments have wanted to challenge this strength of feeling. In this sense, the positions taken by different Canadian governments have no doubt partially reflected their own interests in re-election. However, to understand cultural policy as an instrument of bureaucratic self-perpetuation is to miss the point. Indeed, the point is precisely that cultural issues are important to many Canadians. More importantly, this is so for reasons that cannot be understood through the narrow lens of economic interests. It is only with a deeper understanding of values that the consensus on community-based approaches can properly be understood.

There have, of course, always been vocal dissenters within Canada. The 1920s through to the 1950s, for example, were marked by great dissent within the Canadian parliament about the need for protectionist measures for magazines. Indeed, Prime Ministers Mackenzie King and John Diefenbaker, at different times each gave very traditional market-based defences of freer trade in magazines.[69] However, since a broad consensus emerged in the 1960s, such a defence has been heard much less frequently from Canadian sources. Several academics, such as Steven Globerman, some politicians, a few news commentators, and the Canadian advertising lobby have been the chief exceptions. Even when the Reform Party disagreed with periodicals policy in the 1990s, they usually did not claim that Canadian magazines should not be protected. Instead, they relied on the argument that 'saving' Canadian magazines was not worth an all-out trade war with the United States. Similarly, in opposing limitations on the advertising market, Canadian advertisers have consistently tried to justify their position in terms of the benefits to the Canadian magazine industry. In both cases, opposition was based partly on pragmatic opposition to particular policy instruments and partly in a challenge to community-based principles.

In contrast, American magazine publishers and the US government have (outwardly at least) consistently defended a market-based position. They have persistently refused to recognise that there might be a relevant connection between culture and cultural industries. In all the dealings described above, they have sought to treat periodicals as merely a good like any other, with no other meanings or understandings attached. Not that such a position is without its own rhetoric. As was evident above, the United States hardly hesitates to imply that economic right is on its side, and that Canada is merely being an unruly and selfish trading partner. Even more importantly, the United States is often ready to 'throw its weight around', threatening massive (and often unjustifiable) retaliation as a prelude to (or substitute for) a rules-based solution. Indeed, the rhetoric of the market-based approach often seems to conceal a national commercial strategy that is coincident but not always consistent with the free market. As was the case with the Canadian position, when the rhetoric is peeled away, a different angle on the dispute can be discerned. In the case of the United States, one only has to be reminded of the strong export position of American cultural goods, of the persistent US trade deficit, and of the immense influence of American media giants with Washington DC, to realise that the issue runs deeper than their professed commitment to free trade. In this case, as in many others, free trade rhetoric is the province of the stronger power.[70]

An ethical approach

It is clear from the discussion that market-based and community-based approaches have considerable currency in the debate about Canada–US free trade in periodicals. Moreover, previous chapters have laid out the numerous ethical difficulties associated with the market-based approach to culture. These difficulties are no less present in the American position on trade in periodicals. The ethical status of any given community-based approach, however, is less clear. By the terms of earlier discussions, is the Canadian periodicals policy an ethically justifiable one? If not, what suggestions can be made? The remainder of this chapter will build upon earlier ethical discussions to suggest some key principles for Canadian magazines policy. Subsequently, it will engage with the specific goals and instruments of Canadian policy, offering constructive criticism and suggesting ways in which such policy could become more ethically justifiable.

The analysis developed throughout this book suggests that magazines policy ought to be aimed at meeting the demands of participation and enablement described in Chapter 6. To recap, *enablement* entails that people have substantive opportunities to express their experiences, their needs, their feelings and perspectives on social life in contexts where others can listen.[71] It further entails that people are enabled to develop and exercise their capacities, to meet their needs, and, ultimately, to exercise their freedom and realise their choices.[72] In turn, *participation* entails that people have power over their actions and the conditions of their actions – that they can discuss and decide upon issues concerning the customs, rules, and institutions that affect them. Participation ought to be universal, but also immediate, local, and accessible.[73] In other words, this ethics demands the full participation and inclusion of everyone in society's major institutions and the socially supported substantive opportunity for all to develop and exercise their capacities and realise their choices. Additionally, however, enablement and participation require particular claims about democracy and diversity. These will be briefly set out below.

This book agrees with Young on the importance of democracy in ensuring that people's voices are heard and as an opportunity for the development and exercise of capacities. Furthermore, a deep democracy is one which brings cultural difference into the public sphere, allowing it to become part of public discussion. In this way, democracy is essentially linked to dialogue, and respect for difference. Building on Taylor's relational view of identity, this book has taken a view of dialogue both as a means of intercultural understanding, but also as the process by which the boundaries and substance of culture are defined and renegotiated. To recap, democracy entails that '[a]ll persons should have the right and opportunity to participate in the deliberation and decision-making of the institutions to which their actions contribute or which directly affect their actions'.[74] Furthermore, attempts should be made to ensure that all social groups are adequately represented in decisions affecting them. The demands of full democracy and representativeness may be quite high and, in practice, difficult to achieve. In this light, this book proposes that the demands of radical democracy be taken as an ideal towards which cultural policy ought to be directed. As we will see below, even in this less demanding way, the ideal of democracy nonetheless suggests significant revisions of policy.

Diversity also often arises in discussions of cultural policy. However, it is important to note that there are two important respects in which diversity should be considered. In the first place, it is important to ensure that Canadians have a wide variety of magazines to choose from. In this context, policy should be concerned that there is a wide diversity of cultural output. However, it is important to note that variety is not important for its own sake, but rather to ensure that there exist a large number of different sites for discussion, debate, and sharing of thoughts and interests. This relates to the importance of dialogue, which will be discussed below.

Second, it is important to ensure that the cultural diversity of the Canadian community is represented in the magazine industry. This is important in the sense that magazines are an important site of dialogue for the many social groups within Canada, but also because opportunities for cultural expression are an important element of enablement, as discussed by Young. Indeed, magazines can be included among the 'real participatory structures in which actual people, with their geographical, ethnic, gender, and occupational differences, assert their perspectives on social issues within institutions that encourage the representation of their distinct voices'.[75]

Goals and instruments assessed

Chapter 4 has already suggested that the goal of promoting national identity through culture is flawed and dangerous. Indeed, as was argued in Chapter 4, a focus on the survival of the nation has a strong tendency to essentialise the community and reify the relationship between culture and identity. These approaches assume that the identity of an individual is a singular thing, that it exists in direct relation to a single, uncontested (national) culture which itself is manifest in a single well-defined (and usually political) community. As Chapter 4 emphasised, it is not clear that this concept of the nation is open to substantive revision, nor that it can accommodate extensive cultural pluralism.

The destructive tendencies of the national identity approaches are reinforced by the reliance of the Canadian government on 'Canadian content' requirements as the primary criteria by which the cultural validity of different media is judged. For example, until very recently, magazines were required to contain 75 per cent Canadian content in order to be considered 'Canadian' magazines.[76] In the first place, this approach is restrictive in the sense that many people who consider themselves a part of the Canadian community may be excluded from conversation in that community, simply because they do not meet formal criteria of citizenship. Second, however, this approach limits the extent to which those who would be identified and would self-identify as cultural outsiders can contribute to the Canadian debate on any subject. In this way, it restricts the cultural evolution that is itself an important result of intercultural interaction.

Furthermore, the Canadian government has always considered that Canadian ownership of cultural industries is essential to ensuring that these meet the nationalist goals of Canadian cultural policy. In particular, they have assumed that one important way of ensuring Canadian content is through Canadian ownership. To a certain extent, this is true. Because there are few Canadian multinational entertainment giants, Canadian ownership usually leads to *original* content, although there is no necessary reason why this content should be particularly Canadian. However, Canadian ownership criteria are not the only way to ensure original content. In fact, by confusing ownership with content, they can unnecessarily inhibit intercultural dialogue. For this reason, this analysis is generally sceptical of Canadian ownership criteria. Similarly, given the distribution problems faced by Canadian magazines, this book suggests that steps be taken to ensure adequate access to news-stands for Canadian magazines. This may entail buttressing existing Canadian-owned distribution companies, but should be achieved more directly if possible. Magazines can hardly fulfil their important role in fostering dialogue and ensuring cultural expression if they face such huge difficulties in reaching many potential readers.

Notably, the recent shift in Canadian policy towards original content – content produced for the Canadian market – marks an important step towards a magazine policy that can move beyond exclusively nationalist criteria to accommodate cultural diversity. This is particularly true when original content provisions have replaced *both* existing ownership and content rules. Relying on original content acts to protect a space for discussion and to protect diversity in face of homogenising global influences but it does not do so in a way that prejudges the substance, direction, or participants in cultural exchange.

As a means of achieving the revised goals described above, the idea of preserving some part of Canadian advertising revenue for Canadian magazines is a very good one. Such an approach helps to ensure that there will continue to be a diversity of *both* foreign and domestic magazines available in Canada. Nonetheless, Canadian magazines must still compete with each other and with other media for advertisers. If they wish to be successful, the burden remains on the individual magazines to produce interesting editorial content, thereby attracting subscribers and, in turn, advertisers. In effect, this approach provides the space for Canadian magazines to flourish – and thereby allows Canadian consumers to exercise a real choice – without involving government in the process by which successful magazines are weeded out from unsuccessful ones. However, the one drawback of this approach is that, in pursuing the freedom of magazine industry, it restricts the freedom of Canadian advertisers. Under all the magazine policies pursued by the Canadian government, advertisers have been prevented from selling advertising to foreign publishers. However, there is a strong argument to be made for the fact that advertisers benefit greatly when the Canadian magazine industry is healthy. If the magazine industry were to become smaller and less vigorous, Canadian advertisers would clearly suffer, as would Canadian consumers. In this regard, so long as magazines policy is successful and maintains significant number and range of advertising outlets in Canada, then the freedom of advertisers is not significantly damaged.

In this regard, the Foreign Publishers Advertising Services (FPAS) Act is detrimental in that it allows the Canadian advertising 'pie' to be divided among foreign and Canadian publishers. To be fair, foreign access to Canadian advertising is limited to 18 per cent of total advertising in any given magazine. Nonetheless, critics are right to be point out that 18 per cent of the advertising in several large American magazines could constitute the skimming off of a serious proportion of the overall Canadian advertising market.[77] Indeed, if reality was even to approach this prediction, then the FPAS Act would prove to have been a very foolhardy policy. Not only would the Canadian magazine industry be seriously damaged and Canadian choices and dialogues significantly reduced, but Canadian advertisers would be even more limited in terms of the magazines in which they could place ads.

In contrast to the FPAS Act, Section 19 of the Income Tax Act is a very useful instrument, especially as it has been revised most recently and when it is applied in conjunction with an absolute limit on Canadian advertisements in foreign magazines (such as Bill C-58). In particular, as discussed above, the idea of original content is a crucial one. Further, the concept that different degrees of tax deductibility should apply to ads placed in magazines with different levels of original content is a sophisticated way of rewarding those magazines that make a commitment to producing original content for the Canadian market. Unlike a direct subsidy, Section 19 does not entail government intervention in the process by which certain magazines succeed and others fail. Furthermore, Section 19 allows any magazine from any country to become a 'Canadian' magazine and to enter the dialogue taking place within and about the community. Furthermore, it does not restrict trade in foreign magazines that do not compete for advertising and thereby fosters cultural openness and intercultural penetration.

The new programme of postal subsidies (PAP) has both advantages and disadvantages. The particular distribution problems of Canadian magazines create an inordinate reliance on subscriptions as a source of revenue and a means of maintaining circulation figures. In this regard, it is not unreasonable to provide some sort of assistance to help defray bulk mailing costs for Canadian magazines. However, at the same time, it is not obvious that this assistance is actually *necessary*. In other words, it is not clear that an end to postal subsidies would be so damaging as to cause a precipitous decline in the number or variety of Canadian magazines. Indeed, it seems that the continuation of the postal subsidy programme owes more to insistent lobbying on the part of Canadian magazine publishers, than any demonstrated need for it. Nonetheless, if the Canadian government is to maintain the postal subsidy programme, it ought to make several important changes to its administration.

Currently, postal assistance is available to magazines that meet several criteria. First, in keeping with general cultural ownership provisions, it must be owned and 75 per cent controlled by Canadians. Second, the publisher must have its principal place of business located in Canada and the magazine must be published, typeset, printed, and edited in Canada, by persons resident in Canada.[78] Third, '[a]n eligible publication must also contain a significant portion of original material produced by Canadian citizens or individuals resident in Canada'.[79] In keeping with the thrust of the discussion above, this book disagrees with the thrust of ownership requirements. Furthermore, print-in-Canada requirements seem to be designed to promote the Canadian printing and editing industry. Finally, the criteria concerning original content differ somewhat from the similar provisions of Section 19. In Section 19, originality was defined by the fact that editorial material has not previously or simultaneously been published in a foreign market. This open-endedness provided much of the appeal of Section 19. In contrast, the PAP includes a concern for citizenship or residency – original material must be produced by a Canadian citizen or resident. By adding this criterion, the PAP reinforces the nationalism of earlier Canadian content approaches. If the subsidy programme is continued, it should be revised to centre on the concept of original content set out in Section 19.

Finally, we need to assess the status of current grants policies. In practice, the best means by which to deliver government support to cultural activities generally is through the use of 'arm's length' policies – namely, those which keep the decisions about which cultural activities are valuable at an arm's length from government. Arm's length allocative organisations are already quite common in North America and Europe – for example, the Arts Council in Great Britain and the Canada Council in Canada.[80] However, despite its distance from government, the Canada Council has itself often not met the demands of enablement and participation. In an effort to preserve its own organisational *raison d'être*, the Canada Council has often replicated the drawbacks of a centralised government agency. In the first place, its allocative goals have often remained secret. Furthermore, as Jean Guiot has noted, '[g]rants are convincing arguments to bring about desired behaviour ... on the part of companies which remain chronically dependent on public support'.[81] The argument here is not so much that the Canada Council has aimed to foster such dependence. Instead, it is simply to note that shifting grant-making to a single arts council may not avoid the overcentralisation and opacity characteristic of direct government granting agencies. As a result, I suggest that decisions about arts funding should take place at several different levels, and must incorporate much more localised groups than does the current Canada Council. Every attempt should be made to ensure that these new grant-making bodies are broadly representative of Canadian social groups. Furthermore, they should operate democratically and encourage broad dialogue relating to their activities.

Clearly, the policy suggestions made here are not without their difficulties, nor can they unquestionably ensure that the cultural needs of every individual residing in Canada are adequately met. Nonetheless, the method advocated here clearly offers new insights that both welfare economics and national survival approaches cannot articulate. Furthermore, in assessing the claims made above, it is important to note that these comments are intended only as suggestions for new avenues for policy, not as once-and-for-all solutions to trade disputes concerning magazines. Following Young, these conclusions are meant to 'offer proposals in the ongoing political discussion'.[82] Indeed, it is crucial for both democracy and diversity that there be an inclusive and substantive dialogue about magazine policies. The debate over normative principles and the appropriate way to apply them is ongoing – and these suggestions ought to be treated as one contribution to this process of normative engagement.

In this sense, several important issues become clear. First, this chapter has reinforced the claims of earlier chapters about the importance of market- and community-based approaches in characterising ideas about cultural policy. Second, with a few notable exceptions, the broad Canadian view (especially recently) has been dominated by different strands of the community-based approach and the American view has been characterised by market-based ideas. Indeed, even whether one believes that cultural meanings could possibly have a non-commercial relevance seems to depend on one's initial leanings in the market-based/community-based debate. Third, it is clear that over the years, Canadian culture has gradually become an unavoidably international (or at least bilateral) issue. Whatever proponents of the community-based approach may argue about the need for the community to exclusively decide community issues, this is no longer an option for Canadian periodicals. Indeed, magazines policy is not a matter of domestic regulation alone. Increasingly, the task of Canadian legislators is to find an appropriate balance between Canadian cultural needs and international market requirements. In this realm, American interests and the potential impact on Canada's international trading commitments are now an inescapable part of the policy landscape.

8
Prospects for Post-National Cultural Policy: the Case of the European Union

The previous chapter examined cultural policy at the national level, using Canadian magazines policy as an example. It examined the arguments made by the Canadian and US trade negotiators from the perspective of the market- and community-based approaches. It concluded that the approach taken by American negotiators failed to appreciate the constitutive importance of culture. However, the Canadian perspective is also ethically unsatisfactory and requires greater attention to emancipatory and participatory demands if it is to be ethically defensible.

Given the formative role played by the nation in community-based approaches, it would be tempting to believe that subnational or supranational cultural actions might have a greater chance of supporting participation and emancipation in a way that is less culturally essentialised. This chapter will explore this assertion. It will examine cultural policy at the European level in an attempt to understand whether these policies should be more accurately read in terms of the market-based approach or the community-based approach. It will argue that European attempts at cultural policy demonstrate elements of the national survival approach, underpinned by some familiar liberal assumptions. Combined with European Commission reluctance to interfere in cultural policy at the national level, the result is a cultural policy with confused objectives and uneven impact. Furthermore, the potential for an ethically justifiable cultural policy at the European level has so far not been realised.

European Community cultural policy described

The story of formal European Community involvement in cultural issues begins in 1992.[1] At this time, the Maastricht Treaty establishing the European Community introduced a citizenship of the Union and made changes to two specific articles, thereby formally introducing cultural activity as a legitimate activity of the Community and specifying the purposes of such activity. To Article 3 was added clause (p), which states that the activities of the Community must now include 'a contribution to the education and training of quality and to the flowering of the cultures of the Member States'.[2] Article 128 laid out the objectives and instruments of such activity in further detail. Since it is the definitive article on European cultural activity, it is worth quoting at length:

1. The Community shall contribute to the flowering of the cultures of the Member States, while respecting their national and regional diversity and at the same time bringing the common cultural heritage to the fore.
2. Action by the Community shall be aimed at encouraging cooperation between Member States and, if necessary, supporting and supplementing their action in the following areas:
   - improvement of the knowledge and dissemination of the culture and history of the European peoples;
   - conservation and safeguarding of cultural heritage of European significance;
   - non-commercial cultural exchanges;
   - artistic and literary creation, including in the audiovisual sector.
3. The Community and the Member States shall foster cooperation with third countries and the competent international organisations in the sphere of culture, in particular the Council of Europe.
4. The Community shall take cultural aspects into account in its actions under other provisions of this Treaty, in particular in order to respect and to promote the diversity of its cultures.[3]

The European commitment to Article 3(p) and Article 128 has since been underscored by their inclusion in the Amsterdam Treaty of 1997, although these clauses have now been renumbered as Article 3(q) and Article 151.

Already in the language employed within this Treaty, it is possible to see the outline of some general assumptions that guide European Community thinking on culture. First, it is clear that the state level is very important in considering European-level action towards culture. Not only does the Treaty imply that Member States have culture(s), but it further implies that states are the primary actors in the cultural sphere – the Community[4] shall encourage cooperation between states and shall support and supplement their action in certain key areas. At no point is it suggested that culture ought to be considered independently of the state or that the Community might act independently of states in the cultural arena. Furthermore, much stake is placed on the possibilities inherent in cooperation between states, with all the sense implied of states as unitary actors. Second, and despite the precedence given to states, the Community is keen to acknowledge the possibility of a European culture, based, it seems, mainly on an undefined common European heritage. This is clearly not meant to be a challenge to Member States' cultural authority – it is in fact, presented as non-conflictual action at the European level. As we will see, the principle of subsidiarity effectively prevents any more definite action, while the latent notion of functionalism suggests that the Community may well be using culture instrumentally – to create a community by stealth. These themes will emerge in greater detail when the instruments and objectives of European cultural policy are examined in greater detail below.

Instruments of European cultural activity

Before drawing out the goals of European cultural activity, it is important to briefly examine the several instruments that the European Commission employs. This will give us a sense of the European commitment to cultural policy, and will also help us to draw out and contextualise the objectives of European cultural policy.

(i) Funding programmes

Funding programmes are the central means of European support for cultural activity. From 1994 to 1999, the Commission supported culture through three specific programmes. Raphael (1997–2000) was intended to support cultural heritage. Ariane (1997–98) was to promote literature, books, and reading, while Kaleidoscope was to support cultural creation and cooperation in artistic activities.[5] All three programmes shared a common set of priorities, namely, 'co-operation between operators in the cultural sector; ... public access to and participation in culture; promotion of artistic creation and cultural heritage'.[6] Between 1994 and 1997, 1400 projects were supported, with a total spend of ECU 118,500 – a fairly minimal amount by any standards. Indeed, the Commission itself expressed disappointment with the results of the programmes. Although they did increase transnational cooperation and access to culture, the programmes did not generate any lasting networks of cooperation. Moreover, it was felt that the programmes encouraged a fragmentation of budgetary resources and a corresponding lack of visibility of Community interven-tion.[7] Further, Community cultural action was not focused enough in its use of particular instruments to achieve particular cultural ends.

Following from this evaluation, the Commission decided to imple-ment a more comprehensive framework programme of cultural funding. Notably, in preparing this new programme, the Commission undertook a substantial series of in-depth consultations with Member States, prospective Member States, and European cultural organisations. The result of these consultations is the Culture 2000 programme, a single financing and programming instrument for the period 2000–4 with a total budget of 167 million euros. This programme is specifically geared to promoting cooperation between 'artists, cultural operators and cul-tural institutions in the Member States', with the following objectives:

- the mutual knowledge of the culture and history of the European people, thus revealing their common cultural heritage and encour-aging cultural dialogue;
- encouraging creativity, the international dissemination of culture and greater movement of artists and their creations;
- the promotion of cultural diversity and the development of new forms of cultural expression;
- the contribution of culture to socio-economic development;
- to highlight the European importance of cultural heritage;
- to encourage European cultures in third countries, and dialogue with other countries around the world.[8]

The programme is administered by the European Commission itself, which also lays out specific guidelines for the yearly priorities of the pro-gramme and the consequent areas of eligibility. In 2001, for example, the Commission accepted applications only in respect of the following areas: heritage, artistic, and literary creation and the history and culture of European peoples. Moreover, the Commission further specified the types of projects it would consider. For example, in terms of European cultural heritage, the Commission committed to funding 40 specific projects of one year's duration. Each of these projects was required to involve museum cooperation, travelling exhibitions or 'the European dimension of sub-aquatic archaeology, architecture, archives and the cultural movements ... of the 19th or 20th centuries'.[9] The fact that these requirements are so specific and that the programme is adminis-tered by the Commission itself are worrying developments. This will be discussed further below.

While Culture 2000 is intended to be a very broad programme, it is not the only form of cultural support provided for by the European Community. Several other programmes of industry support will be addressed in the next section. First, however, it is important to discuss European cultural funding through the Regional Development Programmes. In particular, the Commission supports culture through the structural funds which are provided to aid regions which lag behind the Union. Additionally, cultural activities are supported through Article 10 of the European Regional Development Fund (ERDF). In both of these cases, the purpose of cultural support is 'to strengthen economic and social cohesion by contributing to the establishment of networks between the regions and towns of the Union, on the basis of culture and the enhancement of regional and local cultural heritage, with a view to inter-regional cooperation and economic development'.[10] Moreover, while the projects supported can clearly be considered cultural – craft heritage, for example – the Commission is clear that they cannot be considered for support *primarily* because of the cultural dimension. According to the Commission, '[t]he pilot projects for interregional cooperation and economic development in the cultural field ... can be included only under the heading of Community cohesion. This means that they will have to contribute to the development of the least-favoured regions in the Union using the experience and know-how accumulated by more developed regions.'[11] Clearly, the cultural dimension of the projects is of secondary importance to the Commission when it comes to structural funds. Importantly, however, as Juan Delgado Moreira points out, Community expenditure on cultural projects through regional development funds in the year 2000 constitutes nearly 80 times the level of cultural funding provided for through Culture 2000. The Parliament itself admits that its cultural support programmes 'account for only a portion of the Community resources earmarked for culture, most of which are allocated via the Structural Funds'.[12] The implications of directing funding primarily through an economic cohesion programme will be discussed in detail below. First, however, the remaining instruments of cultural policy will be described.

(ii) Industry support and regulation

Two specific industries are not supported by the Culture 2000 programme, namely the audiovisual media and multimedia industries. These are supported by separate programmes designed 'to encourage them to develop a structure and grasp the new opportunities offered by the single market and digital technologies'.[13]

Audiovisual media, including the cinema, are supported by the MEDIA programme and its successors, the MEDIA II and MEDIA PLUS programmes. MEDIA was initiated in 1991 with the aim of strengthening the audiovisual industry by 'providing it with the means to adapt to economic change'.[14] MEDIA does not provide support for audiovisual production, as this was perceived to be the sole responsibility of Member States. Instead, the MEDIA programme was aimed to improve the distribution and promotion of European works – both within Europe and abroad. The MEDIA programme is justified primarily in terms of promoting industrial competitiveness. However, the MEDIA programme clearly has additional effects in terms of promoting wider access to European cultural goods and improving the difficult distribution conditions for European films globally.

Multimedia industries are specifically supported by the eContent programme. Established in 2000, this programme aims to increase the industrial competitiveness of Europe's 'content industries' (e.g. publishing, information industries) by assisting in the production, use, and dissemination of European digital resources. Similarly to the MEDIA programmes, eContent is framed in terms of infant-industry type arguments. The focus of the programme is industrial competitiveness, although there are clearly additional cultural benefits of Commission support.

In addition to these specific support programmes, the Commission is also concerned to ensure that its policies encourage an appropriately competitive environment for all cultural industries. The Community does so through a set of European rules intended to support and supplement national cultural policies. The primary governing principle of all European industry policy is set out in Article 157 of the Treaty of Amsterdam which states that '[t]he Community and Member States shall ensure that the conditions necessary for the competitiveness of the Community's industry exist'.[15] In particular, the Community and Member States should act to speed up the adjustment of industry to structural changes, should encourage an environment favourable to initiative, to cooperation between undertakings, and to innovation. Community rules on the internal market are also intended to apply to the cultural sector. In addition, however, the Treaty of Amsterdam authorises state aid to promote culture, 'where such aid does not affect trading conditions and competition … to an extent that is contrary to the common interest'.[16] More specifically, in the Council Resolution of 12 February 2001 on national aid to the film and audiovisual industries, the Community acknowledges that the European film sector is suffering from conditions of market failure. Moreover, it asserts that 'national aid to the film and audiovisual industries is one of the chief means of ensuring cultural diversity' and that 'the objective of cultural diversity presupposes the industrial fabric necessary to satisfy that objective'.[17] Finally, the Commission perceives that strengthened national industries may lead to a genuinely European audiovisual market. For these reasons, argues the Community, Member States are entitled to aid the audiovisual sector at a national level.

On a smaller scale, the Commission also supports funding of cultural initiatives by the European Investment Bank and actively promotes the development of cultural industries in developing countries through its cooperation agreements and limited support programmes.

All of these industry support programmes resonate strongly with market-based approaches. Indeed, industrial support is the main justification for the programmes discussed above. However, it is not clear that this industrial support is truly a market-based approach. In particular, there is no suggestion that the Commission perceives this assistance to be temporary. The Commission never outwardly refers to market failure, infant industry, or merit goods arguments. Indeed, in the numerous justifications of the programme, a return to industry competitiveness is never discussed. One gets the impression that industrial competitiveness is important on the basis that it will contribute to a diffusion of European culture within Europe and a more successful European cultural industry abroad. Clearly, the European Community is motivated by the jobs and wealth that could be created by enhanced culture industries. More importantly, however, they seem motivated by the prosperity and overall cultural development of the specific European community. On this basis, there is a strong case to be made for the possibility that market-based arguments are simply a form of justification for community-based policies of ongoing industry protection.

(iii) Education and training programmes

Within European comments on culture, education is viewed as playing a key role in access to culture, the development of mutual understanding, and the training of cultural professionals. In its Resolution of 26 July 1996 on access to culture for all, the Council makes the initial claim that 'access to culture for citizens in an operational or user capacity is an essential condition for full participation in society'.[18] However, it also states that improving access to culture is the primary responsibility of the Member States. Nonetheless, there is still a role to be played by the Community in encouraging access to the European dimension of culture. It does this mainly through education and exchange programmes. The Socrates programme, in particular, promotes European cooperation to encourage language learning and European mobility. Specifically, Socrates offers grants to study or teach in another country as well as providing funding for educational institutions to organise teaching projects or educational exchanges.[19] The only condition is that such projects or exchanges must be geared towards promoting knowledge of European cultures. In this respect, it is clear that access to culture through education is perceived to be central to the task of developing mutual understanding.

Additionally, the Commission lends support to cultural and linguistic training programmes through the Leonardo da Vinci vocational training programme. Other programmes, such as Culture 2000 and MEDIA, also have provision to fund the mobility of young artists and the creation of pan-European training courses in dance, music, and to improve skills essential to the audiovisual industry. Finally, the Commission directly funds youth exchanges and education programmes designed specifically to preserve linguistic diversity.[20]

(iv) International negotiations

Finally, the European Union acts bilaterally and multilaterally to secure a satisfactory framework for international trade in cultural goods and adequate protection of intellectual property. In particular, the EU has a mandate in the next round of multilateral negotiations to 'ensure, as in the Uruguay Round, that the Community and its Member States maintain the possibility to preserve and develop their capacity to define and implement their cultural and audiovisual policies for the purpose of preserving their cultural diversity'.[21] The EU also cooperates with the Council of Europe and UNESCO in all areas, but most notably in the areas of heritage protection and cultural diversity.

Clearly, the EU is heavily involved in cultural policy at several levels. Moreover, as has been made clear through a discussion of these instruments, the Union has definite cultural objectives. These, however, were only hinted at in the discussions above. The section which follows will attempt to more systematically distil the stated and unstated objectives of European cultural policy. Following this discussion, the chapter will conclude with a discussion of the ethical implications of European cultural policy.

Objectives and guiding principles

As noted above, since 1992, the Commission, Parliament and Council have published numerous resolutions on cultural activity. Also as discussed above, several formal funding programmes have been implemented, namely Kaleidoscope, Raphael, Ariane, and, most recently, Culture 2000. Through these resolutions and activities, the objectives of European cultural policy have taken shape. Primary among these objectives are the two suggested in the Treaty itself, namely assisting in the flowering of national cultures and improving the knowledge of European culture and history. These will be discussed first, followed by two other, less obvious, objectives.

(i) Assist flowering of national cultures

Beyond the Treaty's assertion that the Community should assist in the flowering of national cultures, there is very little written about this objective. However, it is possible to identify two formative principles which generate this objective and give some insight into its role in European cultural policy-making. In the first place, the desire for national cultures to flourish results from a fundamental beliefs that 'culture is the bedrock on which peoples build their identity', and that 'artistic and cultural freedom of expression and the access of all citizens to culture are fundamental rights'.[22] This conception is notable in that it explicitly links culture with identity and formalises the importance of access of all citizens to culture. It clearly resonates with community-based approaches. However, a full understanding of these commitments depends greatly on the definition of culture which underlies them. As we will see, no firm idea of culture is relied upon by the Community.

The second formative principle which underlies the Community's commitment to national cultures is the principle of subsidiarity. Subsidiarity is one of the central principles of the EU. It essentially provides a division of responsibilities between the Community and the Member States. According to Article 5 of the 1992 Treaty, '[i]n areas which do not fall within its exclusive competence, the Community shall take action ... only and insofar as the objectives of the proposed action cannot be sufficiently achieved by the Member States'.[23] In practice, strict adherence to this principle effectively requires the Community to view culture as located within state-level jurisdiction. The Community must then look for alternative avenues for its cultural activities. In practice, as we have seen above, Community efforts have tended to focus on uncontroversial measures that encourage cultural cooperation and the preservation of heritage. However, we will also see that the Community has hoped that these uncontroversial cultural activities will further the development of a common European culture – a European nation to underpin the European polity.

(ii) Improving knowledge of European culture and history

Improving knowledge of European culture is the second objective that is explicitly mentioned in the Treaty of 1992. In practice, however, much more has been said about this objective than the one discussed above, and one cannot help but get the impression that this is where lies the true cultural enthusiasm of the Community. In fact, improving knowledge of European culture and history has become the basis for the development of a stronger sense of a common European culture. This was clear above in the significant focus on cultural cooperation, on the development of mutual understanding, and the discussion of education. In particular, the Culture 2000 programme is a very important example of the interlinkage of these aims. According to 2002 programme documentation,

> [t]he objectives of the programme are the promotion of a common cultural area characterised by both cultural diversity and a common cultural heritage. Culture 2000 looks to encourage creativity and mobility, public access to culture, the dissemination of art and culture, inter-cultural dialogue, and knowledge of the history of the peoples of Europe.[24]

In this respect, it is clear that the promotion of knowledge of European culture is one small part of a much more ambitious objective.

There is a striking tension in European thinking on a common cultural area. There is, first, the idea of a nascent European identity, which should be nurtured through active education in areas that are common to all Europeans – e.g. common history and culture – and the preservation of specifically European cultural heritage. However, there is equally a view that European uniqueness is born of its diversity. For example, the European Parliament notes in its resolution on cultural cooperation, that 'a European cultural policy which in no way seeks uniformity but can offer an identity born of the encounter between differences is of crucial importance for the development of a collective European consciousness'.[25] At first reading, this would seem to create an impossible uneasiness in European cultural policy. The common catchphrase of 'unity through diversity' does little to specify the normative basis upon which European cultural policy reconciles its crucial commitment to national cultures with its central desire to create a common European cultural area. A further comment by the European Parliament is helpful in understanding how this tension is resolved. In their resolution on cultural cooperation, the Parliament clearly states that 'respect for and promotion of cultural and linguistic diversity and the sharing of a common heritage are a force for the integration and development of human beings'.[26] In this respect, we can understand how the Community believes it can uphold two such different objectives. Furthermore, we can now see how these objectives are reconciled in principle, although, as we will see below, there has been little progress towards a practical substantiation of what is entailed by 'unity through diversity'. In fact, as the European Parliament states, 'it is one of this Parliament's duties to make progress in the search for a common cultural basis, a European civil area, that will increase citizens' sense of belonging to that European area'.[27] Not only does this suggest that the practical basis for a common sense of culture is yet to be fully identified, it also indicates that the search for this cultural basis is perceived to be a crucial element in the creation of a common European polity. The conception of culture and citizenship that are implicated in this discussion will be dealt with below.

(iii) Peace through understanding

Clearly, notions of a 'collective European consciousness' do feature significantly in European Commission statements. However, there is also another, less emphasised reason that the Commission supports increased cultural awareness and improved intercultural dialogue. In particular, the Community also subscribes to the notion that increased awareness of different cultures can foster 'mutual understanding between peoples in the interests of peace'.[28] In terms of good relations within the Union, this Commission statement adds little to other statements on European community-building. It does, however, add some background that explains the Community commitment to cultural exchanges and mobility of culture professionals. However, mutual understanding is key to explaining European cultural policy towards non-Community states, including prospective members. In fact, the EU has signed numerous cooperation agreements with non-member states. These agreements are aimed at 'promoting dialogue and cooperation with the other world cultures; contributing to the profile of European cultures elsewhere in the world; and contributing to cultural development in developing countries'.[29] However, in all of these agreements, there is an underlying belief that 'there would be no such thing as peace were it not for intercultural exchange'.[30] Clearly, there are important parallels between the Commission's comments in this respect and the post-war thinking which underlies the founding of UNESCO – namely that UNESCO must 'contribute to peace and security in the world by promoting collaboration among nations through education, science, culture and communication in order to further universal respect for justice, for the rule of law and for the human rights and fundamental freedoms which are affirmed for the peoples of the world'.[31] As the late twentieth century has clearly demonstrated, however, there is no necessary reason why increased interchanges between cultures will generate peace. Moreover, it has often been argued that the vision of culture which underlies such assertions is unduly essentialist, focusing as it does on discrete cultures being exposed to one another. Unfortunately, however, the Commission offers little more in the way of justification for such a consequentialist analysis, nor does it analyse the ways in which peace through intercultural understanding might actually be brought to fruition.

(iv) Socio-economic integration and economic development

The discussion above has focused on the Community's efforts to enlist both cultural heritage and cultural diversity in the service of community-building. Notably, the Community has been agnostic on the specific nature of the European identity that they hope will flourish. In fact, so strong is the idea of unity through diversity that one might well begin to believe that diversity itself will be the defining and motivating feature of the community. However, this is not completely fair. In other parts of Community literature, there is also a notion that European cultural activity should be used to promote socio-economic integration and social cohesion.

The importance of culture in contributing to economic development was evidenced in the discussion of structural funds as an instrument of cultural support, above, and is further shown through a close reading of European Commission comments. The Parliament asserts that 'culture is an asset in its own right and also makes an important contribution to economic development and helps increase employment'.[32] Similarly, the Council of Europe comments that 'cultural development ... generates employment and economic wealth'.[33] Indeed, in the communications establishing the Culture 2000 programme, the Parliament draws an explicit link between culture and structural policies, arguing that culture ought to be a 'valid component of regional and local development strategies. ... Cultural projects will be eligible if they create jobs and are integrated into local or regional development strategies.'[34]

In addition, the Commission seems to subscribe to the more difficult position that economic development aids social integration, and that culture can play a role in fostering both. In their resolution on cultural cooperation, the European Parliament affirms that 'cultural policy needs to be an integral part of economic and social development, to perform a role of social cohesion and mutual enrichment'.[35] More specifically, Commission notes on preparation of projects indicate that '[p]ilot projects on inter-regional cooperation for economic development in the cultural field should be designed to help develop and disseminate local and regional identities while ... bringing the common cultural heritage to the fore'.[36] Clearly, the Commission believes there to be important links between cultural policy, economic development, and European identity-building. However, as with most Commission communications, the envisaged linkages, and their potential practical embodiments, remain ill-defined.

To recap, this section has claimed that there are four stated objectives of European Community involvement in the cultural sphere, namely the flowering of national cultures, improving knowledge of European culture, peace through understanding, and socio-economic development and integration. The discussion above has drawn out the nature of each of these objectives, hinting also at certain underlying themes and tensions which are revealed by these objectives and the Community interpretation of them. The remainder of this chapter will more critically examine European Community cultural policy, seeking to draw out the multiple understandings of culture which underlie it and the inherent confusion in the Community about the relationship between identity, culture, and community. The ethical implications of the European position will be drawn out, before the chapter concludes with some concrete suggestions for a more ethical European Community approach to culture.

European Community cultural policy examined

The discussion above hinted at certain key tensions in European Community statements on culture. First, there is clearly an unresolved tension between unity and diversity or, phrased differently, between the desire to build a strong and emotive European community and the desire to respect the assumed pre-eminence of the state in the cultural sphere, including the diversity that this is presumed to imply. Second, there is a latent tension between the Community's desire to harness cultural activity as an element of economic development and the desire to build a common European culture as the basis for a future civic European polity. As noted above, this latter conflict is resolved, in principle, at least, by the liberal transnationalist assumption that greater economic development contributes to social integration. Similarly, the assumption that greater cultural understanding leads to peace is never properly examined or justified, but is the glue which binds European culture in service of a peaceful, harmonious European civic community.

Each of these tensions – and, more importantly, the Community's failure to acknowledge them as possible conflicts – belie a failure on the part of the Commission to adequately engage with the substantive issues posed by a foray into the cultural arena. To be clear, one cannot reasonably expect cultural policy-makers to deconstruct their own cultural assumptions to the extent that a scholar would. However, it is not unreasonable to expect that some consideration be given to the numerous meanings of culture and, more importantly, that attention be given to developing a consistent understanding of the role of culture in the good life. Unlike Canadian cultural policy, which was perhaps too focused on the perceived needs of the community, European cultural policy is not focused enough on its founding assumptions. It is a cultural policy which equally acknowledges too many cultural objectives without substantively engaging with any of them. The result is many grand statements, a few uncontroversial actions, and very little by way of a consistent, ethical approach to culture.

(i) Conceptions of culture

Any deeper analysis of European cultural policy begins with an attempt to uncover the various meanings of culture relied upon by the Community. Not surprisingly, few attempts are made by the Community to specifically define culture. One of the few such attempts argues only that 'culture is no longer restricted to "highbrow" culture. Today, the concept also covers popular culture, mass-produced culture, everyday culture. ... [C]ulture is no longer considered a subsidiary activity, but a driving force in society, making for creativity, vitality, dialogue and cohesion.'[37] This statement gives some indication of what is included within the moniker 'culture', but hardly serves as a defining conceptual statement. This is particularly true when one realises that numerous and more varied cultural concepts are repeatedly employed throughout Commission statements. In fact, many of the definitions of culture described in Chapter 2 reappear throughout Commission literature. Culture is variously described as a national characteristic, as heritage, as artistic and literary creation, as industry, as an essential element of a democratic society, as a fundamental right, and a source of vitality, dynamism, and social development. It is alternately something which people create, something which defines a group, something which exists as an independent agent, and something to which one can have access. Moreover, it is not just the random artistic creation of individuals in a diverse society or the imagined community specified by the nation, it often also has a substantive content, as a force for 'democracy and stability'.[38] European culture, particularly, is assumed to be a key element of 'membership of a society founded on freedom, democracy, tolerance and solidarity'.[39] Culture, in this sense, clearly has substantive content – at least in some European Commission documents.

Other scholars have noted the plural definitions of culture in European cultural policy statements. Anne M Cronin notes, for example, that 'European cultural policy documents attempt to navigate between competing definitions of "culture", employing the anthropological sense of culture as shared values and cultural production. ... Yet they also use culture in the sense of a signifying or symbolic system.'[40] She also notes that the common values of Europe are defined as 'freedom of expression and information, cultural diversity and the equal dignity of all human beings'.[41] The European definition of culture is only the starting point of Cronin's argument and, as such, it satisfies the needs of her argument to simply categorise European definitions of culture into these two main schools. Moreover, she does not dwell on the implications of the European attempt to navigate between differing definitions of culture.

In principle, there is nothing harmful about multiple definitions of culture. As this book has no doubt demonstrated, definitions abound – and even the most careful author can be forgiven for mixing his cultural metaphors. The difficulty lies in the fact that each understanding of culture carries with it a certain theoretical and even ontological baggage. In other words, many conceptions of culture also carry an implied vision of the relationship between culture and identity, a sense of the value and specific role of culture in social relations, and, implicitly, a sense of whether culture is constructed or imposed, uniform or diverse, essentialised or constantly evolving. European comments on cultural policy do not do justice to the potential social implications of the definitions that are used.

In the EU context, these difficulties are reinforced by the fact that different policy statements use vastly different conceptions of culture, depending on which concept is most intuitive for the purpose at hand. Little consideration is given to the implications of any particular concept – or, more importantly, to the uneasy partnership of some concepts. For example, where the purpose of supporting culture is to generate jobs, culture is described as a sector, a financial asset, and an industry.[42] However, where the purpose of culture is perceived to be the development of a European sense of belonging, then culture is defined as shared values and a common heritage.[43] Clearly, as the Canadian case showed, it is not easy to promote European culture as a competitive industry and also as a set of specific shared values. This sort of conflict is compounded by the sheer volume of loose definitions of culture relied upon in European policy. Once the implications of these definitions are drawn out, it becomes clear that the EU aim to have an expansive cultural policy has in fact created some potentially serious value conflicts. Moreover, we will see that these latent conflicts can more easily be ignored by the EU because of its implicit reliance on a few myths about liberal citizenship and transnationalism.

(ii) Culture and the good life

Examining European cultural policy through the lens of market-based and community-based approaches will help us to sift through the variety of European pronouncements on culture. By way of a quick reminder, market-based approaches are those which prioritise individual well-being and view culture as a discrete good much like any other. Cultural policies, like many policies, should be structured so as to best promote consumer welfare. In terms of their conception of the good, they are individualist and subjectivist and do not recognise the fundamental relevance of culture in defining human needs and values. In contrast, community-based approaches are those which focus on the benefits of cultural activity for the community – although they vary considerably in terms of how they understand the community and the nature of the good for that community. Where do European cultural policies fit on this spectrum? At first glance, it would seem that certain parts of these policies could be read as market-based (e.g. those which discuss culture as an instrument to assist in the achievement of economic development), while others are incontestably community-based.

Several authors have given consideration to similar questions about the nature of European cultural policy. In particular, some are concerned to show the marketisation or Anglo-Americanisation of European cultural policy. Cronin, for example, argues that the discourse about culture in Europe has come to be dominated by the concept of consumerism. In her words, 'discourses of consumer rights have taken a central place in European policy documents ... cultural freedom is reframed as free access to citizenship rights as *consumer* rights'.[44] Moreover, according to Cronin, placing consumerism at the heart of cultural policy is the mechanism by which the European Commission aims to resolve the tension between unity and diversity. What is implied by Cronin is that the Commission believes it can avoid giving a substantive (and essentialised) form to the common European culture by recasting the issue as one of consumer rights. The duty of government, in this analysis, is simply to ensure adequate competition and free access to cultural goods. People are naturally assumed to choose liberal values.

In this analysis, Cronin is attempting to highlight themes of European cultural policy that would, in the terms of this book, typecast this policy as a stereotypical market-based approach. Indeed, her criticisms draw upon the same critiques that were levelled earlier against the market-based approaches. She argues that a focus on citizens as consumers seeks to erase social barriers, such as class and gender, and create a new conception of consumption as political engagement.[45] The result, according to Cronin, is not the value-neutral, consumer-choice society that is sought by European cultural policy-makers, but instead is a society characterised by new sites of inequality and disenfranchisement.

Indeed, there is much in European Commission policy to lend support to this view. In many documents, culture is very clearly treated as an industry, which must be subject to the same competitive rules as all other industries.[46] Moreover, European support for audiovisual production and distribution is often justified in terms of the need for limited assistance to promote industrial 'catch-up' or to rectify market failure. However, to read European cultural policy through the lens of the anti-interventionist, individualist, and subjectivist market-based approaches would be fundamentally misleading, not least because it would ignore the central importance of the Community itself as the focus of all cultural *and* industrial policy-making. This will be illustrated below.

Like Cronin, Juan Delgado Moreira seeks to highlight the importance of economic considerations in European cultural policy-making. However, unlike Cronin, his analysis demonstrates the way in which the value of economic activity is ultimately located at the community level, not the consumer level. Specifically, Delgado Moreira has argued that economic development and, *through that*, social cohesion are the central purposes of European cultural action. In his 2000 article, 'Cohesion and Citizenship in EU Cultural Policy', he discusses the fact that European spending on cultural projects has mainly taken the form of structural funds disbursed through regional development programmes. The implications of this, according to Delgado Moreira, are twofold. First, because the regional development programmes are focused on local economic development and job creation, funding culture through those programmes leads to a view of European policy in terms of 'a pragmatic justification of culture and citizenship in terms of market efficiency, increased economic productivity and also through the implications for employment, education and the environment'.[47] Moreover, according to Delgado Moreira, the Commission effectively 'emphasizes the economic value of culture' and, correspondingly 'insists on a neutral vision of EU citizenship'.[48] Clearly, this would give strong support to those who would look to justify the relevance of a market-based approach in this context.

However, this is not the end of the story in terms of culture as a means to economic development. In particular, economic and industrial development is of value in this context precisely for its contribution to social cohesion. The centrality of social cohesion as a motivating factor for the European Commission is, in fact, the second, and most key point which Delgado Moreira wishes to make. Specifically, the European approach is described by Moreira as focusing on strengthening 'economic and social cohesion by contributing to the establishment of networks between the regions and towns of the Union, on the basis of culture...with a view to inter-regional cooperation and economic development'.[49] Indeed, the founding treaty of the EU speaks precisely to the connection between cohesion and economic development. In Article 158 (previously Article 130a) entitled 'Economic and Social Cohesion', the Treaty specifies that the Community shall be specifically concerned with strengthening economic and social cohesion. It carries on to state that '[i]n particular, the Community shall aim at reducing disparities between the levels of development of the various regions and the backwardness of the least favoured regions'.[50] In this context, it is clear that although European cultural policy may well be harnessed to purely economic considerations, these economic objectives are themselves completely embedded in the desire to promote a single European community. Indeed, in this respect, the Community evidences the strength of the community-based argument about development. The reader will recall how one strand of community-based thought was focused around the need to support culture to improve the prosperity of the Community. This is the red herring generated by the economic aspects of Community cultural policy.

Although the economic objectives are probably the most misleading of the Community's cultural objectives, they are not the only consideration, as the initial part of this chapter set out to show. The other central, and potentially competing, objective is the development of a common European culture – an 'imagined community' of sorts to support the development of a legitimate European polity and citizenship. Indeed, as Delgado Moreira puts it, 'it would seem that cultural policy in the Union would have more of a "performative" function: increased knowledge and cultural awareness would be destined to complete integration'[51]. The problems with this approach are manifold.

Critique

First, as has been hinted at above, the Union appears initially to be agnostic as to the motivating content of a pan-European common culture. It will be a community defined by rich diversity and a reminiscence of a certain common heritage. However, as a detailed analysis shows, the Community is not as agnostic as it at first appears. Although, as Delgado Moreira notes, the Commission shows a 'failure to address a wider debate about ideas of culture, citizenship and relations between the two',[52] it does nonetheless attempt to give substance to the concept of European citizenship. In fact, it soon becomes clear that there are numerous substantive assumptions underlying the proposition of a common European culture. Most notably, the Commission betrays a strong conviction that common European values include democracy and the respect for freedom and the rule of law. In Delgado Moreira's interpretation, '[t]he Commission sees the economic benefits of transnational cooperation as reinforcing transnational awareness of European cultural heritage, which would provide a civic, liberal nationalism to support a form of liberal citizenship'.[53] It is clear from this that the European Commission view is highly liberal – however, its focus is still the delineated community itself. This is not the individualised liberalism of the market-based approach, with its instrumental conception of state activity. Instead, it is a sort of liberal nationalism – an approach which is comfortable giving primacy to the community *and* espousing diversity precisely because it views liberal values as the only natural basis for that community.[54] With the founding assumptions of Europe so defined, it is not difficult to see how diversity too could be a defining feature of the Union. In fact, a diversity bounded by the liberal rule of law is nothing if not the cornerstone of a healthy liberal democratic polity. Nonetheless, as previous chapters have shown, it is not the fully open and unconstrained diversity that is implied by an initial reading of Community cultural policy. As previous chapters have shown, it contributes little to the development of a deep diversity, based on the mutual recognition of deep difference.

Given that a strong sense of community does underlie European Community thinking, we cannot avoid considering the question of who is in and who is out of the Community under consideration. Moreover, whose values are reflected in the common citizenship, so defined? At the time of the Maastricht Agreement, the Community itself comprised all of the then Member States. At a secondary level, the Community could be seen to be comprised of the nationals of these Member States. That these individuals were community members only in a secondary sense is clear both from the principle of subsidiarity and from the expressed belief of the Community that the cultural lives of Europeans are primarily the responsibility of their states. More importantly, however, are those who are not members – migrants are not yet espoused with the belief in European civilisation, resident non-citizens, and, of course, citizens of states which are yet to be European Member States. In respect of the latter, the Commission is already actively seeking to extend its cultural measures to prospective new Members. It is keenly aware of the potential problems caused by incorporating numerous states who have not had the benefits of several decades of reminding of common European heritage and values. Moreover, the inclusion of these countries in the Union will only add regional disparity to the Union – and hence require greater attention to economic development, if the path to social cohesion is to remain on course. The cultural diversity within these countries could well pose a significant challenge to the European vision of unity through diversity, underlain by liberal democracy. It will be interesting to see if fissures begin to emerge in the European identity as a result. Already, some commentators have noted that there is intra-European dispute surrounding the question of 'whose culture is the new common European culture going to most closely approximate?'[55] Tension in this regard is only likely to increase as the idea of a common culture moves more towards being a concrete reality, with all the practical manifestations of any set of cultural norms.

Secondly, there are significant ethical problems with a theory that defends the primacy of the state as the agent of culture and, additionally, which views cultures as nationally located, discrete units. Not only does this rely upon an essentialist and inflexible view of culture, but it also reinforces the notion that the power to define the community rests with the state – or at least, with the dominant nation. Any view of culture which gives primacy to the state as the repository of community cannot do justice to the complex relationship between identity, culture, and community. It does not recognise culture as both constitutive and yet diverse.

Finally, and most importantly, both the economic and the common culture objectives of European cultural policy-making are seriously flawed because they all seek to use culture instrumentally, as a tool in promoting other community-based objectives. For example, cultural cooperation is not supported for its own sake, nor for its importance in meeting the cultural needs of the Community. Instead, cooperation is promoted as a means to better mutual understanding within Europe, thereby promoting a common European heritage and values and, ultimately supporting a European polity through a civic sense of citizenship. The same is true of education, training, the dissemination of cultural goods, and even access to culture. The latter, for example, should be a key stepping stone to the achievement of full opportunities for cultural expression. In the European case, however, it is presented as yet one more way in which European heritage can be better understood and supported. As was noted above, however, numerous assumptions are required to support such a chain of events – not least the assumptions about the nature of European culture – and not all of them are best-suited to promoting a deep diversity based on the acknowledgement of cultural difference.

Policies

The previous chapter reminded us of the principles that should underlie any discussion of an ethical cultural policy. *Enablement* entails that people have substantive opportunities to express their experiences, their needs, their feelings and perspectives on social life in contexts where others can listen.[56] It further entails that people are enabled to develop and exercise their capacities, to meet their needs, and, ultimately, to exercise their freedom and realise their choices.[57] In turn, *participation* entails that people have power over their actions and the conditions of their actions – that they can discuss and decide upon issues concerning the customs, rules, and institutions that affect them. Participation ought to be universal, but also immediate, local, and accessible.[58] In other words, this ethics demands the full participation and inclusion of everyone in society's major institutions and the socially supported substantive opportunity for all to develop and exercise their capacities and realise their choices. Additionally, however, enablement and participation both require particular claims about democracy and diversity. Democracy entails that '[a]ll persons should have the right and opportunity to participate in the deliberation and decisionmaking of the institutions to which their actions contribute or which directly affect their actions'.[59] Diversity, on the other hand, was held to mean that there should be a wide variety of sites for discussion and debate, and a breadth of 'real participatory structures in which actual people, with their geographical, ethnic, gender, and occupational differences, assert their perspectives on social issues within institutions that encourage the representation of their distinct voices'.[60]

European cultural policy has been particularly poor at encouraging enablement and participation. It has been hampered, on the one hand, by the demands of subsidiarity and, on the other, by the rigid desire to see European funding achieve specific Community-level aims. The discussion below will focus on five key policy instruments – highlighting their ethical problems and suggesting an alternative approach which better meets the demands of enablement and participation.

As noted above, Culture 2000 is intended to be a broad programme of cultural funding aimed at promoting greater cooperation within Europe. In so doing, the programme has the potential to open up substantive opportunities for expression and the development of cultural capacities. Moreover, the programme was developed after a substantial series of consultations, thereby improving the democratic credentials of European cultural policy-making. However, Culture 2000 has been prevented from achieving its emancipatory potential by several things. First, the consultations which established the programme were not democratic in the sense demanded by the ethics of this book. In particular, such consultations focused on Member States and some non-state cultural organisations. As a result, they failed to allow for a true diversity of input and some individuals and groups did not benefit from participation, i.e. exercising input into the cultural conditions of the Union. Second, the Commission should be criticised for administering the programme itself. As earlier chapters noted, a key principle of ensuring more democratic and diverse results from state support for culture is for the state to operate at 'arm's length'. It is a key principle of many cultural policies that the state may grant funds, but should not allow itself to dictate too narrowly the form or substance of successful cultural projects. In fact, such 'closeness' on the part of the state is perceived to be a key element of the more restrictive communitarian approaches. Third, and relatedly, the Commission has set the aims and conditions of the programme so narrowly as to effectively rule out of consideration large swathes of cultural activity in the Union. Not only does this reinforce the sense that the Commission is trying to direct the nature of cultural activity, but it further supports the criticism that Culture 2000 does not adequately encourage a diversity of cultural output and sites of dialogue, nor does it focus enough on generating substantive opportunities for expression and participation. Indeed, if the Commission's cultural support programmes are ever to be more ethically justifiable, it must refrain from justifying them in the terms of European state-building. It must place enablement and participation at the top of the cultural agenda and be prepared to accept the possibility that a European community may not emerge as presently envisaged. Secondly, and as a means of achieving the above, the Commission must delegate its funding programmes to several granting bodies representing the true diversity of the Community.

Similarly, the Commission's focus on access to culture is initially promising, but eventually disappointing from an ethical point of view. Ensuring access to culture is a key element of promoting enablement and participation. Without such access, people will not have opportunities to express themselves, nor will they have an adequate diversity of sites of dialogue. However, it soon becomes clear that, in the terms of the EU, access is only promoted in the very narrow sense of promoting knowledge about other cultures with a view to accessing a common European heritage and culture. This is not wholly problematic, however, if only because the promotion of this kind of access does have a positive side-effect of encouraging understanding and dialogue between different groups. To a limited extent, it brings difference into the public sphere – a positive development from the point of view of participation. Nonetheless, European policy could be improved by a conception of access that did not predetermine the nature of the cultures being accessed (national) or the substance of the result of cultural interaction (a European common identity based on liberal citizenship).

Much of European cultural policy focuses on encouraging cooperation in the cultural sphere, but this too is somewhat problematic and in need of rethinking. The European focus on cooperation at all levels is a move away from the pre-eminence of the state in cultural activity and offers the promise of greater possibilities for participation and even, at a stretch, the inclusion of deep cultural difference in the European public sphere. However, European policy betrays this promise by focusing too much on the aims of cooperation and thinking little about the terms on which such cooperation takes place. In other words, European cultural policy is focused around generating cooperation in specific spheres to generate specific common understandings of European culture. This rigid specificity was criticised above. The further problem under consideration here is that European cultural policy does not adequately consider the implications of which agents cooperate and the terms on which they cooperate. This is not to suggest that the European Commission should act as a cultural policeman, investigating the terms of every cultural engagement. This would be extremely problematic – and contrary to the argument of this book. Rather, the Commission should be concerned to assure itself that the demands of enablement and participation are being met for all people living in the EU region. It should do this by ensuring that support funds are awarded to those who embody difference, including those who may not already have a base of funding and social support. Unfortunately, by maintaining direct control over the purse strings and by awarding funding to those who demonstrate a commitment to furthering the European project, the Commission is unwittingly working against the cause of a truly democratic and diverse cultural policy.

Equally, if European cultural policy is to become more ethically justifiable, it must alter its approach to funding cultural activities through regional development funds. The issue is not so much what these funds are titled, but that they contribute a large source of cultural funding that remains completely outside of the cultural policy remit of the Commission. In other words, such funding is unaccountable from a cultural point of view – it is not expected to support cultural aims and it is clearly not meant to be judged by its effectiveness in achieving any goal but that of increased economic development and cohesion. This is problematic primarily because it implies that a large amount of European spending on culture should not really be considered by the terms of the cultural debate at all. Worse yet, this funding is presently deployed in service of extremely economistic aims. It may still provide opportunities for expression and participation, but is hardly likely to encourage the expression and recognition of difference in the public sphere. In fact, it is not even clear if structural funds are concerned for the development of a public sphere at all. If European cultural policy is to become more ethically justifiable, cultural funding ought not to be hidden under the cloak of regional development. It should be transparent and must strive to resolve key conflicts between the demands of enablement and participation, on the one hand, and the demands of regional development on the other. Treating culture as an industry like any other, while surreptitiously hoping that cultural aid leads to European community and a transnational liberal zone of peace, is not only misleading but could lead to exactly the type of community disparaged by so many liberal critics of communitarianism.

Finally, if all of the above are to be made possible, the Commission (and the Member States) must relinquish the principle of subsidiarity in the cultural sphere. This is not to suggest that Member States should be prevented from taking cultural action at the national level. Far from it – at the very least, the national level remains an important source of funding for cultural endeavour and has incredible power to create ethically justifiable cultural policy. However, the European Community also has great potential to break away from the worst excesses of nationalist communitarianism. With an adequately conceived cultural policy, Europe could act to support and nurture the many cultural outlets and tendencies which do not receive adequate attention from the national state. It could encourage enablement and participation among people who are generally overlooked by the state or whose communities cross state boundaries. As such, it could be an important force in promoting a deep diversity comprised of communities not dependent on the monikers of nationalism for their relevance. Member States, however, would have to accept a greater degree of European 'interference' in their cultural lives. At present, this seems highly unlikely and, combined with European Commission 'essentialisation' of European culture, is the largest barrier to a more ethical European cultural policy.

Conclusion

In concluding this book, I wish to return to several important claims made in the introduction. Specifically, the introduction located this research within several different literatures and, in so doing, set forward several related tasks. First, the introduction claimed that the book would build upon earlier analyses of protectionism – further investigating non-commercial motivations for protectionism, and taking up calls for ethical analysis in IPE. Second, the book would exploit the space for counter-discourse established by neo-Gramscians, while taking an explicitly normative approach. Third, it would show how an adequate emancipatory method for IPE requires taking seriously the meaning and importance of culture. This would be achieved by asking two central questions: (i) what are the ethical premises underlying the conventional approaches to cultural policy; (ii) what legitimate alternatives can we envisage? This book has advanced claims on all of these points.

The relevance of ethics for cultural policy

The argument has shown that differing positions on cultural policy can be understood as normative positions, stemming from different perceptions of the role of culture in social relations, the appropriate criteria for 'good' public policy, and the ideal relationship between culture and economics. The debate was conceptualised in terms of two main approaches – market-based approaches and community-based approaches. Market-based approaches emphasise the centrality of individual welfare, believing that this is best served when the market is functioning properly. Moreover, they believe that it is both possible and desirable for culture to be understood through a market paradigm. They view culture as essentially like any other good, with a market for its creation, its sale, and even its subsidisation. As a result, the question of adequate cultural policy resolves itself into the question of when government can legitimately interfere in the free market. 'Good' policy, in this context, is that which uses (measurable) welfare effects to guide government intervention in the free market.

Community-based approaches to cultural policy all begin from the premise that the good of the community, broadly defined, is the ultimate justification for policy. They believe firmly that cultural activity is itself inescapably social and fulfils important group functions. They stress the benefits to the community of cultural production by, for, and representing that community. However, there are many differences between community-based approaches, not least in their assessments of what constitutes the community and what constitutes the 'good', as well as in their ideas of how this good can be promoted. These differences and their moral relevance were explored in detail.

The ethical inadequacy of economistic and nationalist approaches

The book has further shown that welfare economics and some types of communitarianism provide an ethically unsatisfactory basis upon which to ground cultural policy. In relation to welfare economics, two particular claims are of importance. First, welfare economists do not recognise that their own values are particular. In other words, they do not acknowledge that their own assertions are culturally grounded and have both normative premises and implications. As a result, they are unable to recognise the particularity of their own approach, as well as the possible validity of other approaches based on other moral frameworks. Second, however, when the normative premises of welfare economics are examined in any detail, it becomes clear that these assertions actively work to exclude considerations of culture as morally relevant. Their claims about individual well-being invoke a very strong individualism and a moral subjectivism. Moreover, their analysis is greatly strengthened by a reliance on implicit notions of individual freedom. When these notions are explored, they too invoke very particular claims about individualism, values, and the nature of human self-understandings. Combined, these arguments act to ensure that market-based approaches cannot understand culture as anything more meaningful than just a consumption choice. In effect, they limit the legitimacy of other values and ways of life. In so doing, they foreclose the possibility of a genuine cultural pluralism.

Exposing the ethical limitations of welfare economics as a guide to cultural policy, however, does not imply that the opposing positions, namely community-based approaches, are necessarily defensible. In fact, an important argument of this book is that we can and ought to distinguish between those community-based approaches which are ethically justifiable and those which are not. In this respect, two particular variants of community-based approaches are inadequate as an ethical basis for cultural policy. Approaches that seek their legitimacy in ensuring the survival of the nation should be rejected on the grounds that they rely upon an essentialist understanding of the nation and the community, and that they thereby act to exclude non-national moral sources. Additionally, we should reject some liberal approaches which claim to recognise the fundamental relevance of culture in the constitution of moral personality. The success of this claim depends fundamentally on our acceptance that liberals can consistently uphold two inconsistent claims, namely that culture is ontologically constitutive but can be morally 'optional'. This is not to suggest that there is no middle ground in this debate, but only that it must be approached from a different point of view.

Culture and identity – an ethically justifiable approach

In building towards a new approach, this book has argued that a normatively justifiable approach to culture is one that begins from the ontological primacy of culture in the constitution of identity. Chapter 5 drew on Charles Taylor's work to show what is entailed by understanding culture as integral to identity. It developed a thick conception of moral personhood and showed how such a conception is important for intercultural understanding and, ultimately, freedom. Building on this, and in an attempt to avoid some of Taylor's most serious problems, Chapter 6 relied on Iris Marion Young's work on social justice to develop an ethics which is founded in respect for other cultural forms. This ethics stresses social equality, but broadens it beyond distributive concerns to include the 'full participation and inclusion of everyone in society's major institutions, and the socially supported substantive opportunity for all to develop and exercise their capacities and realize their choices'.[1] Drawing on this ethics, Chapter 6 made the suggestion that a radical democratisation of cultural structures and decision-making bodies at all levels is required.

Implications for policy

Together, these claims constitute a philosophical foundation upon which to discuss appropriate cultural policies. Indeed, this book has made significant efforts in this direction by showing the ways in which the cultural policies of two particular regions might be made more ethically justifiable.

Chapter 7 demonstrated the importance of market- and community-based approaches in characterising ideas about cultural policy in the particular case of Canada–US free trade in magazines. Additionally, the ethical claims of these two approaches were used to highlight the normative assumptions implicit in the debate around free trade in magazines. It is clear that the US position is significantly informed by the market-based approaches, while the broad Canadian view (especially recently) has been dominated by different strands of the community-based approach. In particular, Canadian ideas are significantly reminiscent of the national survival approach. This trend offered ample opportunities for this book to suggest changes in both discourse and policy to ensure that Canadian approaches are supportive of the goals of enablement and participation as set out in the argument of this book.

Chapter 8 considered cultural policy at the European level. It argued that European cultural policy is characterised by elements of the national survival approach, secured by some familiar liberal assumptions. In combination with European Commission reluctance to involve itself in cultural policy at the national level, the result is a cultural policy with confused objectives and uneven impact. Furthermore, as in the Canadian case, the potential for an ethically justifiable cultural policy at the European level has so far not been realised. With an adequately conceived cultural policy, including some of the suggestions made in this chapter, Europe could act to support and nurture the many cultural outlets and tendencies which do not receive adequate attention from the national state. It could encourage enablement and participation among people who are generally overlooked by the state or whose communities cross state boundaries. As such, it could be an important force in encouraging a deep diversity comprised of groups not dependent on the representations of nationalism for their relevance.

Where to from here?

This book has developed and defended a culturally sensitive ethics to guide thinking on cultural policy. In so doing, it has provoked several questions that suggest avenues for further research. First, it is clearly important to address the implications of the argument presented here for cultural policies in other parts of the world, and for other cultural issues. In particular, further research ought first to ask whether the framework developed here could be used to understand other disputes about cultural policy. Even if it was determined that many other cases could not be evaluated according to the demands of this approach without doing any damage to their cultural integrity, we would still have achieved results by understanding our cultural limits. Furthermore, this sense of cultural difference could be the first step towards a productive and transformative intercultural dialogue.

Second, interesting work could be done in understanding cases where the practices or products concerned are less obviously cultural. In particular, it would be interesting to address cultural justifications for certain labour or environmental practices. Further, instances that might appear to us as political corruption or bribery are also 'grey areas' where a cultural analysis would be fraught with difficulties, but might nonetheless be interesting. Indeed, some of these constitute the 'hard' cases raised by the analysis of this book. As with the first set of questions, it is not immediately clear whether and how the approach of this book can be applied to these cases. It bears noting that this uncertainty does not constitute a failing on the part of the book. In this respect, much of the interesting work following on from it consists precisely in analysing this approach, understanding its broader achievements and limitations, and stretching it to see how it can accommodate the 'hard' cases.

Finally, it would be interesting to explore the current and potential effects of the internet for intercultural communication and for cultural policy-making. Indeed, the internet clearly is an important means by which any government's attempts at cultural protectionism may be undermined. However, it also provides a low-cost and highly diffuse means by which a diverse and accessible cultural dialogue can flourish, both within and beyond any given community. In this regard, it is not yet clear how the internet will affect cultural policy generally. Nonetheless, it remains a fascinating subject for further research.

Clearly, this book has raised some questions about the international dimensions of communitarian politics which simply cannot be answered within the context of this work. Nonetheless, it is to be hoped that the book has contributed to the advancement of knowledge in IR and IPE. It has made a metatheoretical case for the importance of critical, normative approaches in IPE. More importantly, however, the book has gone beyond critique. It has developed and defended one particular normative position, showing specifically how it can improve our understanding of particular cases. Finally, in addressing these cases, the book has generated new and relevant policy suggestions.

Notes

1 Introduction

1 David Ricardo, *Principles of Political Economy and Taxation* (London: J.M. Dent & Sons, 1911 [1817]), pp. 82–3.

2 Susan Strange, 'Political Economy and International Relations', in Steve Smith and Ken Booth (eds), *International Relations Theory Today* (Cambridge: Polity, 1995), p. 167.

3 Craig N. Murphy and Roger Tooze, 'Getting beyond the "Common Sense" of the IPE Orthodoxy', in Craig N. Murphy and Roger Tooze (eds), *The New International Political Economy* (Boulder, Colo.: Lynne Rienner, 1991), p. 16.

4 James Mayall, 'Reflections on the "New" Economic Nationalism', *Review of International Studies*, Vol. 10, No. 4 (1984), p. 313.

5 See, for example, Robert O. Keohane, *After Hegemony: Cooperation and Discord in the World Political Economy* (Princeton, NJ: Princeton University Press, 1984).

6 Stephen J. Rosow, 'Echoes of Commercial Society: Liberal Political Theory in Mainstream IPE', in Kurt Burch and Robert A. Denemark (eds), *Constituting International Political Economy* (Boulder, Colo.: Lynne Rienner, 1997), p. 43.

7 James Mayall, 'The Liberal Economy', in James Mayall (ed.), *The Community of States: a Study in International Political Theory* (London: Allen & Unwin, 1982), p. 99.

8 Joseph M. Grieco, *Cooperation among Nations: Europe, America, and Non-Tariff Barriers to Trade* (Ithaca, NY: Cornell University Press, 1990).

9 E.H. Carr, *Nationalism and After* (London: Macmillan, 1968), p. 31.

10 Mayall, 'The Liberal Economy', p. 99.

11 James Mayall, *Nationalism and International Society* (Cambridge: Cambridge University Press, 1990), p. 72.

12 Susan Strange, 'Protectionism and World Politics', *International Organization*, Vol. 39, No. 2 (1985), pp. 233–59.

13 Mayall, 'The Liberal Economy', p. 97.

14 Strange, 'Political Economy and International Relations', p. 171.

15 Joan Robinson, *Economic Philosophy* (Harmondsworth: Penguin Books, 1962), p. 18.

16 Much has been written on this position and the epistemological claims that sustain it. See, for example, Robert W. Cox, 'Gramsci, Hegemony and International Relations: an Essay in Method', in Stephen Gill (ed.), *Gramsci, Historical Materialism and International Relations* (Cambridge: Cambridge University Press, 1993), pp. 49–66; Murphy and Tooze, 'Getting beyond the "Common Sense" of the IPE Orthodoxy'; Ralph Pettman, *Understanding International Political Economy, with Readings for the Fatigued* (Boulder, Colo.: Lynne Rienner, 1996); Roger Tooze, 'Constructive Criticism: Threats, Imperatives, and Opportunities of a Constitutive IPE', in Burch and Denemark (eds), *Constituting International Political Economy*, pp. 207–12; and

Stephen Gill, 'Epistemology, Ontology and the "Italian School"', in Gill (ed.), *Gramsci, Historical Materialism and International Relations*, pp. 21–48.

17   Murphy and Tooze, 'Getting beyond the "Common Sense" of the IPE Orthodoxy', p. 22.

18   Stephen Krasner, 'The Accomplishments of International Political Economy', in Steve Smith, Ken Booth, and Marysia Zalewski (eds), *International Theory: Positivism and Beyond* (Cambridge: Cambridge University Press, 1996), p. 108.

19   There is significant debate about what constitutes positivism. For useful discussion of the relevant issues, see Mark Neufeld, *The Restructuring of International Relations Theory* (Cambridge: Cambridge University Press, 1995), Chapter 2, and Steve Smith, 'Positivism and Beyond', in Smith, Booth, and Zalewski (eds), *International Theory*, especially pp. 17–18.

20   Murphy and Tooze, 'Getting beyond the "Common Sense" of the IPE Orthodoxy', p. 14.

21   Ibid.

22   Indeed, this diversity within the critical camp is emphasised by Chris Brown in his '"Turtles All the Way Down": Anti-Foundationalism, Critical Theory and International Relations', *Millennium: Journal of International Studies*, Vol. 23, No. 2 (1994), pp. 213–36.

23   Ibid., p. 236.

24   Robert Cox, for example, has indicated that he does not identify with any 'school'. See Randall Germain and Michael Kenny, 'International Relations Theory and the New Gramscians', *Review of International Studies*, Vol. 24, No. 1 (1998), p. 4, note 3.

25   Robert W. Cox, 'Social Forces, States and World Orders', in Robert W. Cox with Timothy J. Sinclair, *Approaches to World Order* (Cambridge: Cambridge University Press, 1996), p. 87.

26   Germain and Kenny, 'International Relations Theory and the New Gramscians', p. 4.

27   Mark Rupert, *Producing Hegemony: the Politics of Mass Production and American Global Power* (Cambridge: Cambridge University Press, 1995), p. 26.

28   Robert W. Cox, 'Gramsci, Hegemony and International Relations: an Essay in Method', in Stephen Gill (ed.), *Gramsci, Historical Materialism and International Relations* (Cambridge: Cambridge University Press, 1993), p. 56.

29   Roger Simon, *Gramsci's Political Thought*, revised edition (London: Lawrence and Wishart, 1991), p. 61.

30   Ibid.

31   Rupert, *Producing Hegemony*, p. 28.

32   Stephen Gill, 'Epistemology, Ontology and the "Italian School"', in Gill (ed.), *Gramsci, Historical Materialism and International Relations*, pp. 21–48, p. 21.

33   Ibid., p. 22.

34   Ibid., pp. 22–4.

35   Ibid., p. 25.

36   Ibid., p. 24.

37   Ibid., p. 22.

38   Germain and Kenny, 'International Relations Theory and the New Gramscians', p. 12.

39   Gill, 'Epistemology, Ontology and the "Italian School"', p. 25.

40 Ibid.
41 Isaiah Berlin, 'Does Political Theory Still Exist?', in Peter Laslett and W.G. Runciman (eds), *Philosophy, Politics and Society*, second series (Oxford: Basil Blackwell, 1962), p. 27.
42 Neufeld, *The Restructuring of International Relations Theory*, p. 40.
43 Ibid., p. 46.
44 Ibid., p. 69.
45 Berlin, 'Does Political Theory Still Exist?', p. 8.
46 Ibid.
47 Neufeld, *The Restructuring of International Relations Theory*, p. 2.
48 Robert W. Cox, 'Structural Issues of Global Governance', in Gill (ed.), *Gramsci, Historical Materialism and International Relations*, p. 260.
49 See Michael T. Gibbons, 'Interpretation, Genealogy and Human Agency', in Terence Ball (ed.), *Idioms of Inquiry: Critique and Renewal in Political Science* (Albany, NY: State University of New York Press, 1987), pp. 137–66; Craig Calhoun, *Critical Social Theory: Culture, History and the Challenge of Difference* (Oxford: Blackwell, 1995), especially Chapter 2; Smith, 'Positivism and Beyond'; Neufeld, *The Restructuring of International Relations Theory*, especially Chapter 4; Charles Taylor, 'Interpretation and the Sciences of Man', in Charles Taylor, *Philosophy and the Human Sciences: Philosophical Papers 2* (Cambridge: Cambridge University Press, 1985), pp. 15–57; and Jere Paul Surber, *Culture and Critique: an Introduction to the Critical Discourses of Cultural Studies* (Boulder, Colo.: Westview Press, 1988), Chapter 2.
50 Calhoun, *Critical Social Theory*, p. 63.
51 Ibid.
52 Charles Taylor, 'Irreducibly Social Goods', in Charles Taylor, *Philosophical Arguments* (Cambridge, Mass.: Harvard University Press, 1995), p. 136.
53 Clifford Geertz, *The Interpretation of Cultures* (London: Hutchinson and Company, 1975).
54 This book understands the ontology of a theory to refer to 'the list of sorts of things whose existence is presupposed by that theory'. Rob Martin, *The Philosopher's Dictionary*, second edition (Peterborough: Broadview Press, 1994), p. 166.

2 Contending Views of Culture and the Good Life

1 Steven Globerman, *Cultural Regulation in Canada* (Montreal: The Institute for Research on Public Policy, 1983). See also Steven Globerman and Aidan Vining (eds), *Foreign Ownership and Canada's Feature Film Distribution Sector: an Economic Analysis* (Vancouver: Fraser Institute, 1987); Steven Globerman, 'Price Awareness in the Performing Arts', *Journal of Cultural Economics*, Vol. 2 (1978), pp. 27–42; and S.H. Book and Steven Globerman, *The Audience for the Performing Arts* (Toronto: Ontario Arts Council, 1975).
2 Globerman, *Cultural Regulation*, Chapter 3, especially pp. 60–1.
3 Ibid., p. 85.
4 Ibid., p. 90.
5 See Dick Netzer, *The Subsidized Muse: Public Support for the Arts in the United States* (Cambridge: Cambridge University Press for the Twentieth Century

Fund, 1978); J. Mark Davidson Schuster, 'Arguing for Government Support of the Arts: an American View', in Olin Robison, Robert Freeman, and Charles A. Riley II (eds), *The Arts in the World Economy: Public Policy and Private Philanthropy for a Global Cultural Community* (Hanover, NH: University Press of New England for Salzburg Seminar, 1994), pp. 42–55; and David Cwi, 'Merit Good or Market Failure: Justifying and Analyzing Public Support for the Arts', in Kevin V. Mulcahy and C. Richard Swaim (eds), *Public Policy and the Arts* (Boulder, Colo.: Westview Press, 1982), pp. 59–89.

6   Abraham Rotstein, 'The Use and Misuse of Economics in Cultural Policy', in Rowland Lorimer and Donald C. Wilson (eds), *Communication Canada: Issues in Broadcasting and New Technologies* (Toronto: Kagan and Woo, 1988), p. 142.

7   Michele Trimarchi, 'The Funding Process in a Comparative Perspective: Some Methodological Issues', in Alan Peacock and Ilde Rizzo (eds), *Cultural Economics and Cultural Policies* (Dordrecht: Kluwer Academic Publishers, 1994), p. 24.

8   Globerman, *Cultural Regulation*, p. 4.

9   Ibid., pp. 4–5. Quoted from Statistics Canada, *Culture Statistics*, Vol. 3, No. 9 (Ottawa: Ministry of Supply and Services, 1980), p. 1.

10 James Heilbrun and Charles M. Gray, *The Economics of Art and Culture: an American Perspective* (Cambridge: Cambridge University Press, 1993), p. 97.

11 For more on the principles of welfare economics, see Yew-Kwang Ng, *Welfare Economics: Introduction and Basic Development of Concepts*, revised edition (London: Macmillan, 1983), especially Chapter 1, and Robin Broadway and Neil Bruce, *Welfare Economics* (Oxford: Basil Blackwell, 1984).

12 Globerman, *Cultural Regulation*, pp. 2 and 4.

13 Schuster, 'Arguing for Government Support of the Arts', p. 44, emphasis in original.

14 Cwi, 'Merit Good or Market Failure', p. 74, and Globerman, *Cultural Regulation*, p. 51. This argument originates with Netzer, *The Subsidized Muse*.

15 Globerman, *Cultural Regulation*, p. 51.

16 William Baumol and William Bowen, *Performing Arts: the Economic Dilemma* (Cambridge, Mass.: MIT Press, 1966).

17 Netzer, *The Subsidized Muse*, emphasis in original.

18 Globerman, *Cultural Regulation*, p. 54. See also Cwi, 'Merit Good or Market Failure', p. 76.

19 William C. Apgar and H. James Brown, *Microeconomics and Public Policy* (Glenview, Ill.: Scott, Foresman and Company, 1987), pp. 226–7.

20 See Cwi, 'Merit Good or Market Failure', p. 79.

21 Globerman, *Cultural Regulation*, p. 23.

22 See Franklyn Griffiths, *Strong and Free: Canada and the New Sovereignty* (Toronto: Stoddart Publishing Co. Limited for *Canadian Foreign Policy*, 1996).

23 Globerman, *Cultural Regulation*, p. 42.

24 Apgar and Brown, *Microeconomics and Public Policy*, p. 391.

25 Globerman, *Cultural Regulation*, p. 46.

26 Netzer, *The Subsidized Muse*, p. 23.

27 Ibid.

28 Globerman, *Cultural Regulation*, p. 46.

29 Ibid., p. 47.

30 Netzer, *The Subsidized Muse*, p. 24.
31 Ibid.
32 Globerman, *Cultural Regulation*, p. 48.
33 Cwi, 'Merit Good or Market Failure', pp. 59–89.
34 Ibid., p. 79.
35 Netzer, *The Subsidized Muse*, p. 25.
36 Globerman, *Cultural Regulation*, p. 49.
37 Schuster, 'Arguing for Government Support of the Arts', p. 46.
38 Netzer, *The Subsidized Muse*, p. 18.
39 Globerman, *Cultural Regulation*, p. 27.
40 Ibid.
41 Ibid., p. 33.
42 Netzer, *The Subsidized Muse*, p. 20.
43 Ibid.
44 David Austen-Smith, 'On Justifying Subsidies to the Performing Arts', in William S. Hendon, James L. Shanahan, and Alice J. MacDonald (eds), *Economic Policy for the Arts* (Cambridge, Mass.: ABT Books, 1980), p. 29.
45 Alan Peacock, 'Economics, Cultural Values and Cultural Policies', in Ruth Towse and Abdul Khakee (eds), *Cultural Economics* (Berlin: Springer-Verlag, 1992), p. 10.
46 For the former argument, see ibid.; for the latter, see Cwi, 'Merit Good or Market Failure', pp. 61–4.
47 Globerman, *Cultural Regulation*, p. 37, emphasis added.
48 Schuster, 'Arguing for Government Support of the Arts', p. 51.
49 See Globerman, *Cultural Regulation*.
50 Bernard Ostry, *The Cultural Connection: an Essay on Culture and Government Policy in Canada* (Toronto: McClelland and Stewart, 1978), p. 1.
51 A.W. Johnson, 'Free Trade and Cultural Industries', in Marc Gold and David Leyton-Brown (eds), *Trade-Offs on Free Trade: the Canada–U.S. Free Trade Agreement* (Toronto: The Carswell Company, 1988), p. 350.
52 Ibid., emphasis in original.
53 Ibid., p. 355.
54 Allan Smith, *Canadian Culture, the Canadian State, and the New Continentalism* (Orono, Me: The Canadian–American Center, The University of Maine, 1990), p. 19.
55 Ibid., pp. 20–1.
56 Ibid., p. 8.
57 Ostry, *The Cultural Connection*, p. 204.
58 Ibid., p. 180.
59 Ibid., pp. 4 and 177.
60 Ibid., p. 5. Originally quoted from UNESCO International Fund for the Promotion of Culture, *Information Document, CC/77/CONF.003, IFPC/EXT.2/3* (Paris: UNESCO, 12 August 1977).
61 Ostry, *The Cultural Connection*, p. 5.
62 Paul Audley, 'Cultural Industries Policy: Objectives, Formulation, and Evaluation', in Stuart McFadyen, Colin Hoskins, Adam Finn, and Rowland Lorimer (eds), *Cultural Development in an Open Economy* (Burnaby: Canadian Journal of Communication Corporation (distributed by Wilfred Laurier University Press, Waterloo, 1994)), p. 64.

63   Audley refers to Canada, Department of Communications, *Canadian Voices,*
     Canadian Choices: a New Broadcasting Policy for Canada (Ottawa: Minister of
     Supply and Services Canada, 1988).
64   Abraham Rotstein, 'The Use and Misuse of Economics in Cultural Policy', in
     Rowland Lorimer and Donald C. Wilson (eds), *Communication Canada: Issues*
     in Broadcasting and New Technologies (Toronto: Kagan and Woo, 1988), p. 143.
65   Ibid., p. 144.
66   Ibid., p. 143. Originally from Raymond Breton, 'The Production and Alloca-
     tion of Symbolic Resources: an Analysis of the Linguistic and Ethnocultural
     Fields in Canada', *Canadian Review of Sociology and Anthropology*, Vol. 21, No. 2
     (1984), p. 125.
67   See, for example, Michelle Landsberg's contribution to Laurier LaPierre
     (assembler), *If You Love This Country: Facts and Feelings on Free Trade* (Toronto:
     McClelland and Stewart, 1987), pp. 51–4, and Randall White, *Fur Trade to*
     Free Trade: Putting the Canada–U.S. Trade Agreement in Historical Perspective,
     second edition (Toronto: Dundurn Press, 1988).
68   Griffiths, *Strong and Free*, p. 7.
69   Ibid., p. 9.
70   See Canadian Conference of the Arts, 'Fast Facts on Arts and Culture'
     (Ottawa: Canadian Conference of the Arts, 1995).
71   Marc Raboy, Ivan Bernier, Florian Savageau, and Dave Atkinson, 'Cultural
     Development and the Open Economy: a Democratic Issue and a Challenge
     to Public Policy', in Stuart McFadyen, Colin Hoskins, Adam Finn, and
     Rowland Lorimer (eds), *Cultural Development in an Open Economy* (Burnaby:
     Canadian Journal of Communication Corporation, distributed by Wilfred
     Laurier University Press, Waterloo, 1994).
72   Paul Litt, 'The Massey Commission as Intellectual History: Matthew Arnold
     Meets Jack Kent Cooke', in *Canadian Issues*, Volume IX: *Practising the Arts in*
     Canada, proceedings of the Annual Conference of the Association for
     Canadian Studies, University of Windsor, 31 May–2 June 1988 (Montreal:
     Association for Canadian Studies, 1990), p. 24.
73   Ibid.
74   Matthew Arnold, *Culture and Anarchy* (Cambridge: Cambridge University
     Press, 1981 [1869]), pp. 58–62 and 165–8.
75   Raboy et al., 'Cultural Development and the Open Economy', p. 48.
76   Ibid., p. 45. Originally from Nicholas Garnham, *Contribution to the Project 'Le*
     développement culturel dans un context d'économie ouverte' (Quebec: Centre
     québecois des relations internationales, 1992), pp. 2–3. See also Raboy et al.,
     'Cultural Development and the Open Economy', pp. 52–4.
77   Raboy et al., 'Cultural Development and the Open Economy', p. 51.
78   Ibid., p. 50.
79   Ibid., p. 52.
80   Audley, 'Cultural Industries Policy', p. 85. Originally from Mark Starowicz,
     'Citizens of Video-America: What Happened to Canadian Television in the
     Satellite Age', paper presented at the symposium on Television, Enter-
     tainment and National Culture, sponsored by Duke and Laval Universities,
     Quebec City, 1989, p. 11.
81   Starowicz, 'Citizens of Video-America', p. 12.
82   Ibid., p. 15.

83 Audley, 'Cultural Industries Policy', p. 64.
84 See, for example, David Mitchell, 'Culture as Political Discourse in Canada', in Rowland Lorimer and Donald C. Wilson (eds), *Communication Canada: Issues in Broadcasting and New Technologies* (Toronto: Kagan and Woo, 1988), p. 161.
85 Canada, Federal Cultural Policy Review Committee, *Report* (Ottawa: Ministry of Supply and Services, 1982), p. 68.
86 Ibid., p. 16.
87 Audley, 'Cultural Industries Policy', p. 64.

3   Welfare Economics and the Moral Relevance of Culture

1   See, among others, Tibor R. Machan (ed.), *Business Ethics in the Global Market* (Stanford, Calif.: Hoover Institution Press, 1999); Ian Jones and Michael Pollitt (eds), *The Role of Business Ethics in Economic Performance* (New York: St. Martin's Press, 1998); and Thomas Donaldson and Thomas W. Dunfee (eds), *Ethics in Business and Economics* (Aldershot: Dartmouth Publishers, 1997).
2   See, for example, Partha Dasgupta, 'Trust as a Commodity', in Diego Gambetta (ed.), *Trust: Making and Breaking Cooperative Relations* (Oxford: Basil Blackwell, 1988), pp. 49–72, reprinted in Frank Ackerman, David Kiron, Neva R. Goodwin, Jonathan M. Harris, and Kevin Gallagher (eds), *Human Well-Being and Economic Goals* (Washington, DC: Island Press, 1997), pp. 231–3.
3   See, for example, Charles R. Beitz, *Political Theory and International Relations* (Princeton, NJ: Princeton University Press, 1979), and John Rawls, *A Theory of Justice* (Oxford: Oxford University Press, 1973).
4   For an approach that is similar in its overt consideration of the ethical adequacy of theory, see, among others, Mark Neufeld, *The Restructuring of International Relations Theory* (Cambridge: Cambridge University Press, 1995).
5   Steven E. Rhoads, *The Economist's View of the World: Government, Markets, and Public Policy* (Cambridge: Cambridge University Press, 1985), p. 62.
6   Robin Hahnel and Michael Albert, *Quiet Revolution in Welfare Economics* (Princeton, NJ: Princeton University Press, 1990), p. 15.
7   Rhoads, *The Economist's View of the World*, p. 62. On this point, see also Hahnel and Albert, *Quiet Revolution in Welfare Economics*, p. 15.
8   Rhoads, *The Economist's View of the World*, p. 62.
9   See Hahnel and Albert, *Quiet Revolution in Welfare Economics*, pp. 22–3.
10 Ibid., p. 16.
11 See W. Kip Viscusi, John M. Vernon, and Joseph E. Harrington, Jr, *Economics of Regulation and Antitrust*, second edition (Cambridge, Mass.: The MIT Press, 1995), pp. 73–6.
12 Unusual circumstances include externalities, cases of market failure, and public or merit goods. It is only important to note here that these exceptional cases are accounted for *within* the framework of welfare economics.
13 Neva R. Goodwin, 'Overview Essay to Part I: Interdisciplinary Perspectives on Well-Being', in Ackerman, Kiron, Goodwin, Harris, and Gallagher (eds), *Human Well-Being and Economic Goals*, p. 2, emphasis added. Amartya Sen has made similar criticisms. For a brief version of this argument, see his

On Ethics and Economics (Oxford: Blackwell, 1987), pp. 45–6. Although he is usually perceived to be within the broad 'school' of welfare economics, Sen criticises many of the ideas that underlie this school. Since proponents of market-based approaches to cultural policy do not discuss Sen's work, this chapter will focus only on mainstream welfare economics. It will incorporate Sen's critiques of the mainstream where they are relevant, with the recognition that Sen's position on welfare economics is vastly more sympathetic than that taken by this book.

14   Hahnel and Albert, *Quiet Revolution in Welfare Economics*, p. 15.

15   See, for example, Armen A. Alchian and William R. Allen, *University Economics: Elements of Inquiry* (Belmont, Calif.: Wadsworth Publishing, 1972), pp. 6–7.

16   Charles Taylor, 'Atomism', in Charles Taylor, *Philosophy and the Human Sciences: Philosophical Papers 2* (Cambridge: Cambridge University Press, 1985), p. 206.

17   See, for example, Geoffrey Hodgson, 'Economics, Environmental Policy and the Transcendence of Utilitarianism', in John Foster (ed.), *Valuing Nature? Economics, Ethics, and Environment* (London: Routledge, 1997), p. 49.

18   Milton Friedman, 'The Methodology of Positive Economics', in Friedman, *Essays in Positive Economics* (Chicago, Ill.: University of Chicago Press, 1953), p. 7. Quoted in Hodgson, 'Economics, Environmental Policy and the Transcendence of Utilitarianism', p. 49.

19   Russell Keat, 'Values and Preferences in Neo-classical Environmental Economics', in Foster (ed.), *Valuing Nature?*, p. 45.

20   Charles Taylor, 'Irreducibly Social Goods', in Charles Taylor, *Philosophical Arguments* (Cambridge, Mass.: Harvard University Press, 1995), p. 135.

21   Sen, *On Ethics and Economics*, p. 62.

22   John Foster, 'Introduction', in Foster (ed.), *Valuing Nature?*, p. 12.

23   See, for example, ibid. See also Hodgson, 'Economics, Environmental Policy and the Transcendence of Utilitarianism', p. 53, and Kenneth Arrow, *The Limits of Organization* (New York: Norton, 1974), p. 23. For a contrary argument, see Dasgupta, 'Trust as a Commodity'.

24   Elizabeth Anderson, *Value in Ethics and Economics* (Cambridge, Mass.: Harvard University Press, 1993), p. 4.

25   See, for example, Amartya Sen's distillation of this position in Sen, *On Ethics and Economics*, especially p. 62.

26   See, for example, Foster, 'Introduction', pp. 13–14, and John O'Neill, 'Value Pluralism, Incommensurability, and Institutions', in Foster (ed.), *Valuing Nature?*, p. 82.

27   Taylor, 'Irreducibly Social Goods', p. 142.

28   Ibid., p. 136.

29   Anderson, *Value in Ethics and Economics*, p. 12.

30   For details of this distinction, see Robert Cox, 'Social Forces, States, and World Orders', in Robert W. Cox with Timothy J. Sinclair, *Approaches to World Order* (Cambridge: Cambridge University Press, 1996), p. 88.

31   Ibid.

32   See, for example, Steve Smith, 'Positivism and Beyond', in Steve Smith, Ken Booth and Marysia Zalewski (eds), *International Theory: Positivism and Beyond* (Cambridge: Cambridge University Press, 1996), pp. 11–44; Mark Neufeld, *The Restructuring of International Relations Theory* (Cambridge: Cambridge

University Press, 1995), especially Chapter 1, pp. 9–21; and Jim George, *Discourses of Global Politics: a Critical (Re)Introduction to International Relations* (Boulder, Colo.: Lynne Rienner, 1994), especially pp. 1–39.

33　Cox, 'Social Forces, States, and World Orders', pp. 89–90. A similar argument is powerfully made in Neufeld, *The Restructuring of International Relations Theory*, especially pp. 95–121.

34　Daniel M. Hausman and Michael S. McPherson, 'Taking Ethics Seriously: Economics and Contemporary Moral Philosophy', *Journal of Economic Literature*, Vol. 31, No. 2 (1993), p. 675.

35　It should be noted that these are not the only ethical critiques of welfare economics. However, they are the most important ones for the argument of this book, since they most clearly highlight the cultural difficulties of welfare economics. Another very important critique of economic thinking is that provided by rights-based theories. See, for example, John Rawls, *A Theory of Justice* (Cambridge, Mass.: Harvard University Press, 1971).

36　See, for example, the critiques made by Sen, *On Ethics and Economics*. See also Amartya Sen, 'The Impossibility of a Paretian Liberal', *Journal of Political Economy*, Vol. 78, No. 1 (1970), pp. 152–7, and Charles K. Rowley and Alan T. Peacock, *Welfare Economics: a Liberal Restatement* (New York: John Riley, 1975).

37　On the importance of freedom in economics more generally, see Alan Peacock, *The Political Economy of Economic Freedom* (Cheltenham: Edward Elgar, 1997), especially pp. 19–24. Clearly, freedom was also an important concern for classical economists. On the 'scientisation' of economics in the twentieth century and the corresponding separation of ethics and economics, see Kurt W. Rothschild, *Ethics and Economic Theory: Ideas – Models – Dilemmas* (Aldershot: Edward Elgar, 1993), especially pp. 11–17.

38　Steven Globerman, *Cultural Regulation in Canada* (Montreal: The Institute for Research on Public Policy, 1983), p. 37, and Alan Peacock, 'Economics, Cultural Values and Cultural Policies', in Ruth Towse and Abdul Khakee (eds), *Cultural Economics* (Berlin: Springer-Verlag, 1992), p. 10.

39　See, among others, Chandran Kukathas, *Hayek and Modern Liberalism* (Oxford: Clarendon Press, 1989); John Gray, *Hayek on Liberty*, third edition (London: Routledge, 1998); Calvin Hoy, *A Philosophy of Individual Freedom: the Political Thought of F.A. Hayek* (Westport, Conn.: Greenwood Press, 1984); Roland Kley, *Hayek's Social and Political Thought* (Oxford: Clarendon Press, 1994); Andrew Gamble, *Hayek: the Iron Cage of Liberty* (Cambridge: Polity Press, 1996); Steve Fleetwood, *Hayek's Political Economy: the Socio-Economics of Order* (London: Routledge, 1995); Graham Walker, *The Ethics of F.A. Hayek* (London: University Press of America, 1986); Richard Bellamy, ' "Dethroning Politics": Liberalism, Constitutionalism and Democracy in the Thought of F.A. Hayek', *British Journal of Political Science*, Vol. 24, No. 4 (1994), pp. 419–41; Theodore A. Burczak, 'The Postmodern Moments of F.A. Hayek's Economics', *Economics and Philosophy*, Vol. 10, No. 1 (1994), pp. 31–58; Bruce Caldwell, 'Hayek's Scientific Subjectivism', *Economics and Philosophy*, Vol. 10, No. 1 (1994), pp. 305–13; Razeen Sally, 'Review of F.A. Hayek, *Hayek on Hayek*', *Government and Opposition*, Vol. 30, No. 1 (1995), pp. 131–5; and Lionel Robbins, 'Hayek on Liberty', in Lionel Robbins, *Politics and Economics: Papers in Political Economy* (London: Macmillan, 1963), pp. 91–112.

40   F.A. Hayek, *The Road to Serfdom* (Chicago, Ill.: University of Chicago Press, 1944); F.A. Hayek, *The Constitution of Liberty* (London: Routledge for the University of Chicago, 1960), and F.A. Hayek, 'Individualism: *True and False*', in F.A. Hayek, *Individualism and Economic Order* (London: Routledge and Kegan Paul, 1949), pp. 1–32.

41   See Hayek, *The Constitution of Liberty*, p. 409, and Hayek, *The Road to Serfdom*, p. 262.

42   Hayek, *The Constitution of Liberty*, p. 11.

43   Ibid., p. 133. See also ibid., p. 21.

44   Ibid., pp. 18 and 137.

45   Ibid., p. 25.

46   Ibid., p. 81.

47   Ibid., p. 228.

48   Ibid., p. 43.

49   Ibid., p. 29.

50   Ibid., p. 36.

51   Hayek, *The Road to Serfdom*, p. 19 and Hayek, *The Constitution of Liberty*, p. 160.

52   Hayek, *The Road to Serfdom*, p. 117.

53   Ibid., p. 21.

54   Ibid., pp. 47–8.

55   Hayek, *The Constitution of Liberty*, p. 223.

56   See ibid., Chapter 20.

57   Hayek, *The Road to Serfdom*, p. 117.

58   Hayek, *The Constitution of Liberty*, p. 29.

59   Hayek, *The Road to Serfdom*, p. 41, emphasis added.

60   Hayek, *The Constitution of Liberty*, p. 220.

61   Ibid., p. 140.

62   Ibid., p. 206.

63   Ibid., p. 209.

64   Ibid., p. 152.

65   Ibid., p. 180.

66   Ibid., p. 181.

67   Ibid., p. 206.

68   See, for example Gray, *Hayek on Liberty*, p. 7.

69   On this point, see Caldwell, 'Hayek's Scientific Subjectivism'.

70   Hayek, *The Constitution of Liberty*, p. 94.

71   Ibid., p. 100.

72   Hayek, *The Road to Serfdom*, p. 66.

73   Hayek, 'Individualism', pp. 18–19.

74   Hayek, *The Road to Serfdom*, p. 67.

75   Ibid.

76   Ibid., p. 73.

77   See, for example, Hayek, *The Constitution of Liberty*, p. 96.

78   This critique parallels those made by other critics of liberalism. See, for example, Chantal Mouffe, *The Return of the Political* (London: Verso, 1993); Anne Phillips, 'Dealing with Difference', in Seyla Benhabib (ed.), *Democracy and Difference: Contesting the Boundaries of the Political* (Princeton, NJ: Princeton University Press, 1996), pp. 139–52; and Michael J. Sandel, *Liberalism and the Limits of Justice* (Cambridge: Cambridge University Press, 1982).

79 This point is very closely related to the argument about the priority of the right over the good. For a summary, see Stephen Mulhall and Adam Swift, *Liberals and Communitarians*, second edition (Oxford: Blackwell, 1996), pp. 31–3, 119–21, and 124–6.

80 Ibid., p. vii.

81 See, for example, Hayek, *The Road to Serfdom*, pp. xxiv and xv.

82 Ibid., p. 6. See also Hayek, *The Constitution of Liberty*, pp. 253–66.

83 On this point, see, for example, David Miller, *On Nationality* (Oxford: Oxford University Press, 1995), p. 347.

84 The conflict in Hayek's work between freedom and tradition has been noted by several commentators. See, for example, Caldwell, 'Hayek's Scientific Subjectivism', Burczak, 'The Postmodern Moments of F.A. Hayek's Economics', and Kukathas, *Hayek and Modern Liberalism*. The argument being made here draws upon their observations, but differs substantially from their analysis.

85 Ibid., p. 63.

86 Hayek, *The Road to Serfdom*, p. 231.

87 Hayek, *The Constitution of Liberty*, p. 61.

88 Ibid.

89 Ibid., pp. 66–7.

90 Hayek, *The Road to Serfdom*, p. 223.

91 Hayek, *The Constitution of Liberty*, p. 68.

92 Ibid., p. 231, emphasis added.

93 Ibid., p. 110.

94 For a critical discussion of Hayek's treatment of democracy, see Robbins, 'Hayek on Liberty'.

95 Hayek, *The Constitution of Liberty*, p. 125.

96 Ibid., emphasis added.

97 Ibid., p. 126.

98 Ibid., p. 44.

99 Ibid., p. 81.

100 Ibid., p. 231.

101 Ibid., p. 56.

102 See, for example, Hayek, *The Road to Serfdom*, especially Chapter 12, 'The Socialist Roots of Naziism', pp. 183–98.

103 Hayek, *The Constitution of Liberty*, p. 29.

104 This point is made in a different way by John Gray, *The Moral Foundations of Market Institutions* (London: The IEA Health and Welfare Unit, 1992), pp. 16–17.

4 The Ethics of Culture and Community

1 See, for example, Ronald Dworkin, 'Can a Liberal State Support Art?', in Dworkin, *A Matter of Principle* (Oxford: Oxford University Press, 1985), pp. 221–33; Ronald Dworkin, 'The Foundations of Liberal Equality', in G. Petersen (ed.), *The Tanner Lectures on Human Values*, No. 12, p. 272, note 44; Joseph Raz, *The Morality of Freedom* (Oxford: Oxford University Press, 1986), p. 201; and Charles Taylor, 'Atomism', in *Philosophy and the Human*

Sciences: Philosophical Papers 2 (Cambridge: Cambridge University Press, 1995), p. 205.

2 For an introduction to radical democracy and its points of difference with liberal democracy, see Chantal Mouffe, 'Preface: Democratic Politics Today', in Chantal Mouffe (ed.), *Dimensions of Radical Democracy* (London: Verso, 1992), pp. 1–14.

3 Franklyn Griffiths, *Strong and Free: Canada and the New Sovereignty* (Toronto: Stoddart Publishing Co. Limited for *Canadian Foreign Policy*, 1996), pp. 7 and 9.

4 This view resonates with, for example, Johann Gottfried Herder, Johann Gottlieb Fichte, and more recently, Karl Deutsch. See, for example, Herder, 'Essay on the Origin of Languages', in *On the Origin of Language*, tr. J. Moran and A. Gode (Chicago, Ill.: University of Chicago Press, 1986 [1772]); Fichte, *Addresses to the German Nation*, ed. G.A. Kelly (New York: Harper and Row, 1968); and Deutsch, *Nationalism and Social Communication* (New York: Wiley, 1953). For a sense of the debates about the idea and substance of cultural nationalism, see John Breuilly, 'Race and Ethnicity: a Sociobiological Perspective', *Ethnic and Racial Studies*, Vol. 1, No. 4 (1978), pp. 402–11; John Hutchinson, *The Dynamics of Cultural Nationalism* (London: Allen and Unwin, 1987); Paul Gilbert, *The Philosophy of Nationalism* (Boulder, Colo.: Westview Press, 1998), especially Chapter 7; and Avishai Margalit, 'The Moral Psychology of Nationalism', in Robert McKim and Jeff McMahan (eds), *The Morality of Nationalism* (Oxford: Oxford University Press, 1997), pp. 74–87.

5 I refer to it as a 'so-called' debate to reflect the fact that many liberals and particularly communitarians would not identify themselves as such or perceive themselves to be part of a formal debate. Nonetheless, the concept of a debate is extremely useful for understanding the points at issue. For a good summary of the issues at stake between liberals and communitarians, see Stephen Mulhall and Adam Swift, *Liberals and Communitarians*, second edition (Oxford: Blackwell, 1992).

6 Kymlicka, *Liberalism, Community and Culture*, p. 77.

7 Ibid., p. 78.

8 Yael Tamir, *Liberal Nationalism* (Princeton, NJ: Princeton University Press, 1993), p. 18.

9 Sylvia Bashevkin, *True Patriot Love: the Politics of Canadian Nationalism* (Toronto and Oxford: Oxford University Press, 1991), p. 4.

10 For the arguments surrounding Rawls and constitutive attachments, see Chantal Mouffe, *The Return of the Political* (London: Verso, 1993), especially pp. 41–59. For the cultural precepts of Raz, see his 'Multiculturalism: a Liberal Perspective', in Raz, *Ethics in the Public Domain*, revised edition (Oxford: Clarendon, 1994), pp. 170–91. See also Raz, with Avishai Margalit, 'National Self-Determination', in Raz, *Ethics in the Public Domain*, pp. 125–45, and Raz, *The Morality of Freedom*, especially Chapters 1 and 12. John Gray provides an interesting extension of Raz's ideas in John Gray, *The Moral Foundations of Market Institutions* (London: The IEA Health and Welfare Unit, 1992).

11 See, for example, Michael Sandel, *Liberalism and the Limits of Justice* (Cambridge: Cambridge University Press, 1982), especially pp. 121–2; Sheldon S. Wolin, 'Fugitive Democracy', in Seyla Benhabib (ed.), *Democracy and Difference: Contesting the Boundaries of the Political* (Princeton, NJ: Princeton University Press, 1996), pp. 31–45; and Iris Marion Young, *Justice and the Politics of Difference* (Princeton, NJ: Princeton University Press, 1990).

12 The concept of cultural rights is further explored in Raz, *The Morality of Freedom*, pp. 245–63; Raz, 'Multiculturalism: a Liberal Perspective'; UNESCO, *Cultural Rights and Wrongs* (Paris: UNESCO, 1998); Chandran Kukathas, 'Are There Any Cultural Rights?', *Political Theory*, Vol. 20, No. 1 (1992), pp. 105–39; and the reply by Will Kymlicka, 'The Rights of Minority Cultures: Reply to Kukathas', *Political Theory*, Vol. 20, No. 1 (1992), pp. 140–6.

13 Kymlicka, *Liberalism, Community and Culture*, p. 175, emphasis in original.

14 See Kymlicka's discussion in *Liberalism, Community and Culture*, pp. 177–8, and Will Kymlicka, *Multicultural Citizenship: a Liberal Theory of Minority Rights* (Oxford: Clarendon Press, 1995), pp. 158–63. Kymlicka refers mainly to John Rawls, 'Justice as Fairness: Political not Metaphysical', *Philosophy and Public Affairs*, Vol. 14, No. 3 (1985), pp. 223–51, and Ronald Dworkin, *A Matter of Principle* (Oxford: Oxford University Press, 1985).

15 Kymlicka, *Multicultural Citizenship*.

16 Ibid., p. 177.

17 Ibid., p. 76.

18 Ibid., pp. 18–19.

19 Ibid., pp. 50–1.

20 Ibid., pp. 52–3, emphasis in original.

21 Ibid., p. 95.

22 Ibid.

23 Kymlicka, *Liberalism, Community and Culture*, p. 53.

24 Kymlicka, *Multicultural Citizenship*, p. 83. See Raz, *The Morality of Freedom*, p. 375.

25 Kymlicka, *Liberalism, Community and Culture*, p. 165.

26 Ibid., p. 13.

27 Kymlicka, *Multicultural Citizenship*, p. 83.

28 Ibid., p. 86.

29 Ibid., p. 87.

30 Kymlicka, *Liberalism, Community and Culture*, p. 175, emphasis in original.

31 Kymlicka, *Multicultural Citizenship*, p. 91.

32 Kymlicka, *Liberalism, Community and Culture*, p. 51.

33 See, for example, Charles Taylor, 'What is Human Agency?', in *Human Agency and Language: Philosophical Papers 1* (Cambridge: Cambridge University Press, 1985), pp. 15–44.

34 Kymlicka, *Multicultural Citizenship*, p. 167.

35 For work in this vein, see David Miller, *On Nationality* (Oxford: Oxford University Press, 1995).

36 Kymlicka, *Multicultural Citizenship*, p. 91.

37 Kymlicka, *Liberalism, Community and Culture*, p. 58.

38 Kymlicka, *Multicultural Citizenship*, p. 165.

5 Towards an Ethics for Cultural Policy: Charles Taylor Considered

1 Charles Taylor, 'Introduction', in Taylor, *Human Agency and Language: Philosophical Papers*, Vol. 1 (Cambridge: Cambridge University Press, 1985), p. 1.

2 Ibid.

3   Charles Taylor, 'What is Human Agency', in Taylor, *Human Agency and Language.*

4   Ibid., p. 34. On this point, see also Charles Taylor, *Sources of the Self: the Making of the Modern Identity* (Cambridge, Mass.: Harvard University Press, 1989), Part I.

5   Taylor, 'What is Human Agency', p. 35.

6   Ibid., p. 37.

7   Ibid., p. 38.

8   It should be noted that language, for Taylor, encompasses more than prose. It must include all of the symbolic/expressive creations of man, including poetry, music, art, dance, etc. See Charles Taylor, 'Language and Human Nature', in Taylor, *Human Agency and Language*, p. 233.

9   Taylor, *Sources of the Self*, p. 35.

10 Taylor, 'Language and Human Nature', p. 234.

11 Ibid., p. 231.

12 Ibid., p. 237.

13 Ibid., p. 232. See also Taylor, *Sources of the Self*, pp. 35–6.

14 Charles Taylor, 'Irreducibly Social Goods', in Taylor, *Philosophical Arguments* (Cambridge, Mass.: Harvard University Press, 1995), p. 136.

15 See, for example, Taylor, 'What is Human Agency', p. 40.

16 Charles Taylor, 'Understanding and Ethnocentricity', in Taylor, *Philosophy and the Human Sciences: Philosophical Papers 2* (Cambridge: Cambridge University Press, 1985), pp. 123–4.

17 See Charles Taylor, 'The Politics of Recognition', in Taylor, *Philosophical Arguments*, p. 255.

18 Charles Taylor, 'Theories of Meaning', in Taylor, *Human Agency and Language*, p. 280.

19 Ibid., p. 281.

20 Ibid.

21 Taylor, 'Understanding and Ethnocentricity', pp. 125 and 131.

22 Taylor, 'The Politics of Recognition', p. 256.

23 Taylor, *Sources of the Self*, p. 32. On the question of what is entailed by 'making sense' in this context, see also pp. 8–9 and 27, and Charles Taylor, 'Rationality', in Taylor, *Philosophy and the Human Sciences: Philosophical Papers 2*, p. 151.

24 Taylor, 'The Politics of Recognition', p. 256.

25 Charles Taylor, 'Comparison, History, Truth', in Taylor, *Philosophical Arguments*, p. 151.

26 Ibid., p. 150.

27 Charles Taylor, 'Self-Interpreting Animals', in Taylor, *Human Agency and Language*, pp. 65 and 72.

28 Taylor, 'The Politics of Recognition', p. 225, emphasis in original. See also Charles Taylor, 'Why Do Nations Have to Become States?', in Charles Taylor, *Reconciling the Solitudes: Essays on Canadian Federalism and Nationalism*, ed. Guy Laforest (Montreal and Kingston: McGill-Queen's University Press, 1993), especially pp. 52–3.

29 Taylor, 'The Politics of Recognition', p. 225.

30 See, for example, Charles Taylor, 'Atomism', in Taylor, *Philosophy and the Human Sciences: Philosophical Papers 2*, p. 196 and Taylor, *Sources of the Self*, pp. 82–3.

31 Charles Taylor, 'What's Wrong with Negative Liberty?', in Taylor, *Philosophy and the Human Sciences: Philosophical Papers 2*, pp. 228–9.
32 Charles Taylor, *Hegel and Modern Society* (Cambridge: Cambridge University Press, 1979), p. 160, emphasis in original.
33 Ibid., p. 169.
34 Taylor, 'What's Wrong with Negative Liberty?', p. 229.
35 Charles Taylor, 'Cross-Purposes: the Liberal–Communitarian Debate', in Taylor, *Philosophical Arguments*, p. 192.
36 Ibid.
37 Ibid.
38 Ibid.
39 Taylor, 'Atomism', p. 197.
40 Taylor, 'Understanding and Ethnocentricity', p. 119.
41 Charles Taylor, 'Explanation and Practical Reason', in Taylor, *Philosophical Arguments*, p. 52.
42 Ibid., p. 53.
43 Ibid.
44 Ibid., p. 35. Taylor makes regular references to the 'universal' respect for human life. See, for example, Taylor, *Sources of the Self*, pp. 11–15 and 64–5.
45 Taylor, 'Self-Interpreting Animals', p. 53.
46 Ibid., p. 55.
47 Taylor, 'Comparison, History, Truth', p. 150.
48 Ibid., p. 151.
49 Ibid., p. 152.
50 On error-reducing moves, see especially Taylor, 'Explanation and Practical Reason', pp. 36 and 52.
51 Taylor, 'Comparison, History, Truth', p. 156.
52 Charles Taylor, 'A Canadian Future?', in Taylor with Laforest, *Reconciling the Solitudes*, p. 24.
53 Ibid., p. 35.
54 Charles Taylor, 'Shared and Divergent Values', in Taylor with Laforest, *Reconciling the Solitudes*, pp. 158–61.
55 Ibid., p. 178.
56 Amelie Oksenberg Rorty, 'The Hidden Politics of Cultural Identification', *Political Theory*, Vol. 22, No. 1 (1994), pp. 152–66.
57 Taylor, *Sources of the Self*, p. 28.
58 Rorty, 'The Hidden Politics of Cultural Identification', p. 156.
59 See, for example, William Connolly, 'Pluralism, Multiculturalism and the Nation-State: Rethinking the Connections', *Journal of Political Ideologies*, Vol. 1, No. 1 (1996), pp. 53–74.
60 Charles Taylor, 'Liberal Politics and the Public Sphere', in Taylor, *Philosophy and the Human Sciences: Philosophical Papers 2*, p. 259.
61 Ibid., p. 266.
62 Ibid., p. 276.
63 See, for example, Will Kymlicka, *Multicultural Citizenship: a Liberal Theory of Minority Rights* (Oxford: Clarendon, 1995), p. 91. See also Michael Sandel, *Liberalism and the Limits of Justice* (Cambridge: Cambridge University Press, 1982).

64   On this point, see especially Taylor, 'Irreducibly Social Goods'.
65   Taylor, *Sources of the Self*, p. 28.
66   Ibid., p. 455.
67   Ibid., p. 74.
68   Ibid., p. 510, emphases in original.
69   See, among others, Harvey Mitchell, 'Review Article: Charles Taylor on the Self, Its Languages and Its History', *History of Political Thought*, Vol. 12, No. 2 (1991), p. 357; Quentin Skinner, 'Who Are "We"? Ambiguities of the Modern Self', *Inquiry*, Vol. 34, No. 2 (1991), pp. 133–53; Connolly, 'Pluralism, Multiculturalism and the Nation-State', p. 63; and Judith Shklar, Review of *Sources of the Self*, by Charles Taylor, in *Political Theory*, Vol. 19, No. 1 (1991), pp. 105–9.
70   Taylor, *Sources of the Self*, p. 521.
71   Michael L. Morgan, 'Religion, History and Moral Discourse', in James Tully (ed.), *Philosophy in an Age of Pluralism: the Philosophy of Charles Taylor in Question* (Cambridge: Cambridge University Press, 1994), p. 51.
72   Ibid., emphases in original.
73   Ronald Beiner, 'Hermeneutical Generosity and Social Criticism', *Critical Review*, Vol. 9, No. 4 (1995), p. 455.
74   Ibid., p. 454.
75   On family life, see Taylor, *Sources of the Self*, p. 305; on nationalism, see Taylor, 'Understanding and Ethnocentricity', p. 142; and on Nazism, see Charles Taylor, 'Heidegger and Wittgenstein', in Taylor, *Philosophical Arguments*, p. 76.

6   Social Justice in a Multicultural Context

1   Iris Marion Young, *Justice and the Politics of Difference* (Princeton, NJ: Princeton University Press, 1990), p. 44.
2   Ibid.
3   Ibid., p. 45.
4   Ibid., p. 43. It should be noted that Young does allow for other types of group, most notably interest groups, but since these do not entail the same process of group identification and identity constitution, they do not carry the same moral standing. See ibid., p. 46.
5   Ibid., p. 45.
6   Ibid.
7   Ibid.
8   Ibid.
9   Ibid., p. 46, emphasis in original.
10   Ibid., p. 172.
11   Ibid., p. 46.
12   On Taylor's use of modern, and especially post-structuralist theories of language, see Charles Taylor, *Hegel and Modern Society* (Cambridge: Cambridge University Press, 1979); Charles Taylor, 'Heidegger and Wittgenstein', in Taylor, *Philosophical Arguments* (Cambridge, Mass.: Harvard University Press, 1995), pp. 61–77; and Charles Taylor, 'Heidegger, Language, and Ecology', in Taylor, *Philosophical Arguments*, pp. 100–26.
13   Young, *Justice and the Politics of Difference*, p. 47.

14 Ibid.
15 Ibid., pp. 172–3.
16 Ibid., p. 16.
17 Ibid., p. 24.
18 Ibid., p. 25.
19 Ibid., p. 91.
20 Ibid., p. 37.
21 Ibid., pp. 23, 34, 37, 38, 91, 92, 119, and 121.
22 Ibid., pp. 34, 39, 54, 56, 92, 173, 193, and 251.
23 Ibid., p. 216. Originally from Philip Green, *Retrieving Democracy* (Totowa, NJ: Rowman and Allanheld, 1985), p. 81.
24 Young, *Justice and the Politics of Difference*, p. 222.
25 Ibid., p. 221.
26 Ibid., p. 38.
27 Ibid., p. 40.
28 For a fuller discussion of these five aspects of oppression, see ibid., pp. 48–63.
29 Ibid., p. 50.
30 Ibid., p. 53.
31 Ibid.
32 Ibid., p. 56.
33 Ibid., pp. 58–9.
34 Ibid., p. 60.
35 Ibid., p. 62.
36 Ibid., p. 63.
37 Ibid., p. 34, 37, 38, 73, and 91.
38 Ibid., p. 53, 83, 105, 107, 116, 168, and 173.
39 Ibid., pp. 173 and 252.
40 Ibid., p. 38.
41 Ibid., p. 191.
42 Ibid., p. 92.
43 Ibid.
44 For more on this concept, see the interesting discussion in C.B. Macpherson, *Democratic Theory: Essays in Retrieval* (Oxford: Clarendon Press, 1973), especially pp. 52–7.
45 Young, *Justice and the Politics of Difference*, p. 91.
46 Ibid.
47 Ibid., pp. 99–100.
48 Ibid., p. 100.
49 Ibid., p. 103.
50 Ibid., p. 115.
51 Ibid., p. 161.
52 Ibid., p. 116.
53 Ibid., p. 168, emphasis added.
54 Ibid., p. 119.
55 Ibid.
56 Ibid.
57 Ibid., p. 121.
58 Ibid., p. 120.
59 Ibid., p. 158.

60 Ibid., p. 166.
61 Ibid., p. 184.
62 Ibid., p. 189.
63 Ibid.
64 Greater detail about Giddens' formulation of these three levels is available in Anthony Giddens, *The Constitution of Society: Outline of the Theory of Structuration* (Berkeley and Los Angeles, Calif.: University of California Press, 1984), especially pp. 41–109.
65 Young, *Justice and the Politics of Difference*, pp. 144–5.
66 Ibid., p. 124.
67 Ibid., p. 155.
68 Ibid., p. 66.
69 Ibid., p. 190.
70 Ibid., p. 231.
71 Ibid.
72 Ibid., pp. 238–9.
73 Ibid., p. 240.
74 Ibid.
75 Ibid., p. 252.
76 Ibid.
77 Ibid., pp. 252–3.
78 Ibid., p. 172.
79 Ibid., p. 47.
80 Ibid., p. 40.
81 Giddens, *The Constitution of Society*, p. 49.
82 Young, *Justice and the Politics of Difference*, p. 155.
83 Giddens, *The Constitution of Society*, p. 375.
84 Young, *Justice and the Politics of Difference*, p. 251.

7 Cultural Industries and Cross-Border Trade: Canadian Periodicals Examined

1 Nancy Cebryk, Bob Jenness, and Michael McCracken, *The Canadian Periodical Publishing Industry* (Ottawa: Informetrica, 1994).
2 Canada, *A Question of Balance: Report of the Task Force on the Canadian Magazine Industry* (Ottawa: Minister of Supply and Services Canada, 1994), p. 9.
3 Statistics Canada, *Profile of Canadian Periodicals*, available at http://www.statcan.ca/english/Pgdb/ People/ Culture/arts30.htm
4 See, for example, Isaiah Litvak and Christopher Maule, 'Bill C-58 and the Regulation of Periodicals in Canada, *International Journal*, Vol. 36, No. 1 (1980–81), pp. 70–90; Lon Dubinsky, 'Periodical Publishing', in Michael Dorland (ed.), *The Cultural Industries in Canada: Problems, Policies and Prospects* (Toronto: James Lorimer, 1996), pp. 35–59; and Fraser Sutherland, *The Monthly Epic: a History of Canadian Magazines, 1789–1989* (Markham: Fitzhenry and Whiteside, 1989), pp. 260–3.
5 Canada, Royal Commission on Publications, *Report* (Ottawa: Queen's Printer, 1961), p. 93.

6   Ibid.

7   Isaiah Litvak and Christopher Maule, *Cultural Sovereignty: the Time and Reader's Digest Case in Canada* (New York: Praeger Publishers, 1974), p. 141. Originally from *Hansard*, 24 January 1962.

8   Canada, *A Question of Balance*, p. 63.

9   Art Eggleton, quoted in *The Toronto Star*, 12 March 1996, p. D2.

10 Canada, Department of Communications, *Vital Links: Canadian Cultural Industries* (Ottawa: Ministry of Supply and Services, 1987), p. 11.

11 Ibid.

12 Litvak and Maule, *Cultural Sovereignty*, Appendix E, p. 132. Reprinted from Canada, 'The Income Tax Act', *Revised Statutes of Canada 1952* (Ottawa: Queen's Printer, 1952), Chapter 148.

13 In 1943, *Reader's Digest* became incorporated in Canada and *Time* magazine began printing a special Canadian edition from Chicago. In 1954, *Time* and *Reader's Digest* had secured 18 per cent of the total advertising revenues of the 12 general interest magazines in Canada. By 1955, their share had increased to 37 per cent. Due to this presence, Canadian magazine publishers began pressing for protection as early as 1952. See Litvak and Maule, *Cultural Sovereignty*.

14 Ibid., p. 45.

15 Walter L. Gordon, *A Political Memoir* (Toronto: McLelland and Stewart Limited, 1977), pp. 205–6.

16 Canada, *A Question of Balance*, p. 44.

17 From 1975 to 1989, 'the number of Canadian consumer magazines doubled, and their share of the domestic market increased from 20 per cent to almost 40 per cent, with the top 42 magazines in this country reaching an average of 70 per cent of the Canadian population in any given month'. Canadian Magazine Publishers Association, *The Importance of Section 19 of the Income Tax Act and Tariff Item 9958 to the Canadian Magazine Industry* (Toronto: Canadian Magazine Publishers Association, 1991), p. 4. Moreover, advertising revenues were actually drawn towards magazines and away from other media.

18 *The Toronto Star*, 11 February 1990, p. F1. See also Dubinsky, 'Periodical Publishing', especially pp. 44–5.

19 Statistics Canada, *Periodical Publishing 1990–1991* (Ottawa: Statistics Canada, 1991), p. 5.

20 See the Canadian Periodical Publishers Association, *A Brief to the Federal Cultural Policy Review Committee* (Toronto: Canadian Periodical Publishers Association, no date given), pp. 18–20.

21 See Canada, Department of Communications, *Vital Links*, p. 38.

22 See Melvyn Krauss, *The New Protectionism: the Welfare State and International Trade* (Oxford: Blackwell, 1979) and James Mayall, 'Reflections on the New Economic Nationalism', *Review of International Studies*, Vol. 10, No. 4 (1984), pp. 313–21.

23 Canada, *A Question of Balance*, p. 83.

24 See Litvak and Maule, *Cultural Sovereignty*, and Canada, Royal Commission on Publications, *Report*.

25 Canada, *A Question of Balance*, pp. iv and 27.

26 Ibid., p. v.

27 Ibid.

28 For a summary of all 11 recommendations, see ibid., pp. vi–viii.
29 Ibid., p. vi.
30 Ibid., p. 66.
31 Ibid.
32 *The Ottawa Citizen*, 25 March 1994.
33 *The Toronto Star*, 23 December 1994, p. A1.
34 *The Toronto Star*, 26 March 1994, p. A24.
35 *The Washington Post*, 23 December 1994, p. A17.
36 *The Toronto Star*, 21 December 1994, p. A1.
37 *New York Times*, 22 December 1994, p. D1.
38 *The Montreal Gazette*, 1 February, 1995, p. B2.
39 *The Toronto Star*, 26 September 1995, p. A13.
40 Marte Solberg, MP, quoted in *The Toronto Star*, 26 September 1995, p. A13.
41 *The Toronto Star*, 20 October 1995, p. A12.
42 *The Toronto Star*, 19 October 1995, p. A16.
43 *Financial Times*, 12 March 1996, p. 4. Similar quotes can also be found in *The Washington Post*, 12 March 1996, p. C3.
44 Keith Acheson and Christopher Maule, *Much Ado About Culture: North American Trade Disputes* (Ann Arbor, Mich.: University of Michigan Press, 1999).
45 *The Washington Post*, 12 March 1996, p. C3.
46 *The Toronto Star*, 11 October 1996, p. A25.
47 WTO, *Canada – Certain Measures Concerning Periodicals, Report of the Panel*, 14 March 1997, document number WT/DS31/R, available from http://www.wto.org
48 *The National Journal*, Vol. 28, No. 12 (23 March 1996), p. 648.
49 See WTO, *Canada – Certain Measures Concerning Periodicals, Report of the Panel*, pp. 65–77.
50 'A Blow to Magazines', *Maclean's*, 27 January 1997, p. 58.
51 WTO, *Canada – Certain Measures Concerning Periodicals, Report of the Appellate Body*, 30 June 1997, document number WT/DS31/AB/R, available from http://www.wto.org
52 *The Toronto Star*, 1 July 1997, p. A1.
53 *The Journal of Commerce*, 17 March 1997, p. 1A.
54 USTR Charlene Barshefsky, quoted in *Folio*, 30 November 1998.
55 Quoted in *The Toronto Star*, 1 February 1997, p. F1.
56 *The Ottawa Citizen*, 7 November 1998, p. A3.
57 *The Ottawa Citizen*, 1 December 1998, p. B1.
58 *The Ottawa Citizen*, 10 January 1999, p. C1.
59 *Journal of Commerce*, 14 January 1999, p. 3A. In this context, it should be noted that, unlike the WTO, NAFTA has no formal dispute resolution mechanisms. As a result, any retaliation justified under NAFTA would be costly and time-consuming to reverse.
60 *The Ottawa Citizen*, 30 July 1998, p. A3.
61 Anonymous official quoted in *The Ottawa Citizen*, 13 January 1999, p. C1 and *Journal of Commerce*, 14 January 1999, p. 3A.
62 Quoted in 'Magazine Trade Wars', *Columbia Journalism Review*, January/February (1999), p. 20.
63 Richard Fisher, quoted in *The Ottawa Citizen*, 13 March 1999, p. A3.

64 Interview with Heritage Minister Sheila Copps, reprinted in *The Ottawa Citizen*, 30 January 1999, p. B3.
65 Interview with Sergio Marchi, Canada's International Trade Minister, reprinted in *The Ottawa Citizen*, 9 January 1999, p. B3.
66 Anonymous official, quoted in *The Toronto Star*, 29 April 1999.
67 Acheson and Maule, *Much Ado About Culture*, p. 204.
68 *The Toronto Star*, 16 January 1999, no page given.
69 On King's viewpoint, see Litvak and Maule, *Cultural Sovereignty*, pp. 23–7, and H.F. Angus (ed.), *Canada and Her Great Neighbor: Sociological Surveys of Opinions and Attitudes in Canada Concerning the United States* (Toronto: The Ryerson Press for the Carnegie Endowment for International Peace, 1938), p. 322. On Diefenbaker, see Litvak and Maule, *Cultural Sovereignty*, pp. 64–73.
70 On the notion that free trade is the doctrine of the economic 'top dog', see, for example, J. Gallagher and R. Robinson, 'The Imperialism of Free Trade', *Economic History Review*, Vol. 4, No. 1 (1953).
71 Iris Marion Young, *Justice and the Politics of Difference* (Princeton: Princeton University Press, 1990), p. 91.
72 Ibid., pp. 34, 56, 92, 193.
73 Ibid., pp. 34, 37, 73, 173, 252.
74 Ibid., p. 91.
75 Ibid., p. 116.
76 Litvak and Maule, *Cultural Sovereignty*, Appendix E, p. 132.
77 *The Toronto Star*, 28 May 1999, no page given.
78 Canada, Department of Heritage, 'Publications Assistance Program: Program Description', unpublished document available at http://www.pch.gc.ca/culture/cult_ind/pap/pubs/part1_e.htm
79 Ibid.
80 On arm's length Arts Councils, see John Meisel and Jean Van Loon, 'Cultivating the Bushgarden: Cultural Policy in Canada', in Milton C. Cummings, Jr and Richard S. Katz (eds), *The Patron State: Government and the Arts in Europe, North America, and Japan* (New York and Oxford: Oxford University Press, 1987), pp. 276–310 and Joy Cohnstaedt, 'Shoulder to Fingertip and Points Between in Canadian Cultural Policy', in Andrew Buchwalter (ed.), *Culture and Democracy: Social and Ethical Issues in Public Support for the Arts and Humanities* (Boulder, Colo.: Westview Press, 1992), pp. 169–80.
81 Jean M. Guiot, 'Arts Councils as Organized Anarchies and De Facto Regulatory Agencies: Some Comments on the Bureaucratization of Artistic Production', in Harry-Hillman Chartrand, Claire McCaughey, and William S. Hendon (eds), *Cultural Economics 88: a Canadian Perspective* (Akron, Ohio: The University of Akron for the Association for Cultural Economics, 1989), p. 239.
82 Young, *Justice and the Politics of Difference*, p. 190.

8 Prospects for Post-National Cultural Policy: the Case of the European Union

1 For a history of the limited European actions in the cultural sphere prior to 1992, see Heather Field, 'EU Cultural Policy and the Creation of a Common

European Identity', from *Selected Papers Presented at the 1998 EUSANZ Conference, 'The EU in the Next Millennium'*, Christchurch, New Zealand: 27–30 September, 1998. Available at http://www.pols.canterbury.ac.nz/ECSANZ/papers/Field.htm (Consulted on 19 September 2002.)

2   Treaty establishing the European Union (Treaty of Amsterdam), *Official Journal of the European Communities* (C 340, 10.11.1997), pp. 173–308, Article 3(q). Available at http://www.europa.eu.int/eur-lex/en/treaties/index.html (Consulted on 18 September 2002.)

3   Ibid., Article 151.

4   Throughout this chapter, 'Community' will refer to the European Community in the formal, organisational sense, while 'community' will refer to a more organic group of people, in the sense used by much communitarian literature.

5   Juan M. Delgado Moreira, 'Cohesion and Citizenship in EU Cultural Policy', *Journal of Common Market Studies*, Vol. 38, No. 3, pp. 454–5.

6   'Communication from the Commission to the European Parliament, the Council and the Committee of the Regions'. Available at http://europa.eu.int/en/comm/dg10/culture/program-2000-part1_en.html (Consulted on 10 September 2002.)

7   Ibid.

8   Ibid.

9   Culture 2000 programme – Call for proposals 2001. Available at http://europa.eu.int/comm/culture/eac/culture 2000_en.html (Consulted on 19 September 2002.)

10   Delgado Moreira, 'Cohesion and Citizenship in EU Cultural Policy'. Quoted from European Communities, 'Call for proposals for networks of regional and local authorities wishing to launch joint culturally oriented economic development inter-regional cooperation pilot projects under the terms of Article 10 of the ERDF (95/38)', *Official Journal C253/26*, 29 September 1997.

11   Delgado Moreira, 'Cohesion and Citizenship in EU Cultural Policy'. Quoted from Commission of the European Communities, 'Article 10 ERDF Call for proposals, information note for the preparation of projects'. Available at http://www.inforegio.cec.eu.int/wbpro/prord/art10/cult/cult3_en.htm

12   European Parliament resolution on cultural cooperation in the European Union (2000/2323(INI)), 05/09/2001. Available at http://www3.europarl.eu.int (Consulted on 10 September 2002.)

13   European Commission, 'Europe and Culture: Cultural Industries'. Available at http://europa.eu.int/comm/culture/indus_en.html (Consulted on 9 September 2002.)

14   European Commission, 'Europe and Culture: Support Programmes'. Available at http://europa.eu.int/comm/culture/indus_progr_en.htm (Consulted on 9 September 2002.)

15   Treaty establishing the European Union, Article 157.

16   Ibid., Article 87 (3d).

17   Council resolution of 12 February 2001 on national aid to the film and audiovisual industries, *Official Journal* (2001/C73/02), 6.3.2001. Available at http://www3.europarl.eu.int (Consulted on 10 September 2002.)

18   Council resolution of 25 July 1996 on access to culture for all, *Official Journal* (96/C242/01). Available at http://europa.eu.int (Consulted on 10 September 2002.)

19 European Commission, 'Socrates: Gateway to Education'. Available at http://europa.eu.int/comm/education/socrates/shorten.pdf (Consulted on 17 October 2002.)

20 European Commission, 'Europe and Culture: the Culture Professionals'. Available at http://europa.eu.int/comm/culture/prof_en.htm (Consulted on 9 September 2002.)

21 European Commission, 'Europe and Culture: International Law and Culture'. Available at http://europa.eu.int/comm/culture/reglem_3_en.htm (Consulted on 17 October 2002.)

22 European Parliament resolution on cultural cooperation in the European Union.

23 Treaty establishing the European Union, Article 5.

24 European Community, 'How to Apply for the Culture 2000 Programme?' Available at http://europa.eu.int/comm/culture/eac/c2000condition_en. html (Consulted on 10 September 2002.)

25 European Parliament resolution on cultural cooperation in the European Union.

26 Ibid.

27 Ibid.

28 Ibid.

29 'Communication from the Commission to the European Parliament, the Council and the Committee of the Regions'.

30 European Commission, 'Europe and Culture: International Relations'. Available at http://europa.eu.int/comm/culture/relation_en.htm (Consulted on 9 September 2002.)

31 *Constitution of the United Nations Educational, Scientific and Cultural Organisation*, 1945. Available at http://unesdoc.unesco.org/images/0012/ 001255/125590e.pdf#constitution (Consulted on 23 October 2002.)

32 European Parliament resolution on cultural cooperation in the European Union.

33 Council Resolution of 21 January 2002 on the role of culture in the development of the European Union, *Official Journal*, C32/2, 5 February 2002. Available at http://www.europa.eu.int/eur-lex/en/lif/reg/en_register_1640. html (Consulted on 12 September 2002.)

34 'Proposal for a Parliament and Council Decision establishing a single financing and programming instrument for cultural cooperation (Culture 2000 programme)'. Available at http://europa.eu.int/en/comm/dg10/culture/ program-2000-part2_en.html (Consulted on 9 September 2002.)

35 Ibid.

36 Delgado Moreira, 'Cohesion and Citizenship in EU Cultural Policy', p. 461.

37 'Communication from the Commission to the European Parliament'.

38 European Commission, 'Europe and Culture: Cultural Industries'.

39 'Proposal for a Parliament and Council Decision establishing a single financing and programming instrument for cultural cooperation (Culture 2000 programme)'.

40 Anne M Cronin, 'Consumer Rights/Cultural Rights: a New Politics of European Belonging', *European Journal of Cultural Studies*, Vol. 5, No. 3 (2002), p. 309.

41 Ibid. Quoted from Second Summit of the Council of Europe, *An Action Plan for a United Europe* (Strasbourg: Council of Europe, 1997), p. 49.

42 'Communication from the Commission to the European Parliament'; European Parliament resolution on cultural cooperation in the European Union; and European Commission, European Commission, 'Europe and Culture: Cultural Industries'.

43 European Parliament resolution on cultural cooperation in the European Union. See also Council resolution of 20 January 1997 on the integration of cultural aspects into Community actions, *Official Journal* (C036 05/02/1997), pp. 0004–0005.

44 Cronin, 'Consumer Rights/Cultural Rights', p. 308. Emphasis in original.

45 Ibid., pp. 316–17.

46 See, for example, European Commission, 'Europe and Culture: Cultural Industries'. See also 'Communication from the Commission to the European Parliament'.

47 Delgado Moreira, 'Cohesion and Citizenship in EU Cultural Policy', p. 450.

48 Ibid., p. 467.

49 Ibid., p. 460. Quoted from European Communities, 'Call for Proposals for Networks of Regional and Local Authorities'.

50 Treaty establishing the European Union, Article 158.

51 Delgado Moreira, 'Cohesion and Citizenship in EU Cultural Policy', p. 450.

52 Ibid., p. 466.

53 Ibid.

54 See, for example, Yael Tamir, *Liberal Nationalism* (Princeton, NJ: Princeton University Press, 1993).

55 Field, 'EU Cultural Policy and the Creation of a Common European Identity', p. 1.

56 Iris Marion Young, *Justice and the Politics of Difference* (Princeton: Princeton University Press, 1990), p. 91.

57 Ibid., pp. 34, 56, 92, 193.

58 Ibid., pp. 34, 37, 73, 173, 252.

59 Ibid., p. 91.

60 Ibid., p. 116.

Conclusion

1 Iris Marion Young, *Justice and the Politics of Difference* (Princeton: Princeton University Press, 1990), p. 173.

Bibliography

1. Official publications

Canada, *An Act to Amend the Income Tax Act* (Ottawa: Queen's Printer for Canada, 1976).

—— *The Canada–U.S. Free Trade Agreement* (Canada: Department of External Affairs, 1988).

—— Canadian Heritage News Release, 'Canada and United States Sign Agreement on Periodicals', 4 June 1999.

—— *The Foreign Publishers Advertising Services Act*, available online at: http://www.parl.gc.ca/36/1/parlbus/chambus/house/bills/government/C-55/C-55_4/9 0053bE.html

—— 'The Income Tax Act', *Revised Statutes of Canada 1952* (Ottawa: Queen's Printer, 1952).

—— *A Question of Balance: Report of the Task Force on the Canadian Magazine Industry* (Ottawa: Minister of Supply and Services Canada, 1994).

—— The Cultural Industries Sectoral Advisory Group on International Trade, *Canadian Culture in a Global World* (Ottawa: Department of Foreign Affairs and International Trade, 1999).

Canada, Department of Communications, *Canadian Voices, Canadian Choices: a New Broadcasting Policy for Canada* (Ottawa: Minister of Supply and Services Canada, 1988).

—— *Vital Links: Canadian Cultural Industries* (Ottawa: Ministry of Supply and Services, 1987).

Canada, Department of External Affairs and International Trade, *NAFTA: What's it All About?* (Ottawa: Department of External Affairs and International Trade, 1993).

Canada, Federal Cultural Policy Review Committee, *Report* (Ottawa: Information Services, Department of Communications, 1982).

Canada, Royal Commission on National Development in the Arts, Letters and Sciences, *Report* (Ottawa, 1951).

Canada, Royal Commission on Publications, *Report* (Ottawa: Queen's Printer, 1961).

Canada, Royal Commission on Radio Broadcasting, *Report* (Ottawa: Printer to the King's Most Excellent Majesty, 1929).

Canada, Statistics Canada, *Culture Statistics*, Vol. 3, No. 9 (Ottawa: Ministry of Supply and Services, 1980).

—— *The Daily*, 14 September 1998. Available from www.statcan.ca

—— 'Government Expenditures on Culture, 1989–90', *Culture: Service Bulletin*, Vol. 15, No. 1 (1992), pp. 1–12.

—— *Industry Profile: Periodical Publishing* (Ottawa: Statistics Canada, 1991).

—— *Periodical Publishing 1990–1991* (Ottawa: Statistics Canada, 1991).

European Community, 'Article 10 ERDF Call for proposals, information note for the preparation of projects'. Available at http://www.inforegio.cec.eu.int/wbpro/prord/art10/cult/cult3_en.htm

European Community, 'Call for proposals for networks of regional and local authorities wishing to launch joint culturally oriented economic development inter-regional cooperation pilot projects under the terms of Article 10 of the ERDF (95/38)', *Official Journal*, C253/26, 29 September 1997.

—— 'Communication from the Commission to the European Parliament, the Council and the Committee of the Regions'. Available at http://europa.eu.int/en/comm/dg10/culture/program-2000-part1_en.html

—— Council Resolution of 21 January 2002 on the role of culture in the development of the European Union, *Official Journal*, C32/2, 5 February 2002. Available at http://www.europa.eu.int/eur-lex/en/lif/reg/en_register_1640.html

—— Council resolution of 12 February 2001 on national aid to the film and audiovisual industries, *Official Journal* (2001/C73/02), 6.3.2001. Available at http://www3.europarl.eu.int

—— Council resolution of 20 January 1997 on the integration of cultural aspects into Community actions, *Official Journal* (C036 05/02/1997), pp. 0004–0005.

—— Council resolution of 25 July 1996 on access to culture for all, *Official Journal* (96/C242/01). Available at http://europa.eu.int (Consulted on 10 September 2002.)

—— Culture 2000 programme – Call for proposals 2001. Available at http://europa.eu.int/comm/culture/eac/culture 2000_en.html

—— European Commission, 'Europe and Culture: Cultural Industries'. Available at http://europa.eu.int/comm/culture/indus_en.html

—— European Commission, 'Europe and Culture: the Culture Professionals'. Available at http://europa.eu.int/comm/culture/prof_en.htm

—— European Commission, 'Europe and Culture: International Law and Culture'. Available at http://europa.eu.int/comm/culture/reglem_3_en.htm

—— European Commission, 'Europe and Culture: International Relations'. Available at http://europa.eu.int/comm/culture/relation_en.htm

—— European Commission, 'Europe and Culture: Support Programmes'. Available at http://europa.eu.int/comm/culture/indus_progr_en.htm

—— European Commission, 'Socrates: Gateway to Education'. Available at http://europa.eu.int/comm/education/socrates/shorten.pdf

—— European Community, 'How to Apply for the Culture 2000 Programme?'. Available at http://europa.eu.int/comm/culture/eac/c2000condition_en.html

—— European Parliament resolution on cultural cooperation in the European Union (2000/2323(INI)), 05/09/2001. Available at http://www3.europarl.eu.int

—— Treaty establishing the European Union (Treaty of Amsterdam), *Official Journal of the European Communities* (C 340, 10.11.1997), pp. 173–308.

—— 'Proposal for a Parliament and Council Decision establishing a single financing and programming instrument for cultural cooperation (Culture 2000 programme)'. Available at http://europa.eu.int/en/comm/dg10/culture/program-2000-part2_en.html

UNESCO, *Constitution of the United Nations Educational, Scientific and Cultural Organisation*, 1945. Available at http://unesdoc.unesco.org/images/0012/001255/125590e.pdf#constitution

WTO, *Canada – Certain Measures Concerning Periodicals, Report of the Appellate Body*, 30 June 1997, document number WT/DS31/AB/R. Available from http://www.wto.org

—— *Canada – Certain Measures Concerning Periodicals, Report of the Panel*, 14 March 1997, document number WT/DS31/R. Available from http://www.wto.org

2. Books and journal articles

Acheson, Keith and Maule, Christopher, *Much Ado About Culture: North American Trade Disputes* (Ann Arbor, Mich.: University of Michigan Press, 1999).

Ackerman, Frank, Kiron, David, Goodwin, Neva R., Harris, Jonathan M., and Gallagher, Kevin (eds), *Human Well-Being and Economic Goals* (Washington, DC: Island Press, 1997).

Adorno, Theodor W., *The Culture Industry: Selected Essays on Mass Culture* (London: Routledge, 1991).

Albrow, Martin, *The Global Age: State and Society beyond Modernity* (Cambridge: Polity, 1996).

Alchian, Armen A. and Allen, William R., *University Economics: Elements of Inquiry* (Belmont, Calif.: Wadsworth Publishing, 1972).

Alexander, Jeffrey C. and Seidman, Steven (eds), *Culture and Society: Contemporary Debates* (Cambridge: Cambridge University Press, 1990).

Alleyne, Mark D., *International Power and International Communication* (Basingstoke: Macmillan Press, 1995).

——*News Revolution: Political and Economic Decisions about Global Information* (New York: St. Martin's Press, 1997).

Amaturo, Winifred L., 'Literature and International Relations: the Question of Culture in the Production of International Power', *Millennium: Journal of International Studies*, Vol. 24, No. 1 (1995), pp. 1–25.

Anderson, Benedict, *Imagined Communities* (London: Verso, 1991).

Anderson, Elizabeth, *Value in Ethics and Economics* (Cambridge, Mass.: Harvard University Press, 1993).

Angeles, Peter A., *Dictionary of Philosophy* (London: Harper and Row, 1981).

Angus, H.F. (ed.), *Canada and Her Great Neighbor: Sociological Surveys of Opinions and Attitudes in Canada Concerning the United States* (Toronto: The Ryerson Press for the Carnegie Endowment for International Peace, 1938).

Apgar, William C. and Brown, H. James, *Microeconomics and Public Policy* (Glenview, Ill.: Scott, Foresman and Company, 1987).

Armstrong, Donald, 'Canada–U.S. Free Trade and Canadian Culture', in A.R. Riggs and Tom Velk (eds), *Canadian–American Free Trade: Historical, Political and Economic Dimensions* (Montreal: The Institute for Research on Public Policy, 1987), pp. 185–94.

Arnold, Matthew, *Culture and Anarchy and Other Writings*, ed. S. Collini (Cambridge: Cambridge University Press, 1993 [1869]).

Arrow, Kenneth, *The Limits of Organization* (New York: Norton, 1974).

Ashley, Richard K., 'The Poverty of Neorealism', *International Organization*, Vol. 38, No. 2 (1984), pp. 225–86.

Audley, Paul, *Canada's Cultural Industries: Broadcasting, Publishing, Records and Film* (Toronto: James Lorimer, 1983).

—— 'Cultural Industries Policy: Objectives, Formulation, and Evaluation', in Stuart McFadyen, Colin Hoskins, Adam Finn, and Rowland Lorimer (eds), *Cultural Development in an Open Economy* (Burnaby: Canadian Journal of Communication Corporation (distributed by Wilfred Laurier University Press, Waterloo, 1994), pp. 63–98.

Austen-Smith, David, 'On Justifying Subsidies to the Performing Arts', in William S. Hendon, James L. Shanahan, and Alice J. MacDonald (eds), *Economic Policy for the Arts* (Cambridge, Mass.: ABT Books, 1980), pp. 24–32.

Baldwin, David A., *Economic Statecraft* (Princeton, NJ: Princeton University Press, 1985).

—— 'Money and Power', *Journal of Politics*, Vol. 33 (1971), pp. 578–614.

Baldwin, Elaine, Longhurst, Brian, McCracken, Scott, Ogborn, Miles, and Smith, Greg, *Introducing Cultural Studies* (London: Prentice Hall Europe, 1999).

Bashevkin, Sylvia, *True Patriot Love: the Politics of Canadian Nationalism* (Toronto and Oxford: Oxford University Press, 1991).

Bauman, Zygmunt, 'From Pilgrim to Tourist – or a Short History of Identity', in Stuart Hall and Paul du Gay (eds), *Questions of Cultural Identity* (London: SAGE Publications, 1996), pp. 18–36.

Baumol, William and Bowen, William, *Performing Arts: the Economic Dilemma* (Cambridge, Mass.: MIT Press, 1966).

Beiner, Roland, 'Hermeneutical Generosity and Social Criticism', *Critical Review*, Vol. 9, No. 4 (1995), pp. 447–64.

—— 'Revising the Self', *Critical Review*, Vol. 8, No. 2 (1994), pp. 247–56.

Beitz, Charles, *Political Theory and International Relations* (Princeton, NJ: Princeton University Press, 1979).

Bellamy, Richard, ' "Dethroning Politics": Liberalism, Constitutionalism and Democracy in the Thought of F.A. Hayek', *British Journal of Political Science*, Vol. 24, No. 4 (1994), pp. 419–41.

Benhabib, Seyla (ed.), *Democracy and Difference* (Princeton, NJ: Princeton University Press, 1996).

Bennett, Tony, 'Putting Policy into Cultural Studies', in John Storey (ed.), *What is Cultural Studies: a Reader* (London: Arnold, 1996), pp. 307–21.

Berlin, Isaiah, 'Does Political Theory Still Exist?', in Peter Laslett and W.G. Runciman (eds), *Philosophy, Politics and Society* (second series) (Oxford: Basil Blackwell, 1962), pp. 1–33.

—— 'Two Concepts of Liberty', in Isaiah Berlin, *Four Essays on Liberty* (Oxford: Oxford University Press, 1969), pp. 118–72.

Bernstein, J.M., 'Introduction', in Theodor W. Adorno, *The Culture Industry: Selected Essays on Mass Culture* (London: Routledge, 1991), pp. 1–25.

Bhabha, Homi K., 'Culture's In-Between', in Stuart Hall and Paul du Gay (eds), *Questions of Cultural Identity* (London: SAGE Publications, 1996), pp. 53–60.

Blokland, Hans, *Freedom and Culture in Western Society*, trans. M. O'Loughlin (London: Routledge, 1997).

Book, S.H. and Globerman, Steven, *The Audience for the Performing Arts* (Toronto: Ontario Arts Council, 1975).

Bothwell, Robert, *Canada and the United States: the Politics of Partnership* (Toronto: University of Toronto Press, 1992).

Boucher, Joanne, *Funding Culture: Current Arguments on the Economic Importance of the Arts and Culture*, Ontario Legislative Library Current Issue Paper 158 (Toronto: Legislative Research Service, 1995).

Boyle, Chris, 'Imagining the World Market: IPE and the Task of Social Theory', *Millennium: Journal of International Studies*, Vol. 23, No. 2 (1994), pp. 351–63.

Braybrooke, David, 'Preferences Opposed to the Market: Grasshoppers vs. Ants on Security, Inequality and Justice', in Ellen Frankel Paul, Fred D. Miller Jr, and Jeffrey Paul (eds), *Liberty and Equality* (Oxford: Basil Blackwell, 1985), pp. 101–14.

Brennan, Geoffrey and Buchanan, James, *The Reason of Rules: Constitutional Political Economy* (Cambridge: Cambridge University Press, 1985).

Breton, Raymond, 'The Production and Allocation of Symbolic Resources: an Analysis of the Linguistic and Ethnocultural Fields in Canada', *Canadian Review of Sociology and Anthropology*, Vol. 21, No. 2 (1984), pp. 123–44.

Breuilly, John, 'Race and Ethnicity: a Sociobiological Perspective', *Ethnic and Racial Studies*, Vol. 1, No. 4 (1978), pp. 402–11.

Broadway, Robin and Bruce, Neil, *Welfare Economics* (Oxford: Basil Blackwell, 1984).

Brown, Chris, *International Relations Theory: New Normative Approaches* (Hemel Hempstead: Harvester Wheatsheaf, 1992).

—— ' "Turtles All the Way Down": Anti-Foundationalism, Critical Theory and International Relations', *Millennium: Journal of International Studies*, Vol. 23, No. 2 (1994), pp. 213–36.

Buchanan, Alan, *Ethics, Efficiency, and the Market* (Oxford: Clarendon Press, 1985).

Buchanan, James, *The Limits of Liberty: between Anarchy and Leviathan* (Chicago, Ill.: University of Chicago Press, 1975).

Burczak, Theodore A., 'The Postmodern Moments of F.A. Hayek's Economics', *Economics and Philosophy*, Vol. 10, No. 1 (1994), pp. 31–58.

Caldwell, Bruce, 'Hayek's Scientific Subjectivism', *Economics and Philosophy*, Vol. 10, No. 1 (1994), pp. 305–13.

Calhoun, Craig, *Critical Social Theory: Culture, History and the Challenge of Difference* (Oxford: Blackwell, 1995).

Cameron, Duncan (ed.), *The Free Trade Papers* (Toronto: James Lorimer, 1986).

Camilleri, Joseph A. and Falk, Jim, *The End of Sovereignty? The Politics of a Shrinking and Fragmenting World* (Aldershot: Edward Elgar, 1992).

Canadian Conference of the Arts, 'Fast Facts on Arts and Culture' (Ottawa: Canadian Conference of the Arts, 1995).

—— *A Strategy for Culture* (Ottawa: Canadian Conference of the Arts, 1980).

Canadian Magazine Publishers Association, *Annual Report, 1991–1992* (Toronto: Canadian Magazine Publishers Association, 1992).

—— *Annual Report, 1995–1996* (Toronto: Canadian Magazine Publishers Association, 1996).

—— *Annual Report, 1996–1997* (Toronto: Canadian Magazine Publishers Association, 1997).

—— *Bill C-103 and the Canadian Magazine Industry* (Toronto: Canadian Magazine Publishers Association, 1996).

—— 'The Canadian Magazine Industry: General Statistics' (Toronto: Canadian Magazine Publishers Association, 1994).

—— 'Canadian Magazine Publishing', unpublished paper, 23 May 1989.

—— *The Importance of Section 19 of the Income Tax Act and Tariff Item 9958 to the Canadian Magazine Industry* (Toronto: Canadian Magazine Publishers Association, 1991).

—— *Magazines in Ontario – Fact Sheet* (Toronto: Canadian Magazine Publishers Association, 1991).

—— *Split-Run Editions: the Danger to the Canadian Magazine Publishing Industry and Implications for Tariff Item 9958* (Toronto: Canadian Magazine Publishers Association, 1992).

—— 'WTO Appeal Denied', in *Newsletter*, No. 176 (1997), pp. 1–2.

Canadian Periodical Publishers Association, *A Brief to the Federal Cultural Policy Review Committee* (Toronto: Canadian Periodical Publishers Association, no date available).

Canadian Periodical Publishers Association, *A Brief to the Standing Committee on Broadcasting, Film, and Assistance to the Arts on Bill C-58* (Toronto: Canadian Periodical Publishers Association, no date available).

—— *Severing Vital Links: Report on the Impact of Increasing Postal Rates on Canadian Magazines* (Toronto: Canadian Periodical Publishers Association, 1987).

Caplan, Gerry, 'The Effect of the Proposed Free Trade Agreement on Sovereignty Issues', in Murray G. Smith and Frank Stone (eds), *Assessing the Canada–U.S. Free Trade Agreement* (Halifax: The Institute for Research on Public Policy, 1987), pp. 229–33.

Caporaso, James A. and Levine, David P., *Theories of Political Economy* (Cambridge: Cambridge University Press, 1992).

Carr, E.H., *Nationalism and After* (London: Macmillan, 1968).

Carr, Graham, 'Culture', in Duncan Cameron (ed.), *Canada under Free Trade* (Toronto: James Lorimer, 1993), pp. 203–13.

—— *Trade Liberalization and the Political Economy of Culture: an International Perspective on FTA*, Occasional Paper No. 6, Series in Canadian–American Public Policy (Orono, Me: The Canadian–American Center, The University of Maine, 1991).

Cebryk, Nancy, Jenness, Bob, and McCracken, Michael, *The Canadian Periodical Publishing Industry* (Ottawa: Informetrica, 1994).

Clark, Rt. Hon. Joe, 'Trade Negotiations and Cultural Industries', 15 December 1995, reprinted in Canada, Department of External Affairs, *Canadian Trade Negotiations: Introduction, Selected Documents, Further Reading.*

Clark, Stephen R., 'Taylor's Waking Dream: No One's Reply', *Inquiry*, Vol. 34, No. 2 (1991), pp. 195–215.

Clarkson, Stephen, *Canada and the Reagan Challenge: Crisis and Adjustment 1981–85* (Toronto: James Lorimer and Company, 1985).

Cohnstaedt, Joy, 'Shoulder to Fingertip and Points Between in Canadian Cultural Policy', in Andrew Buchwalter (ed.), *Culture and Democracy: Social and Ethical Issues in Public Support for the Arts and Humanities* (Boulder, Colo.: Westview Press, 1992), pp. 169–80.

Collins, Richard, *Culture, Communication and National Identity: the Case of Canadian Television* (Toronto: University of Toronto Press, 1990).

Connolly, William, *Identity\Difference: Democratic Negotiations of Political Paradox* (Ithaca, NY: Cornell University Press, 1991).

—— 'Pluralism, Multiculturalism and the Nation-State: Rethinking the Connections', *Journal of Political Ideologies*, Vol. 1, No. 1 (1996), pp. 53–74.

Connor, Walker, 'A Nation is a Nation, is a State, in an Ethnic Group, is a ...', *Ethnic and Racial Studies*, Vol. 1, No. 4 (1978), pp. 377–400.

Cook, Ramsay, 'Cultural Nationalism in Canada: an Historical Perspective', in Janice L. Murray (ed.), *Canadian Cultural Nationalism: the Fourth Lester B. Pearson Conference on the Canada–United States Relationship* (New York: New York University Press for the Canadian Institute of International Affairs and the Council on Foreign Relations, 1977), pp. 15–54.

Cooper, Andrew F. (ed.), *Niche Diplomacy: Middle Powers after the Cold War* (Basingstoke: Macmillan, 1997).

Cornell Card, Duncan, *Canada–United States Free Trade and Canadian Cultural Sovereignty* (Montreal: Institute for Research on Public Policy, 1987).

Coughlin, Cletus, Chrystal, K. Alec, and Wood, Geoffrey E., 'Protectionist Trade Policies: a Survey of Theory, Evidence, and Rationale', in Jeffry A. Frieden and David A. Lake, *International Political Economy: Perspectives on Global Power and Wealth*, third edition (New York: St. Martin's Press, 1995), pp. 323–38.

Cox, Robert W., 'Gramsci, Hegemony and International Relations: an Essay in Method', in Stephen Gill (ed.), *Gramsci, Historical Materialism and International Relations* (Cambridge: Cambridge University Press, 1993), pp. 49–66.

—— 'Social Forces, States, and World Orders: Beyond International Relations Theory', in Robert W. Cox with Timothy J. Sinclair, *Approaches to World Order* (Cambridge: Cambridge University Press, 1996), pp. 85–123.

—— 'Structural Issues of Global Governance', in Stephen Gill (ed.), *Gramsci, Historical Materialism and International Relations* (Cambridge: Cambridge University Press, 1993), pp. 259–89.

—— with Sinclair, Timothy J., *Approaches to World Order* (Cambridge: Cambridge University Press, 1996).

Craib, Ian, *Modern Social Theory* (Hemel Hempstead: Harvester Wheatsheaf, 1992).

Crane, Diana, *The Production of Culture: Media and the Urban Arts* (London: SAGE, 1992).

Crean, Susan, 'Cultural Sovereignty: Negotiating the "Non-Negotiable"', in Duncan Cameron (ed.), *The Free Trade Papers* (Toronto: James Lorimer, 1986), pp. 174–81.

Creighton, Donald, *Canada's First Century, 1867–1967* (Toronto: Macmillan of Canada, 1970).

Crispo, John, *Free Trade: the Real Story* (Canada: Gage Educational Publishing, 1988).

Cronin, Anne M, 'Consumer Rights/Cultural Rights: a New Politics of European Belonging', *European Journal of Cultural Studies*, Vol. 5, No. 3 (2002), pp. 307–23.

Cross, Michael S., 'Towards a Definition of North American Culture', in Stephen J. Randall (ed.) with Herman Konrad and Sheldon Silverman, *North America without Borders? Integrating Canada, the United States, and Mexico* (Calgary: University of Calgary Press, 1992), pp. 303–10.

Cunningham, Stuart, 'Cultural Stories from the Point of View of Cultural Policy', in Ann Gray and Jim McGuigan (eds), *Studying Culture: an Introductory Reader*, second edition (London: Arnold, 1997), pp. 306–18.

Curtin, Philip D., *Cross-Cultural Trade in World History* (Cambridge: Cambridge University Press, 1984).

Cutler, A. Claire and Zacher, Mark W. (eds), *Canadian Foreign Policy and International Economic Regimes* (Vancouver: University of British Columbia Press, 1992).

Cwi, David, 'Merit Good or Market Failure: Justifying and Analyzing Public Support for the Arts', in Kevin V. Mulcahy and C. Richard Swaim (eds), *Public Policy and the Arts* (Boulder, Colo.: Westview Press, 1982), pp. 59–89.

Dasgupta, Partha, 'Trust as a Commodity', in Diego Gambetta (ed.), *Trust: Making and Breaking Cooperative Relations* (Oxford: Basil Blackwell, 1988), pp. 49–72, reprinted in Frank Ackerman, David Kiron, Neva R. Goodwin, Jonathan M. Harris, and Kevin Gallagher (eds), *Human Well-Being and Economic Goals* (Washington, DC: Island Press, 1997), pp. 231–3.

Davidson Schuster, J. Mark, 'Arguing for Government Support of the Arts: an American View', in Olin Robison, Robert Freeman, and Charles A. Riley II (eds),

The Arts in the World Economy: Public Policy and Private Philanthropy for a Global Cultural Community (Hanover, NH: University Press of New England for Salzburg Seminar, 1994), pp. 42–55.

Delgado Moreira, Juan M, 'Cohesion and Citizenship in EU Cultural Policy', *Journal of Common Market Studies*, Vol. 38, No. 3 (2000), pp. 454–5.

Deutsch, Karl, *Nationalism and Social Communication* (New York: Wiley, 1953).

Dickey, John Sloan, *Canada and the American Presence: the United States Interest in an Independent Canada* (New York: New York University Press for the Council on Foreign Relations, 1975).

Dixon, Huw D., 'Controversy: Economics and Happiness', *The Economic Journal*, Vol. 107 (1997), pp. 1812–14.

Donaldson, Thomas and Dunfee, Thomas W. (eds), *Ethics in Business and Economics* (Aldershot: Dartmouth Publishers, 1997).

Donelan, Michael, *Elements of International Political Theory* (Oxford: Oxford University Press, 1990).

Doran, Charles F. and Sigler, John H. (eds), *Canada and the U.S.* (Englewood Cliffs, NJ: Prentice-Hall, 1985).

Dorland, Michael, 'Cultural Industries and the Canadian Experience: Reflections on the Emergence of a Field', in Michael Dorland (ed.), *The Cultural Industries in Canada: Problems, Policies and Prospects* (Toronto: James Lorimer, 1996), pp. 347–65.

Dowler, Kevin, 'The Cultural Industries Policy Apparatus', in Michael Dorland (ed.), *The Cultural Industries in Canada: Problems, Policies and Prospects* (Toronto: James Lorimer, 1996), pp. 328–46.

Dubinsky, Lon, 'Periodical Publishing', in Michael Dorland (ed.), *The Cultural Industries in Canada: Problems, Policies and Prospects* (Toronto: James Lorimer, 1996), pp. 35–59.

Dunant, Gwen, *An Investigation of Publisher Promotions at the Newsstand Level* (Toronto: Canadian Magazine Publishers Association, 1995).

Dunne, Timothy, Review of *The Restructuring of International Relations Theory*, by Mark Neufeld, in *International Affairs*, Vol. 72, No. 2 (1996), pp. 357–8.

Dworkin, Gerald, Bermant, Gordon, and Brown, Peter G. (eds), *Markets and Morals* (Washington, DC: Hemisphere Publishing, 1977).

Dworkin, Ronald, 'Can a Liberal State Support Art?', in Ronald Dworkin, *A Matter of Principle* (Oxford: Clarendon Press, 1986), pp. 221–33.

—— 'Foundations of Liberal Equality', in Grethe B. Peterson (ed.), *The Tanner Lectures on Human Values XI* (Salt Lake City, Utah: University of Utah Press, 1990), pp. 3–119.

Ethier, Wilfred J., *Modern International Economics*, third edition (New York: W.W. Norton and Company, 1995).

Featherstone, Mike, Lash, Scott, and Robertson, Roland (eds), *Global Modernities* (London: SAGE, in association with *Theory, Culture & Society*, 1995).

Ferguson, Marjorie and Golding, Peter, *Cultural Studies in Question* (London: SAGE, 1997).

Fichte, Johann Gottlieb, *Addresses to the German Nation*, ed. G.A. Kelly (New York: Harper and Row, 1968).

Field, Heather, 'EU Cultural Policy and the Creation of a Common European Identity', from *Selected Papers Presented at the 1998 EUSANZ Conference, 'The EU in the Next Millennium'*, Christchurch, NZ: 27–30 September 1998. Available at http://www.pols.canterbury.ac.nz/ECSANZ/papers/Field.htm

Fleetwood, Steve, *Hayek's Political Economy: the Socio-Economics of Order* (London: Routledge, 1995).

Foster, John, 'Introduction: Environmental Value and the Scope of Economics', in John Foster (ed.), *Valuing Nature? Economics, Ethics and Environment* (London: Routledge, 1997), pp. 1–17.

—— (ed.), *Valuing Nature? Economics, Ethics, and Environment* (London: Routledge, 1997).

Freiden, Jeffry A. and Lake, David A., *International Political Economy: Perspectives on Global Power and Wealth*, third edition (New York: St. Martin's Press, 1995).

Freiman, Mark J., 'Consumer Sovereignty and National Sovereignty in Domestic and International Broadcasting Regulation', in *Cultures in Collision: the Interaction of Canadian and U.S. Television Broadcast Policies; a Canadian–U.S. Conference on Communications Policy* (New York: Praeger, 1984), pp. 104–21.

Friedman, Milton, *Capitalism and Freedom*, second edition (Chicago, Ill.: University of Chicago Press, 1982).

—— 'The Methodology of Positive Economics', in Milton Friedman, *Essays in Positive Economics* (Chicago, Ill.: University of Chicago Press, 1953), pp. 3–43.

Frost, Mervyn, *Ethics in International Relations: a Constitutive Theory* (Cambridge: Cambridge University Press, 1996).

Gamble, Andrew, *Hayek: the Iron Cage of Liberty* (Cambridge: Polity Press, 1996).

Garnham, Nicholas, *Capitalism and Communication: Global Culture and the Economics of Information* (London: SAGE, 1990).

—— Contribution to the Project 'Le développement culturel dans un context d'économie ouverte' (Quebec: Centre québécois des relations internationales, 1992).

Geertz, Clifford, *The Interpretation of Cultures* (London: Hutchinson and Company, 1975).

Gellner, Ernest, *Conditions of Liberty: Civil Society and Its Rivals* (London: Hamish Hamilton, 1994).

—— 'The Mightier Pen? Edward Said and the Double-Standards of Inside-Out Colonialism', *Times Literary Supplement*, 19 February 1993, and Letters: 19 March, 9 April, 4 June, 11 June 1993.

—— *Nations and Nationalism* (Oxford: Blackwell, 1983).

—— *Plough, Sword and Book: the Structure of Human History* (London: Collins Harvill, 1988).

George, Jim, *Discourses of Global Politics: a Critical (Re)Introduction to International Relations* (Boulder, Colo.: Lynne Rienner, 1994).

Germain, Randall and Kenny, Michael, 'International Relations Theory and the New Gramscians', *Review of International Studies*, Vol. 24, No. 1 (1998), pp. 3–21.

Gibbons, Michael T., 'Interpretation, Genealogy and Human Agency', in Terence Ball (ed.), *Idioms of Inquiry: Critique and Renewal in Political Science* (Albany, NY: State University of New York Press, 1987), pp. 137–66.

Giddens, Anthony, *The Constitution of Society: Outline of the Theory of Structuration* (Berkeley and Los Angeles, Calif.: University of California Press, 1984).

Gilbert, Paul, *The Philosophy of Nationalism* (Boulder, Colo.: Westview Press, 1998).

Gill, Stephen, 'Epistemology, Ontology and the "Italian School"', in Stephen Gill (ed.), *Gramsci, Historical Materialism and International Relations* (Cambridge: Cambridge University Press, 1993), pp. 21–48.

—— 'Two Concepts of International Political Economy', *Review of International Studies*, Vol. 16, No. 4 (1990), pp. 369–81.

Gill, Stephen (ed.), *Gramsci, Historical Materialism and International Relations* (Cambridge: Cambridge University Press, 1993).

Gilpin, Robert, *The Political Economy of International Relations* (Princeton, NJ: Princeton University Press, 1987).

—— *War and Change in World Politics* (Cambridge: Cambridge University Press, 1981).

Globerman, Steven, *Cultural Regulation in Canada* (Montreal: The Institute for Research on Public Policy, 1983).

—— 'Price Awareness in the Performing Arts', *Journal of Cultural Economics*, Vol. 2 (1978), pp. 27–42.

—— and Vining, Aidan, 'Bilateral Cultural Free Trade: the U.S.–Canadian Case', in Fred Thompson (ed.), *Canada–U.S. Interdependence in the Cultural Industries*, proceedings of a conference held at Columbia University (New York: Canadian Studies Program, Columbia University, 1985), pp. 4–26.

—— and Vining, Aidan (eds), *Foreign Ownership and Canada's Feature Film Distribution Sector: an Economic Analysis* (Vancouver: Fraser Institute, 1987).

Gold, Sonia S., 'Consumer Sovereignty and the Performing Arts', in James L. Shanahan, William S. Hendon, Izaak Th., H. Hilhorst, and Jaap van Straalen (eds), *Markets for the Arts* (Akron, Ohio: The University of Akron for the Association for Cultural Economics), pp. 99–111.

Goodwin, Neva R., 'Overview Essay to Part I: Interdisciplinary Perspectives on Well-Being', in Frank Ackerman, David Kiron, Neva R. Goodwin, Jonathan M. Harris, and Kevin Gallagher (eds), *Human Well-Being and Economic Goals* (Washington, DC: Island Press, 1997), pp. 1–14.

Gordon, J. King, *Canada's Role as a Middle Power* (Toronto: Canadian Institute of International Affairs, 1966).

Gordon, Walter L., *A Political Memoir* (Toronto: McLelland and Stewart Limited, 1977).

Gramsci, Antonio, *Pre-Prison Writings*, ed. R. Bellamy, trans. V. Cox (Cambridge: Cambridge University Press, 1994).

Grant, George, *Technology and Empire* (Concord, Ont.: House of Anansi Press, 1969).

Grant, Peter, *The Annotated 1991 Broadcasting Act* (Toronto: McCarthy Tétrault, 1991).

Gray, John, *Hayek on Liberty*, third edition (London: Routledge, 1998).

—— *Liberalism*, second edition (Minneapolis, Minn.: University of Minnesota Press, 1995).

—— *The Moral Foundations of Market Institutions* (London: The IEA Health and Welfare Unit, 1992).

Green, Philip, *Retrieving Democracy* (Totowa, NJ: Rowman and Allanheld, 1985).

Green, T.H., 'Liberal Legislation and Freedom of Contract', in R.L. Nettleship (ed.), *The Works of T.H. Green*, Vol. III (London, 1888).

Grieco, Joseph M., *Cooperation among Nations: Europe, America, and Non-Tariff Barriers to Trade* (Ithaca, NY: Cornell University Press, 1990).

Griffiths, Franklyn, *Strong and Free: Canada and the New Sovereignty* (Toronto: Stoddart Publishing Co. Limited for *Canadian Foreign Policy*, 1996).

Grove-White, Robin, 'The Environmental "Valuation" Controversy', in John Foster (ed.), *Valuing Nature? Economics, Ethics and Environment* (London: Routledge, 1997), pp. 21–31.

Guiot, Jean M., 'Arts Councils as Organized Anarchies and De Facto Regulatory Agencies: Some Comments on the Bureaucratization of Artistic Production', in Harry-Hillman Chartrand, Claire McCaughey, and William S. Hendon (eds), *Cultural Economics 88: a Canadian Perspective* (Akron, Ohio: The University of Akron for the Association for Cultural Economics, 1989), pp. 236–43.

Hahnel, Robin and Albert, Michael, *Quiet Revolution in Welfare Economics* (Princeton, NJ: Princeton University Press, 1990).

Hall, Stuart, 'Introduction: Who Needs Identity?', in Stuart Hall and Paul du Gay (eds), *Questions of Cultural Identity* (London: SAGE Publications, 1996), pp. 1–17.

Halliday, Fred, 'State and Society in International Relations', in Fred Halliday, *Rethinking International Relations* (Basingstoke: Macmillan Press, 1994), pp. 74–93.

Hamlin, Alan P., *Ethics, Economics and the State* (Brighton: Wheatsheaf Books, 1986).

Harmsen, Richard and Subramanian, Arvind, 'Economic Implications of the Uruguay Round', in Naheed Kirmani, with an IMF Staff Team, *International Trade Policies: the Uruguay Round and Beyond*, Vol. II: Background Papers (Washington, DC: IMF, 1994), pp. 1–31.

Hart, Michael, *Decision at Midnight: Inside the Canada–US Free-Trade Negotiations* (Vancouver: UBC Press, 1994).

Haslett, D.W., *Capitalism with Morality* (Oxford: Clarendon, 1994).

Hausman, Daniel M. and McPherson, Michael S., *Economic Analysis and Moral Philosophy* (Cambridge: Cambridge University Press, 1996).

—— 'Economics, Rationality and Ethics', in Daniel Hausman (ed.), *The Philosophy of Economics: an Anthology*, second edition (Cambridge: Cambridge University Press, 1994), pp. 252–77.

—— 'Taking Ethics Seriously: Economics and Contemporary Moral Philosophy', *Journal of Economic Literature*, Vol. 31, No. 2 (1993), pp. 671–731.

Hayek, F.A., *The Constitution of Liberty* (London: Routledge for the University of Chicago, 1960).

—— 'Individualism: True and False', in F.A. Hayek, *Individualism and Economic Order* (London: Routledge and Kegan Paul, 1949), pp. 1–32.

—— *The Road to Serfdom* (Chicago, Ill.: University of Chicago Press, 1944).

Head, John G., *Public Goods and Public Welfare* (Durham, NC: Duke University Press, 1974).

Heilbrun, James and Gray, Charles M., *The Economics of Art and Culture: an American Perspective* (Cambridge: Cambridge University Press, 1993).

Henderson, Michael D. (ed.), *The Future on the Table: Canada and the Free Trade Issue* (Toronto: Masterpress, 1987).

Herder, Johann Gottfried, 'Essay on the Origin of Languages', in *On the Origin of Language*, tr. J. Moran and A. Gode (Chicago, Ill.: University of Chicago Press, 1986).

Hettne, Björn (ed.), *International Political Economy: Understanding Global Disorder* (London: Zed Books, 1995).

Hillmer, Norman and Granatstein, J.L., *Empire to Umpire: Canada and the World to the 1990s* (Toronto: Copp Clark Longman Ltd., 1994).

Hindley, Brian and Messerlin, Patrick A., *Antidumping Industrial Policy: Legalized Protectionism in the WTO and What to Do about It* (Washington, DC: The AEI Press, 1996).

Hirst, Paul and Thompson, Grahame, *Globalization in Question: the International Economy and the Possibilities of Governance* (Cambridge: Polity Press, 1996).

Hodgson, Geoffrey, 'Economics, Environmental Policy and the Transcendence of Utilitarianism', in John Foster (ed.), *Valuing Nature? Economics, Ethics and Environment* (London: Routledge, 1997), pp. 48–63.

Holcombe, Randall G., 'Social Welfare', in John Cready (ed.), *Foundations of Economic Thought* (Oxford: Basil Blackwell, 1990), pp. 159–85.

Holmes, Robert L., 'Nozick on Anarchism', in Jeffrey Paul (ed.), *Reading Nozick: Essays on Anarchy, State and Utopia* (Totowa, NJ: Rowman and Littlefield, 1981), pp. 57–67.

Holquist, Michael, *Dialogism: Bakhtin and His World* (London: Routledge, 1990).

Hoy, Calvin, *A Philosophy of Individual Freedom: the Political Thought of F.A. Hayek* (Westport, Conn.: Greenwood Press, 1984).

Hutcheson, John, 'Culture and Free Trade', in Michael D. Henderson, *The Future on the Table: Canada and the Free Trade Issue* (Toronto: Masterpress, 1987), pp. 101–19.

Hutchinson, John, *The Dynamics of Cultural Nationalism* (London: Allen and Unwin, 1987).

——and Smith, Anthony D. (eds), *Nationalism* (Oxford: Oxford University Press, 1994).

International Affairs, Special Issue on Globalization and International Relations, Vol. 73, No. 3 (1997).

International Federation of the Periodical Press, *Magazine World* (No. 18, 1998), available at http://www.fipp.com/news/1998/18septoct/index.htm#focuscanada

Jackson, Robert H. and James, Alan, 'The Character of Independent Statehood', in Robert H. Jackson and Alan James (eds), *States in a Changing World: a Contemporary Analysis* (Oxford: Clarendon Press, 1993), pp. 3–25.

Jarvis Thompson, Judith, 'Some Ruminations on Rights', in Jeffrey Paul (ed.), *Reading Nozick: Essays on Anarchy, State and Utopia* (Totowa, NJ: Rowman and Littlefield, 1981), pp. 130–47.

Jeffrey, Brooke, *Cultural Policy in Canada: From Massey-Lévesque to Applebaum-Hébert*, Library of Parliament, Backgrounder Report BP-59E (Ottawa: Library of Parliament, 1982).

Jenkins, John J., *Understanding Hume* (Edinburgh: Edinburgh University Press, 1992).

Jenks, Chris, *Culture* (London: Routledge, 1993).

Johnson, A.W., 'Free Trade and Cultural Industries', in Marc Gold and David Leyton-Brown (eds), *Trade-Offs on Free Trade: the Canada–U.S. Free Trade Agreement* (Toronto: The Carswell Company, 1988), pp. 350–60.

Johnson, Jon R. and Schachter, Joel S., 'Culture', in Jon R. Johnson and Joel S. Schachter, *The Free Trade Agreement: a Comprehensive Guide* (Aurora: Canada Law Book Inc., 1988), pp. 139–50.

Jones, Ian and Pollitt, Michael (eds), *The Role of Business Ethics in Economic Performance* (New York: St. Martin's Press, 1998).

Karmis, Dimitrios, 'Cultures autochtones et libéralisme au Canada: les vertus médiatrices du communautarisme libéral de Charles Taylor', *Canadian Journal of Political Science*, Vol. 26, No. 1 (1993), pp. 69–96.

Keachie, Catherine and Pittaway, Kim, 'Federal Policy and Canadian Magazines', *Options Politiques* (January–February 1994), pp. 14–18.

Keat, Russell, 'Values and Preferences in Neo-Classical Environmental Economics', in John Foster (ed.), *Valuing Nature? Economics, Ethics and Environment* (London: Routledge, 1997), pp. 32–47.

Kedourie, Elie, *Nationalism*, fourth edition (Oxford: Blackwell, 1993).

Keohane, Robert O., *After Hegemony: Cooperation and Discord in the World Political Economy* (Princeton, NJ: Princeton University Press, 1984).

—— and Nye, Joseph, *Transnational Relations and World Politics* (Cambridge, Mass.: Harvard University Press, 1972).

Keynes, John Maynard, *The Collected Writings of John Maynard Keynes*, Vol. XVIII: *Activities 1922–32, The End of Reparations*, ed. E. Johnson (Basingstoke: Macmillan for the Royal Economic Society, 1978).

—— *The Collected Writings of John Maynard Keynes*, Vol. XXI: *Activities 1931–1939, World Crises and Policies in Britain and America*, ed. D. Moggridge (Basingstoke: Macmillan for the Royal Economic Society, 1982).

Kindleberger, Charles, *Power and Money: the Economics of International Politics and the Politics of International Economics* (New York: Basic Books, 1970).

Kley, Roland, *Hayek's Social and Political Thought* (Oxford: Clarendon Press, 1994).

Krasner, Stephen, 'The Accomplishments of International Political Economy', in Steve Smith, Ken Booth, and Marysia Zalewski (eds), *International Theory: Positivism and Beyond* (Cambridge: Cambridge University Press, 1996), pp. 108–27.

—— *Structural Conflict: the Third World against Global Liberalism* (Berkeley, Calif.: University of California Press, 1985).

Krause, Jill and Renwick, Neil (eds), *Identities in International Relations* (Basingstoke: Macmillan Press, 1996).

Krauss, Melvyn B., *The New Protectionism: the Welfare State and International Trade* (Oxford: Blackwell, 1979).

Krugman, Paul and Obstfeld, Maurice, *International Economics: Theory and Policy*, second edition (New York: HarperCollins, 1991).

Kukathas, Chandran, 'Are There Any Cultural Rights?', *Political Theory*, Vol. 20, No. 1 (1992), pp. 105–39.

—— *Hayek and Modern Liberalism* (Oxford: Clarendon Press, 1989).

Kymlicka, Will, 'The Ethics of Inarticulacy', *Inquiry*, Vol. 34, No. 2 (1991), pp. 155–82.

—— 'Liberal Individualism and Liberal Neutrality', *Ethics*, Vol. 99, No. 4 (1989), pp. 883–905.

—— *Liberalism, Community and Culture* (Oxford: Clarendon, 1989).

—— *Multicultural Citizenship: a Liberal Theory of Minority Rights* (Oxford: Clarendon, 1995).

—— 'The Rights of Minority Cultures: a Reply to Kukathas', *Political Theory*, Vol. 20, No. 1 (1992), pp. 140–6.

Laclau, Ernesto and Mouffe, Chantal, *Hegemony and Socialist Strategy: Towards a Radical Democratic Politics* (London: Verso, 1985).

Lapid, Yosef, 'Culture's Ship: Returns and Departures in IR Theory', in Yosef Lapid and Friedrich Kratochwil (eds), *The Return of Culture and Identity in IR Theory* (Boulder, Colo.: Lynne Rienner, 1996), pp. 3–20.

—— and Kratochwil, Friedrich (eds), *The Return of Culture and Identity in IR Theory* (Boulder, Colo.: Lynne Rienner, 1996).

LaPierre, Laurier (assembler), *If You Love This Country: Facts and Feelings on Free Trade* (Toronto: McClelland and Stewart, 1987).

Lester, Malcolm, 'Free Trade and Canadian Book Publishing', in Marc Gold and David Leyton-Brown (eds), *Trade-Offs on Free Trade: the Canada–U.S. Free Trade Agreement* (Toronto: The Carswell Company, 1988), pp. 361–4.

Lingle, Christopher, 'Public Choice and Public Funding of the Arts', in Ruth Towse and Abdul Khakee (eds), *Cultural Economics* (Berlin: Springer-Verlag, 1992), pp. 21–30.

Linklater, Andrew, 'The Achievements of Critical Theory', in Steve Smith, Ken Booth, and Marysia Zalewski (eds), *International Theory: Positivism and Beyond* (Cambridge: Cambridge University Press, 1996), pp. 279–98.

—— *The Transformation of Political Community: Ethical Foundations of the Post-Westphalian Era* (Cambridge: Polity Press, 1998).

Lipset, Seymour Martin, *Continental Divide: the Values and Institutions of the US and Canada* (London and New York: Routledge, 1990).

Lipsey Richard G., and York, Robert C., *Evaluating the Free Trade Deal: a Guided Tour through the Canada–U.S. Agreement* (Scarborough: Prentice-Hall for the C.D. Howe Institute, 1988).

——, Steiner, Peter O., Purvis, Douglas D., and Courant, Paul N., *Macroeconomics*, ninth edition (New York: Harper and Row, 1990).

Litt, Paul, 'The Massey Commission as Intellectual History: Matthew Arnold Meets Jack Kent Cooke', *Canadian Issues*, Vol. IX: *Practising the Arts in Canada*, proceedings of the Annual Conference of the Association for Canadian Studies, University of Windsor, 31 May–2 June 1988 (Montreal: Association for Canadian Studies, 1990), pp. 23–34.

—— *The Muses, the Masses, and the Massey Commission* (Toronto: University of Toronto Press, 1992).

Litvak, Isaiah and Maule, Christopher, 'Bill C-58 and the Regulation of Periodicals in Canada', *International Journal*, Vol. 36, No. 1 (1980–81), pp. 70–90.

—— *Cultural Sovereignty: the Time and Reader's Digest Case in Canada* (New York: Praeger Publishers, 1974).

—— *The Impact of Bill C-58 on English Language Periodicals in Canada* (Ottawa: Secretary of State, 1978).

Lorimer, Roland M. and McNulty, Jean, *Mass Communication in Canada*, third edition (Oxford and Toronto: Oxford University Press, 1996).

—— with Duxbury, Nancy, 'Of Culture, the Economy, Cultural Production, and Cultural Producers: an Orientation', in Stuart McFadyen, Colin Hoskins, Adam Finn, and Rowland Lorimer (eds), *Cultural Development in an Open Economy* (Burnaby: Canadian Journal of Communication Corporation (distributed by Wilfred Laurier University Press, Waterloo), 1994), pp. 5–35.

Löw-Beer, Martin, 'Living a Life and the Problem of Existential Impossibility', *Inquiry*, Vol. 34, No. 2 (1991), pp. 217–36.

McAnany, Emile G. and Wilkinson, Kenton T., *Mass Media and Free Trade: NAFTA and the Cultural Industries* (Austin, Tex.: University of Texas Press, 1996).

McBride, Stephen and Shields, John, *Dismantling a Nation: Canada and the New World Order* (Halifax: Fernwood, 1993).

McCarthy and McCarthy (Barristers and Solicitors), *The Canada–United States Free Trade Agreement: an Analysis* (Toronto, January 1998).

McDowell, Duncan, 'The Trade Policies of Canada's Grits and Tories, 1840–1988', in Charles F. Doran and Gregory P. Marchildon (eds), *The NAFTA Puzzle: Political Parties and Trade in North America* (Boulder, Colo.: Westview Press, 1994), pp. 87–116.

Machan, Tibor R. (ed.), *Business Ethics in the Global Market* (Stanford, Calif.: Hoover Institution Press, 1999).

McNeil Lowry, W. (ed.), *The Arts and Public Policy in the United States* (Englewood Cliffs, NJ: Prentice-Hall for the American Assembly, Columbia University, 1984).

Macpherson, C.B., *Democratic Theory: Essays in Retrieval* (Oxford: Clarendon Press, 1973).

Marchak, M.P., 'The Ideology of Free Trade: a Response to Smith', *Canadian Public Policy*, Vol. 15, No. 2 (1989), pp. 220–5.

Margalit, Avishai, 'The Moral Psychology of Nationalism', in Robert McKim and Jeff McMahan (eds), *The Morality of Nationalism* (Oxford: Oxford University Press, 1997), pp. 74–87.

Martin, Rob, *The Philosopher's Dictionary*, second edition (Peterborough: Broadview Press, 1994).

Masters, Donald C., *The Reciprocity Treaty of 1854* (London, New York, and Toronto: Longmans, Green and Co., 1937).

Mayall, James, 'The Liberal Economy', in James Mayall (ed.), *The Community of States: a Study in International Political Theory* (London: Allen & Unwin, 1982), pp. 96–111.

——*Nationalism and International Society* (Cambridge: Cambridge University Press, 1990).

——'Reflections on the "New" Economic Nationalism', *Review of International Studies*, Vol. 10, No. 4 (1984), pp. 313–21.

Meiksins Wood, Ellen, 'The Separation of the Economic and the Political in Capitalism', *New Left Review*, No. 127 (May/June 1981), pp. 66–95.

Meisel, John and Van Loon, Jean, 'Cultivating the Bushgarden: Cultural Policy in Canada', in Milton C. Cummings, Jr and Richard S. Katz (eds), *The Patron State: Government and the Arts in Europe, North America, and Japan* (New York and Oxford: Oxford University Press, 1987), pp. 276–310.

Mill, J.S., *Utilitarianism*, ed. H.B. Acton (London: J.M. Dent & Sons, 1972 [1863]).

Miller, David, *On Nationality* (Oxford: Oxford University Press, 1995).

Mitchell, David, 'Culture as Political Discourse in Canada', in Rowland Lorimer and Donald C. Wilson (eds), *Communication Canada: Issues in Broadcasting and New Technologies* (Toronto: Kagan and Woo, 1988), pp. 157–74.

Mitchell, Harvey, 'Review Article: Charles Taylor on the Self, Its Languages and Its History', *History of Political Thought*, Vol. 12, No. 2 (1991), pp. 335–58.

Mittelman, James H. (ed.), *Globalization: Critical Reflections* (Boulder, Colo.: Lynne Rienner, 1996).

Moffett, Samuel E., *The Americanization of Canada* (PhD Thesis, Columbia University, 1907; Toronto: University of Toronto Press, 1972).

Morgan, Michael L., 'Religion, History and Moral Discourse', in James Tully (ed.), *Philosophy in an Age of Pluralism: the Philosophy of Charles Taylor in Question* (Cambridge: Cambridge University Press, 1994), pp. 49–66.

Morrow, Raymond A., with Brown, David D., *Critical Theory and Methodology* (Thousand Oaks, Calif.: SAGE, 1994).

Mouffe, Chantal, 'Preface: Democratic Politics Today', in Chantal Mouffe (ed.), *Dimensions of Radical Democracy* (London: Verso, 1992), pp. 1–14.

——*The Return of the Political* (London: Verso, 1993).

——(ed.), *Dimensions of Radical Democracy* (London: Verso, 1992).

Mulcahy, Kevin V., 'Government and the Arts in the United States', in Milton C. Cummings, Jr and Richard S. Katz (eds), *The Patron State: Government and the*

Arts in Europe, North America, and Japan (New York and Oxford: Oxford University Press, 1987), pp. 311–32.

Mulhall, Stephen and Swift, Adam, *Liberals and Communitarians*, second edition (Oxford: Blackwell, 1996).

Murphy, Craig N. and Tooze, Roger, 'Getting Beyond the "Common Sense" of the IPE Orthodoxy', in Craig N. Murphy and Roger Tooze (eds), *The New International Political Economy* (Boulder, Colo.: Lynne Rienner, 1991), pp. 11–31.

——(eds), *The New International Political Economy* (Boulder, Colo.: Lynne Rienner, 1991).

Murray, Janice L. (ed.), *Canadian Cultural Nationalism* (New York: New York University Press, 1977).

Nagel, Thomas, 'Libertarianism without Foundations', in Jeffrey Paul (ed.), *Reading Nozick: Essays on Anarchy, State and Utopia* (Totowa, NJ: Rowman and Littlefield, 1981), pp. 191–205.

Nardin, Terry and Mapel, David (eds), *Traditions of International Ethics* (Cambridge: Cambridge University Press, 1992).

Netzer, Dick, *The Subsidized Muse: Public Support for the Arts in the United States* (Cambridge: Cambridge University Press for the Twentieth Century Fund, 1978).

Neufeld, Mark, 'Critical Interventions: New Directions in IR Theory', *International Journal*, Vol. 51 (Winter 1995–96), pp. 148–54.

——'Interpretation and the "Science" of International Relations', *Review of International Studies*, Vol. 19, No. 1 (1993), pp. 39–61.

——*The Restructuring of International Relations Theory* (Cambridge: Cambridge University Press, 1995).

——Review of *The Return of Culture and Identity in IR Theory*, edited by Yosef Lapid and Friedrich Kratochwil, in *American Political Science Review*, Vol. 91, No. 1 (1997), pp. 238–9.

Ng, Yew-Kwang, *Welfare Economics: Introduction and Basic Development of Concepts*, revised edition (London: Macmillan, 1983).

Norval, Aletta, 'Rethinking Ethnicity: Identification, Hybridity and Democracy', in Paris Yeros (ed.), *Ethnicity and Nationalism in Africa* (Basingstoke: Macmillan Press, 1998), pp. 81–100.

Nozick, Robert, *Anarchy, State and Utopia* (New York: Basic Books, 1974).

O'Donnell, R.M., *Keynes: Philosophy, Economics and Politics* (Basingstoke: Macmillan Press, 1989).

Oksenberg Rorty, Amelie, 'The Hidden Politics of Cultural Identification', *Political Theory*, Vol. 22, No. 1 (1994), pp. 152–66.

O'Neill, John, 'Value Pluralism, Incommensurability and Institutions', in John Foster (ed.), *Valuing Nature? Economics, Ethics, and Environment* (London: Routledge, 1997), pp. 75–88.

Ontario, Legislative Research Service, *Final Editions? Split-Run Editions and Canada's Ailing Magazine Industry*, prepared by E. Israel (Toronto: The Queen's Printer for Ontario, 1993).

Ontario, Ministry of Culture, Tourism and Recreation, *The Business of Culture: a Report to the Advisory Committee on a Cultural Industries Sectoral Strategy* (Toronto: The Queen's Printer for Ontario, 1994).

Ostry, Bernard, 'Canada–U.S. Interdependence in the Cultural Industries', in Fred Thompson (ed.), *Canada–U.S. Interdependence in the Cultural Industries*, proceedings of a conference held at Columbia University (New York: Canadian Studies Program, Columbia University, 1985).

—— *The Cultural Connection: an Essay on Culture and Government Policy in Canada* (Toronto: McClelland and Stewart, 1978).

Owram, Douglas, 'The NDP and Free Trade: Facing the American Capitalist Empire', in Charles F. Doran and Gregory P. Marchildon (eds), *The NAFTA Puzzle: Political Parties and Trade in North America* (Boulder, Colo.: Westview Press, 1994), pp. 117–42.

Park, Julian (ed.), *The Culture of Contemporary Canada* (Toronto: The Ryerson Press and Ithaca, NY: Cornell University Press, 1957).

Patten, Alan, 'The Republican Critique of Liberalism', *British Journal of Political Science*, Vol. 26, No. 1 (1996), pp. 25–44.

Paul, Jeffrey (ed.), *Reading Nozick: Essays on Anarchy, State and Utopia* (Totowa, NJ: Rowman and Littlefield, 1981).

Peacock, Alan, 'Economics, Cultural Values and Cultural Policies', in Ruth Towse and Abdul Khakee (eds), *Cultural Economics* (Berlin: Springer-Verlag, 1992), pp. 9–20.

—— *The Political Economy of Economic Freedom* (Cheltenham: Edward Elgar, 1997).

Pelletier, Gérard, *L'aventure du pouvoir, 1968–1975* (Quebec: Les éditions internationales Alain Stanké, 1992).

Pettman, Ralph, *Understanding International Political Economy, with Readings for the Fatigued* (Boulder, Colo.: Lynne Rienner, 1996).

Phillips, Anne, 'Dealing with Difference', in Seyla Benhabib (ed.), *Democracy and Difference: Contesting the Boundaries of the Political* (Princeton, NJ: Princeton University Press, 1996), pp. 139–52.

Polanyi, Karl, *The Great Transformation: the Political and Economic Origins of Our Time* (Boston, Mass.: Beacon Press, 1944).

Raboy, Marc, Bernier, Ivan, Savageau, Florian, and Atkinson, Dave, 'Cultural Development and the Open Economy: a Democratic Issue and a Challenge to Public Policy', in Stuart McFadyen, Colin Hoskins, Adam Finn, and Rowland Lorimer (eds), *Cultural Development in an Open Economy* (Burnaby: Canadian Journal of Communication Corporation, distributed by Wilfred Laurier University Press, Waterloo, 1994), pp. 37–61.

Rawls, John, 'Justice as Fairness: Political not Metaphysical', *Philosophy and Public Affairs*, Vol. 14, No. 3 (1985), pp. 223–51.

—— *A Theory of Justice* (Oxford: Oxford University Press, 1973).

Raz, Joseph, *Ethics in the Public Domain* (Oxford: Clarendon, 1994).

—— *The Morality of Freedom* (Oxford: Clarendon, 1986).

—— 'Multiculturalism: a Liberal Perspective', in Joseph Raz, *Ethics in the Public Domain*, revised edition (Oxford: Clarendon, 1994), pp. 170–91.

—— with Margalit, Avishai, 'National Self-Determination', in Joseph Raz, *Ethics in the Public Domain*, revised edition (Oxford: Clarendon, 1994), pp. 125–45.

Rhoads, Steven E., *The Economist's View of the World: Government, Markets, and Public Policy* (Cambridge: CUP, 1985).

Ricardo, David, *Principles of Political Economy and Taxation* (London: J.M. Dent & Sons, 1911 [1817]).

Ritchie, Gordon, *Wrestling with the Elephant* (Toronto: Macfarlane, Walter and Ross, 1997).

Robbins, Lionel (Lord), *Politics and Economics: Papers in Political Economy* (London: Macmillan and Co., 1963).

Robertson, Roland, *Globalization: Social Theory and Global Culture* (London: SAGE, 1992).

Robinson, Joan, *Economic Philosophy* (Harmondsworth: Penguin Books, 1962).

Rosen, Michael, 'Must We Return to Moral Realism?', *Inquiry*, Vol. 34, No. 2 (1991), pp. 183–94.

Rosenberg, Justin, *The Empire of Civil Society: a Critique of the Realist Theory of International Relations* (London: Verso, 1994).

—— 'The International Imagination: IR Theory and Classic Social Analysis', *Millennium: Journal of International Studies*, Vol. 23, No. 1 (1994), pp. 85–108.

Rosow, Stephen J., 'Echoes of Commercial Society: Liberal Political Theory in Mainstream IPE', in Kurt Burch and Robert A. Denemark (eds), *Constituting International Political Economy* (Boulder, Colo.: Lynne Rienner, 1997).

Rothschild, Kurt W., *Ethics and Economic Theory: Ideas – Models – Dilemmas* (Aldershot: Edward Elgar, 1993).

Rotstein, Abraham, 'The Use and Misuse of Economics in Cultural Policy', in Rowland Lorimer and Donald C. Wilson (eds), *Communication Canada: Issues in Broadcasting and New Technologies* (Toronto: Kagan and Woo, 1988), pp. 140–56.

Rowley, Charles K. and Peacock, Alan T., *Welfare Economics: a Liberal Restatement* (New York: John Wiley and Sons, 1975).

Rupert, Mark, *Producing Hegemony: the Politics of Mass Production and American Global Power* (Cambridge: Cambridge University Press, 1995).

Ryan, Cheyney C., 'Yours, Mine, and Ours: Property Rights and Individual Liberty', in Jeffrey Paul (ed.), *Reading Nozick: Essays on Anarchy, State and Utopia* (Totowa, NJ: Rowman and Littlefield, 1981), pp. 323–43.

Said, Edward, *Orientalism*, second edition (London: Penguin, 1995).

—— *Representations of the Intellectual: the 1993 Reith Lectures* (London: Vintage, 1994).

Sally, Razeen, Review of *Hayek on Hayek*, by F.A. Hayek, in *Government and Opposition*, Vol. 30, No. 1 (1995), pp. 131–5.

Salutin, Rick, 'Culture and the Deal: Another Broken Promise', in Marc Gold and David Leyton-Brown (eds), *Trade-Offs on Free Trade: the Canada–U.S. Free Trade Agreement* (Toronto: The Carswell Company, 1988), pp. 365–9.

Sandel, Michael J., *Liberalism and the Limits of Justice* (Cambridge: Cambridge University Press, 1982).

Saward, Michael, *The Terms of Democracy* (Cambridge: Polity Press, 1998).

Scanlon, Thomas, 'Nozick on Rights, Liberty, and Property', in Jeffrey Paul (ed.), *Reading Nozick: Essays on Anarchy, State and Utopia* (Totowa, NJ: Rowman and Littlefield, 1981), pp. 107–29.

Scannell, Paddy, Schlesinger, Philip, and Sparks, Colin, *Culture and Power: a Media, Culture and Society Reader* (London: SAGE, 1992).

Schafer, D. Paul, *Aspects of Canadian Cultural Policy* (Paris: UNESCO, 1976).

—— *Canada's International Cultural Relations*, second edition (Toronto: D. Paul Schafer for World Culture Project, 1997).

—— and Fortier, André, *Review of Federal Policies for the Arts in Canada (1944–1988)* (Ottawa: The Canadian Conference of the Arts, 1989).

Scheffler, Samuel, 'Natural Rights, Equality, and the Minimal State', in Jeffrey Paul (ed.), *Reading Nozick: Essays on Anarchy, State and Utopia* (Totowa, NJ: Rowman and Littlefield, 1981), pp. 148–68.

Schnapper, Dominique, 'Citizenship and National Identity in Europe', *Nations and Nationalism*, Vol. 8, No. 1 (2002), pp. 1–14.

Scholte, Jan Aart, 'Globalisation and Collective Identities', in Jill Krause and Neil Renwick (eds), *Identities in International Relations* (Basingstoke: Macmillan Press, 1996), pp. 38–78.

Scitovsky, Tibor, 'Arts in the Affluent Society: What's Wrong with the Arts is What's Wrong with Society', *American Economic Review*, Vol. 62 (May 1972), pp. 62–9.

—— 'Subsidies for the Arts: the Economic Argument', in James L. Shanahan, William S. Hendon, Izaak Th. H. Hilhorst, and Jaap van Straalen (eds), *Economic Support for the Arts* (Akron, Ohio: The University of Akron for the Association for Cultural Economics, 1983), pp. 15–25.

Seglow, Jonathan, 'Goodness in an Age of Pluralism: On Charles Taylor's Moral Theory', *Res Publica*, Vol. 2, No. 2 (1996), pp. 163–80.

Sen, Amartya, 'The Impossibility of a Paretian Liberal', *Journal of Political Economy*, Vol. 78, No. 1 (1970), pp. 152–7.

—— *On Ethics and Economics* (Oxford: Blackwell, 1987).

—— and Williams, Bernard (eds), *Utilitarianism and Beyond* (Cambridge: Cambridge University Press, 1982).

Shaw, Douglas V., Hendon, William S., and Owen, Virginia Lee (eds), *Cultural Economics 88: an American Perspective* (Akron, Ohio: The University of Akron for the Association for Cultural Economics, 1989).

Shklar, Judith, Review of *Sources of the Self*, by Charles Taylor, in *Political Theory*, Vol. 19, No. 1 (1991), pp. 105–9.

Silverman, Sheldon A., 'Reflections on the Cultural Impact of a North American Free Trade Agreement', in Stephen J. Randall (ed.) with Herman Konrad and Sheldon Silverman, *North America without Borders? Integrating Canada, the United States, and Mexico* (Calgary: University of Calgary Press, 1992), pp. 307–12.

Simon, Roger, *Gramsci's Political Thought*, revised edition (London: Lawrence and Wishart, 1991).

Singer, Peter, 'The Right to Be Rich or Poor', in Jeffrey Paul (ed.), *Reading Nozick: Essays on Anarchy, State and Utopia* (Totowa, NJ: Rowman and Littlefield, 1981), pp. 37–53.

Sjostedt, Gunnar and Sundelius, Bengt (eds), *Free Trade – Managed Trade? Perspectives on a Realistic International Order* (Boulder, Colo.: Westview Press, 1985).

Skinner, Quentin, 'Who Are "We"? Ambiguities of the Modern Self', *Inquiry*, Vol. 34, No. 2 (1991), pp. 133–53.

Smart, J.J.C. and Williams, Bernard, *Utilitarianism: For and Against* (Cambridge: Cambridge University Press, 1973).

Smiers, Joost, 'The Role of the European Community Concerning the Cultural Article 151 in the Treaty of Amsterdam', Research Paper, Utrecht School of the Arts, April 2002.

Smith, Adam, *An Inquiry into the Nature and Causes of the Wealth of Nations*, Book I (Oxford: Clarendon, 1976 [1784]).

Smith, Allan, *Canadian Culture, the Canadian State, and the New Continentalism* (Orono, Me: The Canadian–American Center, The University of Maine, 1990).

Smith, Anthony D., *Nations and Nationalism in a Global Era* (Cambridge: Polity, 1995).

Smith, I. Norman, *The Journal Men* (Toronto: McLelland and Stewart, 1974).

Smith, M.R., 'A Sociological Appraisal of the FTA', *Canadian Public Policy*, Vol. 15, No. 1 (1989), pp. 57–71.

Smith, Murray G. and Stone, Frank (eds), *Assessing the Canada–U.S. Free Trade Agreement* (Halifax: The Institute for Research on Public Policy, 1987).

Smith, Steve, 'Positivism and Beyond', in Steve Smith, Ken Booth, and Marysia Zalewski (eds), *International Theory: Positivism and Beyond* (Cambridge: Cambridge University Press, 1996), pp. 11–44.

Solomon, Robert C., *A Better Way to Think about Business: How Personal Integrity Leads to Corporate Success* (Oxford and New York: Oxford University Press, 1999).

Spero, Joan Edelman, *The Politics of International Economic Relations*, fourth edition (London: Unwin Hyman Ltd, 1990).

Stone, Frank, *Canada, the GATT and the International Trade System*, second edition (Halifax: The Institute for Research on Public Policy, 1992).

Storey, John, *An Introduction to Cultural Theory and Popular Culture*, second edition (Hemel Hempstead: Harvester Wheatsheaf, 1993).

Strange, Susan, 'The Persistent Myth of Lost Hegemony', *International Organization*, Vol. 41, No. 4 (1987), pp. 551–74.

——'Political Economy and International Relations', in Steve Smith and Ken Booth, *International Relations Theory Today* (Cambridge: Polity, 1995), pp. 154–74.

—— 'Protectionism and World Politics', *International Organization*, Vol. 39, No. 2 (1985), pp. 233–59.

——*States and Markets*, second edition (London: Pinter, 1994).

Surber, Jere Paul, *Culture and Critique: an Introduction to the Critical Discourses of Cultural Studies* (Boulder, Colo.: Westview Press, 1988).

Sutherland, Fraser, *The Monthly Epic: a History of Canadian Magazines, 1789–1989* (Markham: Fitzhenry and Whiteside, 1989).

Swanson, Roger Frank, 'Canadian Cultural Nationalism and the U.S. Public Interest', in Janice L. Murray (ed.), *Canadian Cultural Nationalism: the Fourth Lester B. Pearson Conference on the Canada–United States Relationship* (New York: New York University Press for the Canadian Institute of International Affairs and the Council on Foreign Relations, 1977), pp. 55–82.

Tamir, Yael, *Liberal Nationalism* (Princeton, NJ: Princeton University Press, 1993).

Taylor, Charles, 'Can Liberalism Be Communitarian?', *Critical Review*, Vol. 8, No. 2 (1994), pp. 257–62.

—— 'Comments and Replies', *Inquiry*, Vol. 34, No. 2 (1991), pp. 237–54.

——*Hegel and Modern Society* (Cambridge: Cambridge University Press, 1979).

——*Human Agency and Language: Philosophical Papers 1* (Cambridge: Cambridge University Press, 1985).

——*Philosophical Arguments* (Cambridge, Mass.: Harvard University Press, 1995).

——*Philosophy and the Human Sciences: Philosophical Papers 2* (Cambridge: Cambridge University Press, 1985).

——*Reconciling the Solitudes: Essays on Canadian Federalism and Nationalism*, ed. G. Laforest (Montreal and Kingston: McGill-Queen's University Press, 1993).

——*Sources of the Self: the Making of the Modern Identity* (Cambridge, Mass.: Harvard University Press, 1989).

Thompson, John B., *Ideology and Modern Culture* (Cambridge: Polity, 1990).

Thompson, John Herd, 'Canada's Quest for Cultural Sovereignty: Protection, Promotion, and Popular Culture', in Stephen J. Randall (ed.) with Herman Konrad and Sheldon Silverman, *North America without Borders? Integrating Canada, the United States, and Mexico* (Calgary: University of Calgary Press, 1992), pp. 269–84.

—— and Randall, Stephen J., *Canada and the United States: Ambivalent Allies*, second edition (Athens, Ga: The University of Georgia Press, 1997).

Tomlinson, John, *Cultural Imperialism: a Critical Introduction* (London: Pinter Publishers, 1991).

Tooze, Roger, 'Constructive Criticism: Threats, Imperatives, and Opportunities of a Constitutive IPE', in Kurt Burch and Robert A. Denemark (eds), *Constituting International Political Economy* (Boulder, Colo.: Lynne Rienner, 1997), pp. 207–12.

Towse, Ruth (ed.), *Cultural Economics: the Arts, the Heritage, and the Media Industries*, 2 vols (Lyme, NH: Edward Elgar, 1997).

—— and Khakee, Abdul (eds), *Cultural Economics* (Berlin: Springer-Verlag, 1992).

Trentmann, Frank, 'Political Culture and Political Economy: Interest, Ideology and Free Trade', *Review of International Political Economy*, Vol. 5, No. 2 (1998), pp. 217–51.

Trimarchi, Michele, 'The Funding Process in a Comparative Perspective: Some Methodological Issues', in Alan Peacock and Ilde Rizzo (eds), *Cultural Economics and Cultural Policies* (Dordrecht: Kluwer Academic Publishers, 1994), pp. 23–31.

Tully, James (ed.), *Philosophy in an Age of Pluralism: the Philosophy of Charles Taylor in Question* (Cambridge: Cambridge University Press, 1994).

Tumlir, Jan, *Protectionism: Trade Policy in Democratic Societies* (Washington, DC: American Enterprise Institute for Public Policy Research, 1985).

Turner, Graeme, *British Cultural Studies: an Introduction* (Boston, Mass.: Unwin Hyman, 1990).

UNESCO International Fund for the Promotion of Culture, *Information Document*, CC/77/CONF.003, IFPC/EXT.2/3 (Paris: UNESCO, 12 August 1977).

—— *Cultural Rights and Wrongs* (Paris: UNESCO, 1998).

United States, The Congress of the United States, Congressional Budget Office, *How the GATT Affects U.S. Antidumping and Countervailing Duty Policy* (Washington, DC: US Government Printing Office, 1994).

van den Hoek, A. W., *Cultural Diversity and the Ideology of Development: UNESCO's Role in the International Debate on the Cultural Dimension of Development* (Leiden: UNESCO, 1988).

Varian, Hal R., *Intermediate Microeconomics: a Modern Approach*, second edition (New York: W.W. Norton and Company, 1990).

Vipond, Mary, 'Canadian Nationalism and the Plight of Canadian Magazines in the 1920s', *Canadian Historical Review*, Vol. 58, No. 1 (1977), pp. 43–63.

Viscusi, W. Kip, Vernon, John M., and Harrington, Joseph E., *Economics of Regulation and Antitrust*, second edition (Cambridge, Mass.: The MIT Press, 1998).

Waite, P.B., *Canada 1874–1896: Arduous Destiny* (Toronto: McClelland and Stewart, 1971).

Waldron, Jeremy, *The Right to Private Property* (Oxford: Clarendon, 1988).

Walker, Graham, *The Ethics of F.A. Hayek* (London: University Press of America, 1986).

Walker, R.B.J., *Inside/Outside: International Relations as Political Theory* (Cambridge: Cambridge University Press, 1993).

—— *One World, Many Worlds: Struggles for a Just World Peace* (Boulder, Colo.: Lynne Rienner Publishers, 1988).

—— 'Social Movements/World Politics', *Millennium: Journal of International Studies*, Vol. 23, No. 3 (1994), pp. 669–700.

—— 'Sovereignty, Identity, Community: Reflections on the Horizons of Contemporary Political Practice', in R.B.J. Walker and Saul Mendlovitz (eds), *Contending Sovereignties: Redefining Political Community* (Boulder, Colo.: Lynne Rienner, 1990), pp. 159–85.

—— (ed.), *Culture, Ideology and World Order* (Boulder, Colo.: Westview Press, 1984).

Walzer, Michael, *Spheres of Justice: a Defense of Pluralism and Equality* (New York: Basic Books, 1983).

Warner, Donald F., *The Idea of Continental Union: Agitation for the Annexation of Canada to the United States, 1849–1893* (Lexington, Ky: University of Kentucky Press, 1960).

Warnock, John W., 'All the News It Pays to Print', in Ian Lumsden (ed.), *Close the 49th Parallel Etc: the Americanization of Canada* (Toronto: University of Toronto Press, 1970), pp. 117–34.

—— *Free Trade and the New Right Agenda* (Vancouver: New Star Books, 1988).

Weber, Max, *Economy and Society*, ed. G. Roth and C. Wittich (New York: Bedminster Press, 1968).

—— *The Protestant Ethic and the Spirit of Capitalism*, second edition, trans. T. Parsons (London: Routledge, 1992).

Weisskopf, Walter A., 'The Moral Predicament of the Market Economy', in Gerald Dworkin, Gordon Bermant, and Peter G. Brown (eds), *Markets and Morals* (Washington, DC: Hemisphere Publishing, 1977), pp. 33–41.

Wheeler, Mark, 'Research Note: the "Undeclared War" Part II', *European Journal of Communication*, Vol. 15, No. 2 (2000), pp. 253–62.

White, Randall, *Fur Trade to Free Trade: Putting the Canada–U.S. Trade Agreement in Historical Perspective*, second edition (Toronto: Dundurn Press, 1988).

Wildavsky, Ben, 'Culture Clashes', *The National Journal*, Vol. 28, No. 12 (23 March 1996).

Wilden, A., *The Imaginary Canadian* (Vancouver: Pulp Press, 1980).

Williams, Bernard, 'The Minimal State', in Jeffrey Paul (ed.), *Reading Nozick: Essays on Anarchy, State and Utopia* (Totowa, NJ: Rowman and Littlefield, 1981), pp. 27–36.

Williams, Raymond, *Culture* (London: Fontana, 1981).

—— *Keywords: a Vocabulary of Culture and Society* (London: Fontana, 1983).

Winters, Alan L., *International Economics*, fourth edition (London and New York: Routledge, 1992).

Wolff, Jonathan, *Robert Nozick: Property, Justice and the Minimal State* (Stanford, Calif.: Stanford University Press, 1991).

Wolff, Robert Paul, 'Robert Nozick's Derivation of the Minimal State', in Jeffrey Paul (ed.), *Reading Nozick: Essays on Anarchy, State and Utopia* (Totowa, NJ: Rowman and Littlefield, 1981), pp. 77–104.

Wolin, Sheldon S., 'Fugitive Democracy', in Seyla Benhabib (ed.), *Democracy and Difference: Contesting the Boundaries of the Political* (Princeton, NJ: Princeton University Press, 1996), pp. 31–45.

Woodcock, George, *Strange Bedfellows: the State and the Arts in Canada* (Vancouver: Douglas and McIntyre, 1985).
Young, Iris Marion, *Justice and the Politics of Difference* (Princeton, NJ: Princeton University Press, 1990).
Youngs, Gillian, 'Beyond the "Inside/Outside" Divide', in Jill Krause and Neil Renwick (eds), *Identities in International Relations* (Basingstoke: Macmillan Press, 1996), pp. 22–37.

3. Newspapers and newsmagazines

The Buffalo News
The Economist
Financial Times
Folio
Journal of Commerce
Maclean's
The Montreal Gazette
The New York Times
The Ottawa Citizen
The San Diego Union – Tribune
Strategy
The Toronto Star
The Washington Post

Index